T0090699

THE GLOBAL WAR ON CHRISTIANS

THE

GL⊕BAL
WAR
ON CHRISTIANS

Dispatches from the Front Lines of
Anti-Christian Persecution

John L. Allen Jr.

IMAGE

New York

Library of Congress Cataloging-in-Publication data is available upon request.

ISBN 978-0-7704-3737-4
eBook ISBN 978-0-7704-3736-7

Book design by Ruth Lee
Cover design by FORT

First Paperback Edition

146056540

This book is dedicated to *Laura Hebert Frazier*, my grandmother, who died at the age of ninety-eight as the manuscript was being written. I doubt she would have read the finished product, even if her short-term memory hadn't pretty much evaporated by the end. She was always proud of my work, but not always eager to consume it. She would often say my writing is too long and too complicated, and people who've stumbled across my stuff over the years might well share that assessment. Even if it wasn't necessarily her cup of tea, everything in this book, and whatever else I've accomplished, in many ways is the fruit of her inspiration, support, and love. St. Laura, pray for us!

Contents

Preface to the 2016 Edition

When this book was first published in 2013, the idea of anti-Christian persecution as a legitimate category of human rights concern was still something of a stretch for many people in the West, long accustomed to thinking of institutional Christianity as powerful and privileged and therefore relatively immune to real danger. At most, Westerners tended to think of actual violence against Christians as something isolated and uncommon and to find claims of widespread anti-Christian prejudice overheated, driven more by the wars of culture in Europe and North America than by realities on the ground. In the early round of media appearances I did for the book, the first question almost invariably was, "Is there really such a thing as a war on Christians?"

Not long after the book appeared, however, the "Islamic State" declared a caliphate in Iraqi and Syrian territory under its control, unleashing a brutal offensive in the Plains of Nineveh that left thousands of Christians and Yazidis dead and hundreds of thousands in exile. During the assault, churches and monasteries were destroyed, centuries-old Christian manuscripts were burned, and scores of Christians were killed, often in staggeringly brutal fashion—flogged to death, beheaded, and, in at least a few cases, reportedly crucified. The city of Mosul, which has had a Christian presence stretching all the way back to the second century, today is essentially a Christian-free zone. In June 2014, the city's archbishop announced that for the first time in more than 1,800 years, no Sunday Mass would be celebrated in Mosul. Iraqi Christians suffered these hardships cheek by jowl with Yazidis, neighbors who practice an ancient syncretistic form of monotheism.

At almost exactly the same time in another part of the world, a group of Boko Haram militants attacked a government secondary school in the town of Chibok in Nigeria's northern Borno State, kidnapping almost 300 teenage girls, most of them Christians. The cry of "Bring Back Our Girls!" went viral, becoming an international cause célèbre and throwing a spotlight on the atrocities associated with Boko Haram, an extremist Islamic movement whose name literally means "Western education is prohibited." While its violence exempts no one, much of it undeniably has an anti-Christian edge. The Protestant watchdog group Open Doors reported that 2,484 Christians were killed in Nigeria between November 1, 2013, and October 31, 2014, making it the world's most dangerous nation for Christians during that reporting period. The carnage extended into 2015, especially in the northern Plateau State, where attacks by Boko Haram–style militants on rural Christian farmers have become so stunningly common that body counts are offered in summary fashion on the evening news alongside the day's stock market activity and tomorrow's weather.

While it seems perverse to ascribe a silver lining to the rise of ISIS and Boko Haram, the movements at least have had the effect of making denial about anti-Christian persecution impossible to sustain. By now, it has become a settled fact for most clear-eyed observers that these forces are explicitly hostile to Christians, and that Christians at risk from them merit the same security and human rights concern as other groups, whether defined by religion or other factors, that have long been the targets of similar hate campaigns.

There is a risk, however, that the horrors associated with these two movements may leave the bigger picture out of focus. While Islamic fundamentalism is indeed the world's leading manufacturer of anti-Christian hatred, it is hardly the only threat facing the faith. In the early twenty-first century there are 2.3 billion Christians in the world, scattered in every nook and cranny of the planet, and they experience a bewildering variety of forms of persecution. In Latin America, where Christianity represents an overwhelming social majority, Christians nevertheless are being martyred for their stands in favor of social justice and human rights, often falling victim to narco-terrorists and paramilitary bands. In parts of Asia, Christians run afoul of other forms of religious fundamentalism, such as the rise of Hindu nationalist forces in India. In other places, such as China, North Korea, and Myanmar, Christians are seen as threats to the hold on power of various kinds of police states.

To put the point as clearly as possible, today's war on Christians is a global phenomenon, and it cannot be reduced simply to a chapter in the "clash of civilizations" between Islam and the West. The truth is that radical Islam could fall off the face of the earth tomorrow, and it would not mean that Christians face no further danger. Instead they are at risk due to a complex cocktail of forces and one-size-fits-all diagnoses or solutions won't fly.

In the first part of 2015, I and a colleague from *Crux* and the *Boston Globe*, Inés San Martín, traveled to five countries in an effort to tell the stories of Christianity's new martyrs. We began in El Salvador, where Christian activists and pastors are in danger from the *maras*, violent criminal gangs that have given the country the world's highest murder rate, and then Colombia, where thousands of Christian clergy and laity have perished amid the world's longest-running civil war. We moved on to Egypt, where the sizable Christian minority is routinely hassled and targeted by extremist Muslim currents despite pledges of protection from the country's military-backed government. We visited India, where the "saffronization" of the country, referring to a drive to enforce strong Hindu values and practices, under a government with close ties to radical Hindu nationalists has left the Christian minority alarmed, and where violent attacks against Christians have become so routine as to pass almost unnoticed. We ended up in Nigeria, trying to unwrap the complexities of the Boko Haram movement and the way it's split both Muslims and Christians apart in Africa's largest nation but also brought them together in surprising and often deeply moving ways.

For one illustrative story out of countless others, we met Sister Meena Lalita Barwa, a Catholic nun of the Servite order who was in Kandhamal in eastern India in 2008 when a violent anti-Christian pogrom broke out that eventually left 100 people dead and thousands injured and homeless. She and a local priest, the Rev. Thomas Chellen, were dragged into the streets by frenzied attackers shouting "Kill Christians!" The assailants tried to force Chellen to rape Barwa, and when he refused, they beat him savagely, stopping only because they thought he was dead. At least one man raped Barwa—she lost consciousness and can't recall whether others joined in the assault—and she was then paraded through the streets of the village semi-naked in a final act of humiliation.

Barwa is what Indians call a "tribal," meaning a member of one of the country's original indigenous peoples, groups that typically face severe social prejudice and chronic underdevelopment. Now 37, Barwa is pursuing a law degree in order to fight for justice for other victims of similar violence.

She's adopted a unique spiritual perspective on the tragedy she experienced seven years ago.

"Because Jesus Christ wasn't a woman, there were certain kinds of suffering he couldn't experience in his own body in order to save the world," she says. "I like to think I helped to complete his sacrifice."

While Barwa's experience was harrowing, it's anything but rare. In India, one monitoring body estimates that for the first half of 2015, there was at least one violent attack against Christians somewhere in the country every week. Around the world, the low-end estimate for the number of new Christian martyrs every year in the early twenty-first century is in the low thousands, which works out to roughly one new casualty every hour.

To be sure, Christians are not the only group suffering, as no one has any monopoly on martyrdom. Certainly too, Christians concerned about the fate of their coreligionists ought to be equally engaged on behalf of other vulnerable populations, because building a movement in defense of human rights and religious freedom will never succeed if it's seen as a matter of confessional self-interest. All that said, it remains the case that too often the suffering of Christians is enveloped in silence, in part because it defies the Western narrative of Christianity as the architect of oppression rather than its victim; in part because these Christians are often poor, illiterate, and isolated, rendering them all but invisible; and in part because the forces putting them at risk are often maddeningly complex, causing many observers to despair of ever being able to understand the situation, let alone to change it.

The Global War on Christians is an effort to break the silence—not in order to stoke a twenty-first-century version of the Crusades or to make converts to the faith, but to place anti-Christian persecution among the towering human rights challenges of our time, one that requires no religious conviction to recognize, and one which merits the engagement of the broadest possible humanitarian coalition. As citizens, building that coalition is a matter of both civic duty and self-interest, since religious violence is the single most destabilizing force on the planet today. For Christians, however, coming to the aid of their vulnerable brothers and sisters in the faith is also a spiritual imperative, one that can no longer be delayed.

Acknowledgments

Over the course of my career, I've had many occasions to come into firsthand contact with victims of anti-Christian violence and persecution. I've met Christian refugees from Syria attending an open-air papal Mass on Beirut's waterfront, people who have no idea if they'll ever be able to go home and whose most desperate message they wanted to relay to the West was, "Don't forget about us!" I've stood in the ruins of bombed churches in Nigeria and spoken with a Nigerian evangelical pastor named James Wuye who once led an armed Christian militia into pitched battles with Muslims, losing his right hand in the process, and who today partners with a Nigerian imam in promoting peace and reconciliation. I've sat in rectories in Eastern Europe listening to Christian clergy, both Orthodox and Catholic, describe their experiences in Soviet gulags. Several of these clergy still bore the physical scars of the experience, in the form of limps where their legs had been shattered, coughs from untreated diseases, and gnarled digits where the fingers on their hands used to administer blessings had been broken. I've interviewed a twentysomething Chaldean Catholic refugee from Iraq named Fatima, a survivor of the siege of the Basilica of Our Lady of Salvation in Baghdad on October 31, 2010. She made it through by playing dead, pulling the corpses of two slain Christian friends over her on the church floor and waiting for four hours for the church to be liberated, thinking every moment might be her last. While I am not an expert on religious persecution, it's fair to say these personal experiences inspired this book and shaped my approach to it.

That said, the vast majority of the detailed accounts I summarize throughout this book are not the fruit of my own reporting. While I don't cite individual source material, because doing so would be too cumbersome, I want to acknowledge the main organizations, media outlets, and individual experts upon whom I've relied:

- The annual World Watch List published by Open Doors, which provides a global overview of anti-Christian persecution during the year under consideration, and country-by-country accounts of places where Christians face the gravest danger.

- Aid to the Church in Need, a widely respected Catholic relief organization based in Germany, which also publishes occasional reviews of anti-Christian persecution, including detailed incident reports from a variety of different countries.

- Fides, the Vatican's missionary news agency, which publishes an annual report on Catholic pastoral workers killed around the world during the previous year, including bishops, priests, brothers, deacons, nuns, and laywomen and -men who worked professionally for the Catholic Church.

- Asia News, another Catholic news agency sponsored by the Pontifical Institute for Foreign Missions and directed by Fr. Bernardo Cervellera, a dynamic Italian who, among other things, is one of the best Sinologists in the Catholic world. In my experience, Asia News probably does the best job, day in and day out, of documenting cases of anti-Christian persecution in the developing world, not just of Catholics but of all stripes of Christians.

- Forum 18, a Norwegian human rights organization that promotes religious freedom, and which is especially adept at monitoring the situation in the former Soviet sphere. Its regular news bulletins and analyses are extremely useful for understanding what's happening in that part of the world.

- Nina Shea, Paul Marshall, and others at the Hudson Institute, who have done yeoman's work over the last two decades to bring the issue of anti-Christian persecution to the forefront of American consciousness, and who continue to provide regular dispatches and overviews.

- The Pew Forum on Religion and Public Life in Washington, D.C., which provides the most reliable hard data on religious harassment and persecution around the world.

- The Center for the Study of Global Christianity at Gordon-Conwell Theological Seminary in South Hamilton, Massachusetts, which has pioneered the statistical investigation of Christian martyrdom and remains the lone serious source for estimates of the number of contemporary martyrs.

- The Catholic Near East Welfare Association (CNEWA), which has almost a century of experience delivering humanitarian and pastoral support to the churches of the Middle East, assisting not just Catholics but people of all faiths, and whose personnel often know the lay of the land better than anyone.

- Francesca Paci, a veteran print and broadcast journalist in Italy, whose 2011 book *Dove muoiono i Cristiani* (Where Christians are dying), published by Mondadori, was so good that I almost decided not to write this one. Communications 101, however, teaches us that sometimes the key to getting a point across is repetition. I hope this book accomplishes in English some of what Paci achieved in Italian.

Obviously, any misrepresentation or inaccuracies in the presentation of the incidents described in these pages is my fault alone and shouldn't be attributed to any of the organizations or individuals listed above.

Looking back, it's often hard to know exactly where the inspiration for a book came from, but I can date with precision the first time I considered global anti-Christian persecution as a possible topic. It was during a 2009 conversation with Cardinal Timothy Dolan of New York, who mused that perhaps Christians haven't roused themselves to confront the problem because we don't have our own Holocaust literature. He meant that Christians haven't told the stories of their new martyrs in a compelling way, in the same fashion that Jewish authors have described the horrors of the Shoah. This book is my own small contribution to a budding Christian genre dedicated to telling these stories, and I want to thank Cardinal Dolan for that nudge.

I'd like to take this chance to express gratitude to the team at Image, including Gary Jansen, Johanna Inwood, Carrie Freimuth, and their colleagues. As I've had the opportunity to say to them personally, they are "the best, the very best," and this book would not exist without their support. As always with my book projects, thanks also go to the editorial team at the *National Catholic Reporter* for tolerating both my growing obsession with the subject of anti-Christian persecution and my occasional absences to produce the manuscript.

Finally, the most profound thanks go to my wife, Shannon, and our beloved pug, Ellis, without whom . . . well, they're my *sine quo nihil*—without whom, nothing.

INTRODUCTION

This book is about the most dramatic religion story of the early twenty-first century, yet one that most people in the West have little idea is even happening: the global war on Christians. We're not talking about a metaphorical "war on religion" in Europe and the United States, fought on symbolic terrain such as whether it's okay to erect a nativity scene on the courthouse steps, but a rising tide of legal oppression, social harassment, and direct physical violence, with Christians as its leading victims. However counterintuitive it may seem in light of popular stereotypes of Christianity as a powerful and sometimes oppressive social force, Christians today indisputably are the most persecuted religious body on the planet, and too often their new martyrs suffer in silence.

The Me'eter military camp and prison, located in the Eritrean desert off the coast of the Red Sea, is a compelling place to begin the tale.

The prison's signature bit of cruelty is the use of crude metal shipping containers to hold inmates, with so many people forced into these 40-by-38-foot spaces, designed to transport commercial cargo, that prisoners typically have no room to lie down and barely enough to sit. The metal exacerbates the desert temperatures, which means bone-chilling cold at night and wilting heat during the day. When the sun is at its peak, temperatures inside the containers are believed to reach 115 degrees Fahrenheit or higher. One former inmate, lucky enough to be released after serving up a coerced confession, described the containers as "giant ovens baking people alive." Because prisoners are given little water, they sometimes end up drinking their own scant sweat and urine to stay alive.

When not in lockdown, prisoners are forced into pointless exercises such as counting grains of sand in the desert at midday, and scores die of heatstroke and dehydration. There are no toilets inside the containers, just crude buckets overflowing with urine and feces, placing inmates at risk of infection with diseases such as cholera and diphtheria. Prisoners have no contact with their families or friends, no legal representation, and no medical care. Forms of torture at Me'eter (also transliterated as "Meiter" and "Mitire") include making inmates kneel on a tree trunk and beating the soles of their feet with rubber hoses; hanging prisoners by their arms and exposing them to the sun, sometimes for forty-eight hours or more; and forcing prisoners to walk barefoot over stones and thorns, with beatings for not going fast enough. Survivors say sexual abuse is also common.

Me'eter was opened in 2009 by Eritrea's single-party regime, controlled by the People's Front for Democracy and Justice, and is still going strong, despite the fact its horrors are well documented. Diplomatic cables released in 2011 by WikiLeaks reveal that U.S. officials had interviewed escapees from Eritrea's concentration camps and passed along reports to the State Department.

Here's how one female survivor described life at night inside the shipping containers in a 2009 book:

> A single candle flickers, its flame barely illuminating the darkness. They never burn for more than two hours after the door is locked; there's not enough oxygen to keep the flame alive. The air is thick with a dirty metallic tang, the ever-present stench of the bucket in the corner, and the smell of close-pressed, unwashed bodies. Despite the proximity of so many people, it's freezing cold.

This survivor described being forced to squat on her haunches and lift three different sizes of rocks while moving them from one side of her body to another, over and over again. At one point she was tossed into a container with a female inmate who had been beaten so badly her uterus was actually hanging outside her body. The survivor desperately tried to push the uterus back in, but cries for help went unanswered and the woman died in agonizing pain.

The unavoidable question is why the abuse at Me'eter doesn't arouse the same horror and intense public fascination as the celebrated atrocities that unfolded at Abu Ghraib, for instance, or at Guantanamo Bay. Why hasn't there been the same avalanche of investigations, media exposés, protest marches, pop culture references, and the other typical indices of scandal? Why isn't the whole world abuzz with outrage over the grotesque violations of human rights at Me'eter?

In part it's because Abu Ghraib and Guantanamo Bay were operated by the United States, a country that styles itself a champion of democracy and the rule of law. Nobody really has the same expectations of Eritrea, a one-party state ruled since 1993 by a strongman who prevailed in a bloody civil war. More basically, however, the difference comes down to this: Abu Ghraib and Guantanamo Bay formed chapters in a war everyone cared about, meaning the U.S.-led "war on terror," while Me'eter is an equally dramatic chapter in a war that almost no one is aware is even being waged.

SNAPSHOTS OF A GLOBAL WAR

For all intents and purposes, Me'eter is a concentration camp for Christians. It's a military complex converted to house religious prisoners, most of whom adhere to a branch of Christianity not authorized by the state. While precise counts are elusive, most estimates say that somewhere between two thousand and three thousand Christians are presently languishing in Eritrean prisons because of their religious beliefs. The testimony quoted above comes from an evangelical gospel singer named Helen Berhane, an Eritrean Christian jailed from 2004 to 2006 after refusing to sign a pledge promising not to engage in religious activities. She was released thanks to a worldwide pressure campaign, but most of her fellow Christians haven't been so lucky.

Eritrea is far from an isolated case. The evangelical group Open Doors, devoted to monitoring anti-Christian persecution, estimates that one hundred million Christians worldwide presently face interrogation, arrest, torture, or even death because of their religious convictions. Protestant scholar Todd Johnson of Gordon-Conwell Theological Seminary, an expert on religious demography, has pegged the number of Christians killed per year from 2000 to 2010 at one hundred thousand. That works out to eleven Christians killed every hour, every day, throughout the past decade. Some experts question that number, but even the low-end estimate puts the number of Christians killed every day on the basis of religious hatred at twenty, almost one per hour.

This is a truly ecumenical scourge, in the sense that it afflicts evangelicals, mainline Protestants, Anglicans, Orthodox, Catholics, and Pentecostals alike. All denominations have their martyrs, and all are more or less equally at risk. A 2011 report from the Catholic humanitarian group Aid to the Church in Need described the worldwide assault on Christians as "a human rights disaster of epic proportions."

Though such language could seem to smack of hyperbole, consider these snapshots of what's happening:

- In Baghdad, Iraq, Islamic militants stormed the Syrian Catholic cathedral of Our Lady of Salvation on October 31, 2010, killing the two priests celebrating Mass and leaving a total of fifty-eight people dead. Though shocking, the assault was far from unprecedented: of the sixty-five Christian churches in Baghdad, forty have been bombed at least once since the beginning of the 2003 U.S.-led invasion. The effect of this campaign of violence and intimidation has been devastating for Christianity in the country. At the time of the first Gulf War in 1991, Iraq boasted a flourishing Christian population of at least 1.5 million. Today the high-end estimate for the number of Christians left is around 500,000, and many believe it could be as low as 150,000. Most of these Iraqi Christians have gone into exile, but a staggering number have been killed.

- India's northeastern state of Orissa was the scene of the most violent anti-Christian pogrom of the early twenty-first century. In 2008, a series of riots ended with as many as five hundred Christians killed, many hacked to death by machete-wielding Hindu radicals; thousands more were injured, and at least fifty thousand were left homeless. Many Christians fled to hastily prepared displacement camps, where some languished for two years or more. An estimated five thousand Christian homes, along with 350 churches and schools, were destroyed. A Catholic nun, Sr. Meena Barwa, was raped during the mayhem, then marched naked through the streets and beaten. Police sympathetic to the radicals discouraged the nun from filing a report and declined to arrest her attackers.

- In Burma, members of the Chin and Karen ethnic groups, who are strongly Christian, are considered dissidents by the regime and routinely subjected to imprisonment, torture, forced labor, and murder. In October 2010, the Burmese military launched helicopter strikes in territories where the country's Christians are concentrated. A Burmese air force source told reporters that the junta had declared these areas "black zones," where military personnel were authorized to attack and kill Christian targets on sight. Though there are no precise counts, thousands of Burmese Christians are believed to have been killed in the offensive.

- In Nigeria, the militant Islamic movement Boko Haram is held responsible for almost three thousand deaths since 2009, including eight hundred fatalities in 2012 alone. The movement has made a specialty out of targeting Christians and their churches, and in some cases they seem determined to drive Christians completely out of parts of the country. In December 2011, local Boko Haram spokespeople announced that all Christians in Nigeria's northern Yobe and Borno states had three days to get out, and followed up with a spate of church bombings on January 5–6, 2012, which left at least twenty-six Christians dead, as well as two separate shooting sprees in which eight more Christians died. In the aftermath, hundreds of Christians fled the area, and many are still displaced. Over Christmas 2012, at least fifteen Christians are believed to have had their throats cut by Boko Haram assailants.

- North Korea is widely considered the most dangerous place in the world to be a Christian; roughly a quarter of the country's two hundred thousand to four hundred thousand Christians are believed to be living in forced-labor camps because of their refusal to join the national cult around founder Kim Il Sung. The anti-Christian animus is so strong that even people with Christian grandparents are frozen out of the most important jobs—a grand irony, given that Kim Il Sung's mother was a Presbyterian deaconess. Since the armistice in 1953 that stabilized the division of the peninsula, some three hundred thousand Christians in North Korea have simply disappeared and are presumed to be dead.

Subsequent chapters will recount similar episodes from other parts of the world, but the point should already be clear: in a remarkable number of global neighborhoods, being a Christian is hazardous to your health.

The ways and means of this war on Christians vary, but at its most extreme it's a form of religious cleansing designed to wipe Christians off a particular part of the map. Take the case of southeastern Turkey, a zone bordering Syria where today Kurds and militant Turkish nationalists vie for control. At the beginning of the twentieth century there was a flourishing community of half a million Aramaic-speaking Christians in the area, keeping alive the language traditionally thought to have been spoken by Christ. By the end of the century, the Aramaic Christian population had shriveled to twenty-five hundred due both to violent persecution and to the daily pressures of de jure and de facto discrimination, and most people believe it's only a question of time before it becomes an artifact of history.

Nura Ardin, eighty-five, is one such exile. He recently told journalists that his family stayed in the area as long as his oldest son was alive, because the son had made a promise to the local bishop to remain as long as the bishop did. Upon hearing of that vow, Ardin said, Turkish nationalists raided the family's home one night in 1986 and shot his oldest son to death, whereupon the rest of the family decided to cut their losses and get out. Walking through southeastern Turkey's ghost towns of empty Christian villages, one has the feeling that here the war on Christians is basically already over.

THE RHETORIC OF WAR

"War" is probably the most overused term in politics, especially in the United States. Americans call pretty much everything a war—"war on poverty," "war on drugs," "war on terror," "culture wars," even a slightly self-parodying "war on Christmas." During the 2012 election, several more alleged wars emerged, including a "war on women" and a "war on religion." Generally such rhetoric is an invitation to hysteria. Believing that you don't just disagree with someone but are at war with them makes it far more difficult to find common ground. After all, nobody wants to be the Neville Chamberlain of the war on Christmas.

Before going further, therefore, we must clearly identify the risks of describing the pattern of religious violence summarized above as a "war."

- Calling it a "war" could suggest a degree of coordination to anti-Christian persecution that simply doesn't exist. There's no single enemy, and the problem can't be solved with a single strategic approach.
- Using the imagery of war could come off as a call to arms, a way of urging Christians to stop turning the other cheek. The last thing the world needs is a contemporary version of the Crusader armies of yore, armed with AK-47 assault rifles and rocket-propelled grenades.
- Overheated rhetoric could inflame the situation, making life even more perilous for Christians who already carry a bull's-eye on their backs.

- Because "war" is so overused, cynics might regard talk of a "war on Christians" as just another bit of spin, a slogan cooked up to serve someone's political interests.

Even with those cautions acknowledged, the question remains: What other word are we supposed to use? We're talking about a massive, worldwide pattern of violence and oppression directed against a specific group of people, often explicitly understood by its perpetrators as part of a broader cultural and spiritual struggle. Granted, slapping the label "war" on political disagreements is often an exaggeration. By the same token, feckless reluctance to call something a "war" when it plainly is can also be counterproductive. Among other things, failure to call this a "war" can inhibit people from facing the situation with the necessary sense of urgency.

Although reasonable observers might be willing to accept that widespread religious violence constitutes a genuine war, they may still balk at a specific focus on Christians as its victims. Again, let's tick off the most obvious reservations.

- Followers of other religions are suffering too. Many thoughtful Christian leaders in Nigeria hesitate to frame Boko Haram in terms of Christian/Muslim conflict, in part because its largest pool of victims is actually composed of fellow Muslims. Similarly, while Syria's Christians are paying a steep price, so too are other religious and ethnic groups in the country. Factions of the rebel alliance have taken up the chant "Christians to Lebanon, and Alawites to the sea!"
- Talking too much about a war "on Christians" could make the defense of religious freedom seem like a parochial matter of Christian self-interest, rather than principled support for the human rights of all people.
- Too much emphasis on Christians may fuel suspicions that advocacy of religious freedom is another chapter in Western colonialism, or a covert plot to promote Christian proselytism. Those perceptions are already strong in some quarters, and act as a trigger for violence.

Once again, even in the teeth of these hazards, there are compelling reasons for talking about a war "on Christians." As we will see in the next chapter, the leading estimate holds that 80 percent of all acts of religious discrimination in the world today are directed at Christians. If the defense of human rights and religious freedom is to mean anything, its cutting edge has to be formed by robust concern for the fate of these Christians. If the rhetoric of a war "on Christians" wakes people up to that reality, it will have served a purpose.

THE "WAR ON RELIGION" AND THE WAR ON CHRISTIANS

Precisely because the language of "war" is tossed around so readily, it's important at the outset to make a clear distinction between two different conflicts in which perceived assaults on Christianity are involved.

- The "global war on Christians," meaning violence and overt persecution directed at individual Christians as well as their churches and other institutions on the basis of their religious faith, the works of charity they perform, or the virtues they exhibit.
- A "war on religion" in the West, a phrase that many commentators in Europe and North America use to refer to what they see as a growing climate of secular hostility to religion, and to Christianity in particular. It usually involves tensions over the ability of faith-based institutions to both be true to their creeds and play a robust public role, rather than direct assaults on individuals.

In drawing this distinction, I'm aware that many thoughtful Christians don't believe it's ultimately tenable. Some Christian intellectuals believe that what's going on in Western culture today is the first wave of a more violent assault on religion. Cardinal Francis George of Chicago memorably expressed where he believes Western society is heading in 2010: "I expect to die in bed, my successor will die in prison, and his successor will die a martyr in the public square." (Not often quoted is George's more hopeful footnote after the reference to the martyred bishop: "His successor will pick up the shards of a ruined society and slowly help rebuild civilization, as the church has done so often in human history.")

Without passing judgment on such forecasts, the subject matter of this book is the literal war on Christians already under way in other parts of the world. Readers looking for a close examination of today's church/state tensions in the United States and Europe, which the Catholic bishops of America have characterized in terms of an "ever more frequent assault and ever more rapid erosion" of religious liberty, will not find it here.

I make this choice for two reasons, the first of which is unabashedly political. Matters such as the Obama administration's insurance mandates, which require faith-based groups to cover contraception and sterilization, divide even the most rational of souls. I don't want those divisions to get in the way of forming consensus about the global war on Christians, because while reasonable minds may draw differing conclusions over insurance policy, there ought to be no such disagreement when innocent people are being shot, tortured, imprisoned, or threatened.

Here's an example of seemingly improbable alliances. In 2011 and again in 2013, a bill to create a special-envoy position within the U.S. State Department to advocate for religious minorities in the Middle East and South Central Asia was introduced by two members of Congress: Frank Wolf, a Virginia Republican, and Anna Eshoo, a California Democrat. In many ways, they're a political odd couple. Wolf is a strong pro-lifer, given a 100 percent score by the National Right to Life Committee; Eshoo is pro-choice, rated 100 percent by the National Abortion Rights Action League. Wolf voted for the Defense of Marriage Act, while Eshoo, a major gay rights supporter, opposed it. They've split over the budget, health care reform, and many other contentious issues. Yet when it comes to defending Christians at risk, they're in agreement. Wolf has long been a leader on religious freedom, sending a letter in early January 2013 to three hundred Protestant and Catholic leaders pleading with them to become more outspoken "on behalf of the persecuted church around the world." Eshoo is the only member of

Congress of Assyrian descent and is cofounder of its Religious Minorities in the Middle East caucus. She's authored an amendment to the Foreign Relations Act insisting that "special attention should be paid to the welfare of Chaldo-Assyrians and other indigenous Christians in Iraq." I want this book to contribute to holding such disparate coalitions together, avoiding anything that might split them apart.

The second reason for distinguishing a Western "war on religion" from the global war on Christians is moral. However harassed believers in the West may feel, their difficulties pale in comparison with the threats to life and limb faced by Christians in other global neighborhoods. The agony of those truly at risk has been ignored for too long, and it would be tragic—in the classic language of Christian moral theology, it would be scandalous—if metaphorical battles at home, however necessary it may be to fight them, distracted Western Christians from engaging in the very real war being waged abroad.

As a footnote, wherever one stands on the "war on religion," there is a silver lining to those perceptions. Part of the reason Christians in the West have been slow to recognize the scope and scale of anti-Christian violence is because they have no personal experience of persecution. Today, however, a growing number of Christians in Europe and North America have come to see themselves as part of an oppressed minority. For our purposes, the extent to which those impressions are merited is almost irrelevant; in terms of popular psychology, they have the potential to make Christians more concerned about, and sympathetic to, persecution in other places.

LETTING OURSELVES OFF THE HOOK?

Another reason why some people are uncomfortable with the imagery of a "war on Christians" is concern that a narrative of Christian victimization may let those of us in the West off the hook too easily. Iraq is the most commonly cited example. Complaints about anti-Christian violence in Iraq, critics object, glosses over the fact that it was two ill-advised American wars in the country that created the chaos, waged by an administration that frequently invoked Christian values to justify its policies. If we truly want to protect Christians from harm, these critics suggest, don't we have to consider the foreign policy and lifestyle choices in the West that often tempt people to turn their Christian neighbors into convenient targets?

Rhetoric about a "war on Christians" can be used that way, and it's a mistake. Nothing in this book should be interpreted as an excuse for short-circuiting hard questions about equity in international relations, in the use of force, or in contemporary models of development. Pope Paul VI said in 1972, "If you want peace, work for justice," and his insight remains as valid today as it was at the height of the war in Vietnam.

There's an intra-Christian version of this criticism, which holds that making a fetish out of Christian suffering risks overlooking the responsibility Christians themselves sometimes bear for creating conditions of conflict. For instance, haven't the churches over the centuries sometimes allowed themselves to be co-opted by political systems in exchange for power and privilege, offering a de facto blessing for situations of injustice? Don't Christians sometimes engage in overly aggressive forms of proselytism that court retribution? Don't triumphalist Christian theologies of *extra ecclesiam nulla salus*, "outside the church there is no salvation," sometimes inflame resentments among followers of other faiths?

Once again, nothing in this book should obstruct conversation within, and among, the churches over these subjects. While no other global religion arguably has done greater public penance over the sins of its past and present than Christianity, the church still remains *semper reformanda*, always to be reformed. Yet also once again, the failures of either institutional churches or of individual Christians cannot justify indiscriminate violence and harassment. The logic cuts both ways: the global war on Christians is no excuse for avoiding tough debates over Christian doctrine and practice, but equally, those debates are no excuse for ignoring the global war on Christians.

IS IT REALLY "ANTI-CHRISTIAN"?

A final objection to claims of a war on Christians is that such language is overly simplistic, because the forces that drive the violence often have little to do with religion. When wealthy landowners in Brazil gun down Christian activists supporting the property rights of indigenous people, for instance, or militias in the Congo murder preachers and catechists because they stand in the way of recruitment or plunder, the architects of the violence are hardly driven by religious conviction. Once again, there's merit to the concern. The mere fact that Christians are harmed someplace does not ipso facto mean they were harmed because they are Christian. It's equally fallacious both to dismiss religion as a causal factor and to privilege it over others.

At the same time, a one-sided focus on the motives of the perpetrators of violence can also produce a badly skewed picture. When someone is threatened or harmed, there are actually two questions to ask: First, what are the motives of the attackers? Second, did the victim make choices that placed himself or herself at risk, and if so, why? Generally, most people focus only on the first in assessing whether something counts as religious violence. For Catholics, that instinct is actually encoded in their theology. Classically, the church has only recognized martyrs if they were killed *in odium fidei*, meaning "in [explicit] hatred of the faith." Let's take two cases, however, that illustrate why this way of seeing things doesn't bring the full picture into view.

First: A businessman who happens to be Christian is on his way to a meeting to negotiate a deal, and he's walking down the street in what's usually a safe neighborhood. He's mugged by a thief looking to make a quick score, getting roughed up in the process.

Second: A Pentecostal preacher is walking down the street on his way to church in a neighborhood known for drug trafficking and gang violence. He understands the risks but believes continuing his ministry in an otherwise abandoned community is what God is calling him to do. The preacher is mugged, getting roughed up in the process. (In some parts of Latin America, by the way, this is almost a daily occurrence.)

Most people would say the businessman did not suffer because of his Christian beliefs but the pastor did—even though the motives of the party inflicting the violence are precisely the same.

Aside from logical cogency, here's a further argument for taking a more expansive view of anti-Christian persecution. Many experts believe that a society's treatment of Christians is a harbinger of its track record on human rights across the board. Because Christians today are distributed across the planet, because they're disproportionately women and nonwhite, because they often belong to other at-risk groups (such as ethnic and linguistic minorities), and because they're often found in the forefront of efforts for political and economic liberalization, the way a society treats its Christians is a fairly reliable test of its overall approach to the protection of minorities and the rule of law. To ignore threats against Christians because they're not explicitly religious is, therefore, to miss the forest for the trees.

Admittedly, it can be dangerous to describe something as a religious conflict when other forces are also involved. To take the best-known example, one can get an overheated impression of animosity between Muslims and Christians by focusing only on the religious identity of jihadists in the Middle East, without considering the political, economic, and cultural factors that also foment violence. Accurate diagnosis is a key to cure. If Christians are being targeted in Sri Lanka, for instance, not primarily because of their religious affiliation but because of lingering ethnic and political tensions related to that nation's civil war, protecting them may require solutions that have more to do with statecraft than with confessional rivalry.

At the same time, it cheapens the witness of legions of victims of persecution and violence to suggest their suffering doesn't count as "religious" simply because their oppressors aren't directly motivated by religious concerns. There are signs that many Christian churches are moving toward a more balanced understanding. On May 25, 2013, Fr. Giuseppe "Pino" Puglisi was beatified by the Catholic Church as a martyr, having been killed in 1993 for challenging the Mafia's hold on his Palermo neighborhood, Brancaccio. The motives of his assassins may not have had anything to do with Christianity, but Puglisi's certainly did.

Here's the bottom line, expressed in a sound bite: in assessing the scope and scale of today's war on Christians, it's not enough to consider what was in the mind of the person pulling the trigger—we also have to ponder what was in the heart of the believer getting shot.

WHY THE SILENCE?

Back in 1997, American author Paul Marshall said that anti-Christian persecution had been "all but totally ignored by the world at large." To be sure, the situation has changed in the sixteen years since Marshall's classic work *Their Blood Cries Out*. A cluster of advocacy groups and relief organizations has emerged, and from time to time anti-Christian persecution has drawn coverage in major news outlets such as the *Economist*, *Newsweek*, and *Commentary*. On the whole, however, the war on Christians remains the world's best-kept secret. As recently as 2011, Italian journalist Francesca Paci—who writes for the Italian media market, which probably pays more attention to Christian topics than almost any other culture on earth, given the massive footprint of the Vatican—said about the fate of persecuted Christians in places such as Iraq, Algeria, and India: "We ignore too many things, and even more indefensibly, we pretend not to see too many things."

In 2011, the Catholic Patriarch of Jerusalem, Fouad Twal, addressed the crisis facing Arab Christianity in the Middle East during a conference in London. He bluntly asked: "Does anybody hear our cry? How many atrocities must we endure before somebody, somewhere, comes to our aid?" Those are questions that deserve answers, and understanding the motives for the silence about the global war on Christians is a good place to begin.

Explaining the Silence in the Secular Milieu

In the secular milieu, several factors intersect to explain the relative indifference toward the global persecution of Christians. First is the basic point that some secularists have little personal experience of religion and can be strikingly ignorant on religious subjects. There's also a reflexive hostility to institutional religion, especially Christianity, in some sectors of secular opinion. People conditioned by such views are inclined to see Christianity as the agent of repression, not its victim. Say "religious persecution," and the images that come to mind are the Crusades, the Inquisition, the wars of religion, Bruno and Savonarola, the Salem witch trials—all chapters of history in which Christianity is cast as the villain. For many such folks today, "Christianity" means an all-male gerontocracy in Rome cracking down on progressive American nuns, or intemperate evangelicals seeking to restrict a woman's right to choose or a gay's right to marry.

Victims of the global war on Christians challenge this narrative head-on, because they show Christianity not as the oppressor but as the oppressed. By 2012, almost two-thirds of the 2.2 billion Christians in the world lived outside of the West, and that share should reach three-quarters by midcentury. These Christians often carry a double or triple stigma, representing not only a faith that arouses suspicion but also an oppressed ethnic group (such as the Karen or Chin in Burma) or social class (such as Dalit converts in India, who may be as much as 60 percent of the country's Christian population). Given the facts on the ground, it's time for secular thought to get past the *Da Vinci Code*. Today's Christians aren't the ones dispatching mad assassins; more often than not, they're the ones fleeing the assassins others have dispatched.

For many people, the war on Christians is also simply too far away. Today's martyrs often go to their deaths in Sri Lanka, the Maldive Islands, and Sudan—places that many people in the West would struggle to find on a map, to say nothing of feeling a personal investment in what's happening there. The war on Christians is also incredibly complex, with no simple explanation and no simple remedy to advocate. What might work to combat Buddhist extremism in Bangladesh may be unsuited to deal with narcoterrorists in Colombia.

A further reason for paralysis is suggested by French intellectual Régis Debray, a veteran leftist who fought alongside Che Guevara. Debray observes that anti-Christian persecution falls squarely into the political blind spot of the West. The victims, Debray argues, are "too Christian" to excite the left, "too foreign" to interest the right. Western politics also encourages people to see only part of the picture. Conservatives pounce on every outrage by Islamic radicals but shrink from condemning the way Israeli security policies often suck the life out of Arab Christianity. Liberals celebrate the martyrs to right-wing regimes in Latin America but are often unwilling to acknowledge the reality of anti-Christian hatred in the Hamas-controlled Gaza Strip, or the way that leftist regimes often make Christians their first targets.

Explaining the Silence in the Churches

It might be disappointing that secular circles haven't seized on anti-Christian persecution, but it's probably not terribly surprising. What's less obvious is why mainstream Western Christianity hasn't focused on it. It's probably a safe bet that one could visit a variety of different Christian denominations over an extended period of time before hearing a sermon devoted to the subject of the global war on Christians, or finding an adult faith formation group studying it, or reading about it while browsing the collection of literature in the back of a church. At the political and social levels, the churches of the West have not yet driven anti-Christian persecution to the top of anybody's to-do list, despite expending enormous resources on other questions.

How do we account for the apparent paradox that the most compelling Christian narrative of the early twenty-first century has seemingly been lost on a broad swath of Christian consciousness?

One reason has already been mentioned, which is that Christians in Western societies generally have no personal experience of persecution. I'm a good example. I grew up a Catholic in western Kansas during the 1970s and 1980s, and the closest I ever came to suffering for the faith was eating fish sticks or macaroni and cheese on Fridays during Lent. When I first began to encounter reports about anti-Christian violence, my initial reaction was to regard them as rare and exceptional, not as evidence of something pervasive or systematic. Though we won't pursue the point here, there may be a parallel with the climate of denial many victims of sexual abuse in Christian churches experienced when they first came forward; even when people believed the individual reports, they had a hard time seeing them as part of a larger pattern.

There's also a broad tendency in Western societies, one that has reached inside many Christian denominations as well, to see the primary function of religion as promoting inner peace and tranquility. Hearing accounts of how Muslim radicals in Egypt pour sulfuric acid on the wrists of Coptic Christians in order to eviscerate the tattooed crosses most Copts wear is not exactly conducive to inner peace. It's disturbing and uncomfortable, and perhaps not what some Christians in the West are seeking.

Christians are also shaped by the societies in which they live, and American Christians in particular often reflect the somewhat myopically domestic outlook of the broader culture. When most American Christians talk about "the church," what they usually mean is the American church. When they say "the clergy," they mean American clergy, and when they say "the laity," they mean American laity. Browse a collection of recent titles by Christian authors in the United States, and whether their sympathies lie on the left, on the right, or in the center, the common denominator is often that their imaginations end at the water's edge.

On a more practical note, most churches are nonprofit operations facing chronically limited resources, and the need to pay the electric bill, fix the roof, and pay the pastor's salary sometimes overwhelms everything else. Further, there's "good-cause fatigue" among many church-goers, who are routinely hit up to support every humanitarian and spiritual endeavor under the sun, and after a while they simply start tuning out anything that strikes them as another sales pitch.

As an additional factor, most Christian denominations have expended enormous resources in recent decades on building interfaith dialogues. That's a welcome advance from the antagonism and fear toward other faiths that once dominated Christian psychology, but it also runs the risk of "interfaith correctness." Some Christians may be reluctant to speak out about the difficulties facing Arab Christians in Israel for fear of disrupting Christian/Jewish relations; others may be hesitant to challenge Muslims about the oppression of Christians in Islamic societies for fear of stoking a "clash of civilizations." While responsibility for the global war on Christians should not be imputed to entire religions, timidity about putting real issues on the table in interfaith dialogue is also a factor in explaining why Christians don't engage the global war with greater verve.

Finally, there's one more force at work. A distressing share of Christian time and treasure today is eaten up by internal battles, making it difficult to galvanize a unified response on anything. Not only is that point true across denominational lines, but it's become increasingly the case even within denominations. If Christians are to come together to respond effectively to the global war on their sisters and brothers in the faith, one preliminary challenge will be to break through tribalization—to foster a "post-tribal" mind-set in which the things that unite Christians are seen as more important than the fractures that divide them.

TIME TO WAKE UP

These factors may amount to explanations, but they're not excuses. It's well past time for the world, especially its Christians, to wake up.

No faith commitment is required to see the plight of persecuted Christians as an urgent human rights priority. Just as one didn't need to be Jewish to be concerned with the fate of dissident Soviet Jews in the 1960s and 1970s, and one didn't need to be black to feel outrage over South African apartheid in the 1980s, one doesn't have to be a Christian today to be appalled by the widespread torture and murder of Christians.

Yet for Christians, there's a special obligation. In theological parlance, one might say that Christians have a "vocation" to come to the aid of their suffering sisters and brothers. Though the various denominations understand baptism somewhat differently, all share a conviction that through baptism we're incorporated into the Body of Christ, so that the suffering of any part of that body, anywhere, is our pain too. St. Paul in his letter to the Galatians issues this charge: "So then, while we have the opportunity, let us do good to all, but especially to those who belong to the family of the faith." The question facing the Christian conscience today is, does that mean anything, or is it just a bit of pious rhetoric?

At a more practical level, Christians also have a responsibility because in many cases they're the only ones in a position to do anything. Victims of the global war on Christians are often reluctant to report what's happened, to press legal charges, or to reveal their suffering to the media. They fear blowback for speaking out and will only discuss their experiences with people they trust, meaning fellow believers. Christians are often the only people in a position to collect reports of what's really happening on the ground, and the only ones who can build relationships with victims in order to bring them into the conversation about the most effective way to respond.

Aside from the moral and spiritual imperatives, there are three other reasons why making this a core concern in the early twenty-first century would be good for the Christian soul.

First, the defense of persecuted Christians could be a major boon to the ecumenical movement, meaning the push to put the divided Christian family back together again. In the twentieth century, pioneers of the ecumenical movement were powerfully influenced by the experience of the Soviet gulags and the Nazi concentration camps, where Catholic, Orthodox, and Protestant Christians formed a common fellowship of suffering. The same experience is unfolding today, and it could have a similarly dramatic ecumenical impact. Second, the defense of persecuted Christians could also help believers in the West get past their internal fights. Third, the testimony of the martyrs has a unique spiritual power, so the better known their stories are in popular Christian consciousness, the healthier global Christianity will be.

HOPE AND PERSPECTIVE

My first personal taste of this spiritual punch came in June 2001, while I was covering Pope John Paul II's trip to Ukraine. During the Soviet era, the Greek Catholic Church in Ukraine was the largest illegal religious body in the world, and in percentage terms no nation produced more martyrs. John Paul went to Ukraine in part to honor their memory and in part to celebrate the church's renaissance following the collapse of the Soviet system. On June 26, he celebrated a huge outdoor Mass in an arena normally used for horse races, which on this day was packed with a million people who had braved strong rain and mud.

Before I reached the heart of the crowd, I happened to see a young woman off by herself weeping quietly. Curious, I approached and asked if she would mind telling me what she was feeling. In halting English, she told me that her grandfather had been a Greek Catholic priest. (The Greek Catholic Church in Ukraine is one of twenty-two Eastern churches in communion with Rome, and most have married clergy.) He had been rounded up and packed off to the gulags, and because he refused to renounce his faith, he was beaten, starved, and tortured, and he eventually died in prison. He was actually nailed upside down to the prison wall, in a grotesque parody of the crucifixion. After telling me the story, the young woman explained why she was crying: "I'm imagining what my grandfather must be feeling today looking down from heaven and seeing the Holy Father standing on Ukrainian soil."

That moment had a lasting impact. What she brought home for me is that beyond all the frustrations Christians feel—beyond the scandals, crises, and failures that frequently mar the churches—there's something so precious about faith in Christ and membership in the church that, when push comes to shove, ordinary people will pay in blood rather than let it go. That insight has sustained me when I've been tempted to despair, and it's also given me a deeper sense of what's truly important. I know that similar experiences have had the same impact on others. The martyrs, in other words, offer us the two most precious commodities in the spiritual life: hope and perspective.

In the end, I can do no better to drive home the case than to quote Francesa Paci from her book *Dove muoiono i Cristiani* (Where Christians are dying). Her reference to the Vatican reflects its centrality in Italian psychology, but otherwise her points are universally applicable.

Christians are dying in Orissa, in Iraq, in the Brazilian Amazon, but above all they're dying in the indifference of so many who, not wanting to seem clericalist, simply minimize what's happening. Their response is predictable: "Why doesn't the Vatican do something about it?" If that's the case, I ask my conscience, then why should I worry about the fate of the Gypsies instead of referring the problem to Romania or the former Yugoslavia? Why should I concern myself with child soldiers in sub-Saharan Africa who are so far away from me? Why should I support campaigns against hunger or AIDS, or express solidarity with peoples without a homeland such as the Palestinians? Neither does the attempt work to justify this scant attention with the contradictions of the Church, beginning with the awful stories of pedophile priests. What do Pakistani Christians condemned to death for

preferring the Gospel over the Qur'an have to do with the evil
desires of those priests, or the omertà that for a long time shame-
fully protected them? It would be like ignoring the desperation of
the immigrants who arrive at our shores in search of a better life
with the argument that some of them will end up as delinquents.

Paci has it exactly right. This book's burden is to tell the stories of
the global war on Christians and to debunk the myths that too often
surround it.

PART ONE

Anti-Christian Persecution
Around the World

This section begins with an overview of the threats facing Christians and offers a series of snapshots from the front lines of the global war. The focus is limited to the past twenty years, meaning since 1993, and in most cases the examples date from the opening years of this century. To be clear, this is far from a comprehensive account. As the next chapter illustrates, estimates of the annual casualties in this global war range from a high of 100,000 to a low of 7,300. Even if we take the low-end number, it would work out to 146,000 new Christian martyrs over the past twenty years. If the higher end estimates turn out to be closer to the truth, then we're talking about 2 million. In either case, telling all these stories would be impossible. Moreover, one doesn't have to die to be a victim of the global war. Helen Berhane and other inmates lucky enough to survive Eritrea's Me'eter concentration camp are not literally martyrs, but they are victims—and once again, the count of such folks is simply too high to be captured in its entirety.

Instead, this section provides representative examples of the kinds of suffering Christians around the world endure—legal harassment, social discrimination, arbitrary detention and imprisonment, torture, physical assault and injury, and, all too often, death. The aim is to strike a balance between telling a sufficient number of stories that the scale of the global war becomes clear, without compounding examples to such a degree that readers become numb to the human realities. In every case, the stories are intended to offer pieces of a bigger picture, and the omission of certain victims or atrocities should not suggest that those people do not count.

In similar fashion, these chapters do not deal with all the countries in a given continent, but simply offer a few examples of the more intense conflict zones. The omission of a certain nation or region should not suggest that it's trouble free, or that the sufferings endured by its Christians don't count as part of the global war. For instance, there's no chapter on the Pacific Islands, but that doesn't make Pastor Ruimar Duarte DePaiva, his wife, Margareth, and their son, Larisson, any less noteworthy as victims of anti-Christian violence. Members of the Seventh-day Adventist Church, they were hacked to death with machetes in Palaua, Micronesia, in 2003. Similarly, the omission of the Pacific Islands doesn't mean that a standoff in 2005 between the Methodist Church and the Fijian army, when commanders threatened to order soldiers to stop being Methodists because of church leaders' support for a national reconciliation commission intended to establish the truth about a 2000 coup, wasn't a potentially dramatic chapter in this global war.

If my aim had been to present a comprehensive list of anti-Christian harassment, this book would never have been finished. Every day I worked on it, fresh accounts from various parts of the world arrived in emails, letters, news accounts, and phone calls. I was often reminded of the ending of the Gospel of John: "There are also many other things that Jesus did, but if these were to be described individually, I do not think the whole world would contain the books that would be written." Much the same could be said about the individual stories that make up the global war on Christians.

I do not provide individual footnotes with the original sources of the reports for the cases described in the chapters that follow. There are too many, and publishing all the bibliographical information documenting these accounts would become unwieldy. In virtually every instance, all one has to do is to enter the name of the victim, or keywords about the incident, into any Internet search engine, and the original source material will come up quickly. The problem in the global war on Christians is not that no one is reporting what's happening. It's rather that far too few people are paying attention.

1

OVERVIEW

Having recalled the story of Abu Ghraib in the introduction, here's another echo from the "war on terror": waterboarding. Though the procedure is nobody's idea of a good time, officials of the Bush administration famously insisted that it's not a form of torture after it was revealed that American interrogators were using it on extrajudicial prisoners—even though Japanese soldiers actually had been hanged by the United States during World War II for using similar techniques on American prisoners. Waterboarding was banned by the Obama administration in 2009, yet to this day some experts continue to defend it. More broadly, "torture" remains a tricky word to define with precision, with most people falling back on the classic Potter Stewart test for obscenity: "I know it when I see it."

If it's tough to achieve consensus about what constitutes torture, agreement is even more elusive with terms such as "repression," "persecution," "harassment," and "discrimination." If we're going to try to document a global war on Christians that includes such terminology, we'd best begin with as much clarity as we can reasonably achieve about what those words mean, although forewarned is forearmed: in determining whether a particular incident counts as part of the global war on Christians, quite often we'll still be operating on the premise of knowing it when we see it.

To begin, here's what many experts regard as the best generalized definition of anti-Christian persecution, which was crafted by Protestant scholar Charles L. Tieszen in 2008: "Any unjust action of mild to intense levels of hostility, directed at Christians of varying levels of commitment and resulting in varying levels of harm, with religion, namely the identification of its victims as 'Christian,' as the primary motivator."

What exactly does that "mild to intense" hostility look like? The Barnabas Fund is a U.K.-based international, interdenominational body founded in 1993 to support persecuted Christians. In 2006, the fund attempted to classify the main categories of persecution faced by Christians, especially in societies in which they're a minority. In effect, these ten forms of harassment and persecution are the primary weapons in the global war on Christians.

1. *Societal discrimination.* In general, "societal discrimination" refers to de facto, rather than de jure, restrictions on religious freedom. For instance, social pressures are often directed at Christian women in majority-Muslim societies to convert to Islam if they marry a Muslim man. Reports from the Gaza Strip, to take one example, indicate that the pressure against mixed Muslim/Christian marriages has become so intense in recent years that such couples are often having children out of wedlock, and in some cases subsequently abandoning them, rather than enduring the backlash of becoming legally married.

2. *Institutional discrimination.* For instance, difficulties in obtaining zoning permits to either build or repair Christian churches, as a means of trying to inhibit the normal pastoral life of Christianity. In Belarus, for instance, ordinances prohibit any religious activity in a building if it's not's zoned for it, and Pentecostal pastors have said that officials generally refuse permission to zone their buildings for worship.

3. *Employment discrimination.* The number of Christians eligible for certain categories of employment is often limited, if they're not shut out altogether. In Egypt, for instance, it's long been difficult for members of the Coptic Christian minority to obtain senior positions either in the military or in the public sector. As of 2010, there was no Coptic university president or dean in Egypt.

4. *Legal discrimination.* Denying Christians and other religious minorities access to the courts, denying them legal representation when charged with crimes, or making it difficult for Christians to make reports and pursue justice when a crime has been committed against them. In certain Indian states, for instance, there are chronic complaints that police and prosecutors are slow to investigate offenses committed against Christians by Hindu radicals.

5. *Suppression of Christian missionary activity.* In some cases, Christians may be tolerated if they keep to themselves, but any effort to spread the Christian message or to expand Christianity's footprint in a region will meet with persecution. That's often the case in societies in which national or cultural identity is tied to another religion, or where there's a strong undercurrent of suspicion about the West. Iran, for instance, routinely arrests Christian missionaries and deports or incarcerates them. Theoretically, Christians, Jews, and Zoroastrians are free to practice their faith, but any proselytism is forbidden.

6. *Suppression of conversion to Christianity.* Most common in countries with "blasphemy" or "apostasy" laws, these legal measures effectively criminalize conversion from one religion to another, typically Islam to Christianity. In such societies, converts often live a sort of catacomb existence, hesitant to reveal their new religious affiliation even to family and close friends.

7. *Forced conversion from Christianity.* The use of force to compel someone to renounce the Christian faith may be done

formally by the state, informally by social actors, or through a combination of both. In India, for instance, Hindu radicals have staged massive "reconversion" ceremonies in rural areas in which Christians are effectively compelled to embrace Hinduism, and these events are often organized in cooperation with local police and security authorities.

8. *Suppression of corporate worship.* This form of intimidation refers to restricting the ability of Christians to worship together, either in a formal church setting or informally in public areas or in private homes. Authorities both in China and in Saudi Arabia, for instance, routinely raid the services of Christian "house churches"—unregistered churches that typically meet in someone's private home—usually tossing the pastors into jail (before deporting them if they're foreign nationals) and subjecting the congregation to various sanctions and forms of harassment.

9. *Violence against individuals.* Violence directed at individual believers can be delivered either through the power of the state—arrest, isolation, torture of both the physical and the psychological sort, execution, and so on—or through social actors, such as the radical Boko Haram movement in Nigeria. This is the most common form of the global war on Christians, as well as the most lethal.

10. *Community oppression.* This refers to violence directed at an entire community, such as the assault on Our Lady of Salvation Syrian Catholic cathedral in Baghdad, Iraq, on October 31, 2010, which left fifty-eight people dead. Violence at the community level can be carried out either by the state or by social forces, the latter sometimes with the connivance of the state.

THE MOST PERSECUTED GROUP

Two of the world's leading demographers of religion, David B. Barrett and Todd Johnson, have performed an exhaustive statistical analysis of Christian martyrdom, reaching the conclusion that there have been seventy million martyrs since the time of Christ. Of that total, fully half, or forty-five million, went to their deaths in the twentieth century, most of them falling victim to either Communism or National Socialism. More Christians were killed because of their faith in the twentieth century than in all previous centuries combined.

This boom in religious violence is still very much a growth industry. Christians today are, by some order of magnitude, the most persecuted religious body on the planet, suffering not just martyrdom but all the forms of intimidation and oppression mentioned above in record numbers. That's not a hunch, or a theory, or an anecdotal impression, but an undisputed empirical fact of life. Confirmation comes from multiple sources, all respected observers of either the human rights scene or the global religious landscape.

Christians Are the Target of 80 Percent of All Discrimination

The Internationale Gesellschaft für Menschenrechte (International Society for Human Rights) is a Frankfurt, Germany-based nongovernmental organization (NGO) founded in 1972 to track human rights violations in the Soviet Union. Today the organization has approximately thirty thousand members in thirty-eight countries and has expanded its brief to cover other sorts of human rights issues. In 2011, for instance, the society issued a report documenting how German technology was being used by authoritarian regimes in various parts of the world to monitor and harass their dissidents, including in cyberspace. Notably, this is a secular NGO, not a confessional outfit operated by a Christian denomination or a consortium of churches.

In September 2009, the chairman of the International Society for Human Rights, Martin Lessenthin, estimated that 80 percent of all acts of religious discrimination in the world today are directed against Christians, citing the results of a survey carried out among staff and members of his organization, and saying those findings dovetail with conclusions reached by his colleagues at other human rights observatories. Lessenthin emphasized that the raw numbers of Christians experiencing discrimination are higher in part simply because Christianity is the largest religious body on earth, with 2.2 billion adherents, and even where Christians are most taking it on the chin, such as China, followers of other religious traditions also are suffering—members of Falun Gong, for instance, and Muslim Uyghurs. Nonetheless, Lessenthin predicted that as several worrying trends continue to unfold, such as the press in many Muslim societies for the application of shariah law, the number of Christians suffering some form of discrimination is likely to continue to grow.

Discrimination Occurs in 139 Countries

The Pew Forum on Religion and Public Life is a widely respected secular think tank in Washington, D.C., not sponsored by any church or confessional organization. In September 2012, the Pew Forum issued a report documenting what it described as a "rising tide of restrictions on religion" around the world. Among other things, the report concluded that Christians faced harassment, either de jure or de facto, in a higher number of countries than the followers of any other religion. At some point between 2006 and 2010, according to the report, Christians had been harassed in a total of 139 nations, which is almost three-quarters of all the countries on earth. Muslims, by way of contrast, faced harassment in 121 nations, Jews in 85, followers of folk religions in 43, Hindus in 30, and Buddhists in 21.

According to the Pew analysis, Christians were harassed by government officials or organizations in 95 countries during the year ending in mid-2010, while they faced discrimination by nonstate actors, either groups or individuals, in 77 nations. Muslims were also more likely to be harassed by governments than by social actors, but Jews were more likely to face social discrimination (64 nations) than state-sponsored harassment (only 21 nations.) In terms of trends over time, the Pew analysis found a slight increase in the number of nations where Christians suffered social harassment (from 74 in 2007 and 70 in 2009 to 77 in 2010), and a more sizable increase in countries where Christians faced government harassment (from 79 in 2007 and 71 in 2009 to 95 in 2010—that 24-nation jump from 2009 to 2010 represents a fairly impressive 33 percent growth).

Overall, the Pew Forum report found that restrictions on religious freedom are rising in each of the five major regions of the world, and that 37 percent of nations have "high" or "very high" restrictions, up from 31 percent a year ago, representing a six-point spike in just twelve months. Three-quarters of the world's population, meaning 5.25 billion people, live in countries with significant restrictions on religious freedom. That too was up from the previous year, when 70 percent of the world's population lived in such societies. Notably, the Pew findings suggest that restrictions are rising not only in countries that already had a tough climate for religious freedom, such as North Korea or Saudi Arabia, but also in places that previously had a pretty good track record, such as Switzerland and the United States. America was one of sixteen nations whose scores for government and social restrictions jumped by more than a point.

Sixteen for Sixteen

The United States Commission on International Religious Freedom is a bipartisan federal commission set up in 1998 under President Bill Clinton, a Democrat. Its mandate is to track violations of religious freedom around the world, and each year it publishes a report on May 1 flagging a list of countries of special concern. In its 2012 document, the commission identified sixteen such nations, which it charged with "heinous and systematic" offenses, including torture, imprisonment, and murder. While all sorts of different religious communities suffered in these countries, according to the report, only one group found itself under attack in all sixteen of the world's worst offenders: Christians.

The countries flagged by the commission were Burma, China, North Korea, Egypt, Eritrea, Iran, Iraq, Nigeria, Pakistan, Saudi Arabia, Sudan, Tajikistan, Turkey, Turkmenistan, Uzbekistan, and Vietnam. Aside from imprisonment, arrest, and torture, the report documented multiple other ways in which religious freedom was under assault in these countries, including discriminatory policies in housing and employment, pervasive monitoring and surveillance by security agencies, school textbooks that include crudely bigoted depictions of minority religious groups, and the discriminatory enforcement of "blasphemy laws" to charge members of certain religions with criminal offenses. Overall, the commission's bottom line was that in each of these societies, religious minorities are "to a chilling extent, in trouble."

Attacks Have Jumped by 309 Percent

The National Consortium for the Study of Terrorism and Responses to Terrorism (known by the acronym START) was established in 2005 by the U.S. Department of Homeland Security and is based at the University of Maryland. Obviously not a religious outfit, it tries to understand the origins of terrorism as well as its social and psychological impact, and among other things the consortium tracks patterns in terrorist violence around the world. In 2011, the consortium concluded that in Africa, Asia, and the Middle East, Christians outpaced all other groups in terms of the frequency with which they faced terrorist attacks.

In 2003, the consortium found, Christians were explicitly attacked by terrorists in Africa, Asia, and the Middle East eleven times, while in 2010 Christians faced forty-five such assaults. As the START analysis points out, that represents a fairly stunning growth rate of 309 percent in just seven years. Those findings have since made the rounds: they were cited by the Vatican's representative to the United Nations in Geneva, Archbishop Silvano Tomasi, during a high-profile speech in March 2012, and were also made into a chart and published alongside Ayaan Hirsi Ali's provocative February 13, 2012, cover story for *Newsweek* magazine, titled "The Rise of Christophobia."

One Hundred Million Have Been Persecuted

The evangelical advocacy and relief organization Open Doors has been providing aid to persecuted Christians since it was founded in 1955 by a Dutch Protestant named Andrew van der Bijl, better known as "Brother Andrew," who began by smuggling Bibles into the Soviet sphere. Today it's become one of the world's best-known organizations tracking anti-Christian persecution, issuing each January an annual watch list of the top fifty countries in which Christians are at risk. The Open Doors estimate, based on decades of tracking the realities of persecution in some of the darkest corners of the earth, is that roughly one hundred million Christians today suffer interrogation, arrest, and even death for their faith, with the bulk located in Asia and the Middle East. The overall total makes Christians the most at-risk group for violations of religious freedom.

Hundreds of Millions More Suffer Discrimination

Though this estimate is now sixteen years old, conservative religious freedom advocate Paul Marshall concluded in 1997 that there were two hundred million Christians at that time suffering "massacre, rape, torture, slavery, beatings, mutilations, and imprisonment," as well as "pervasive patterns of extortion, harassment, family division, and crippling discrimination in employment and education." Marshall further concluded that there were four hundred million Christians in the world subject to "discrimination and legal impediments," the vast majority of whom, he wrote, live in non-Western cultures. Though developments since that estimate was crafted would doubtless change the raw numbers, such as a rough end to the slaughter in Sudan and the declaration of independence of strongly Christian South Sudan in 2011, the overall picture presented by Marshall remains more or less the same.

The Situation in the Middle East

In January 2013, Fr. John E. Kozar, a longtime expert on the Middle East and the secretary of the Catholic Near East Welfare Association, estimated that there are twenty-five million Christians in the Middle East alone "exposed to situations of poverty, and victims of war and persecution." Kozar was speaking at a meeting of the Equestrian Order of the Holy Sepulcher of Jerusalem, a Catholic organization devoted to supporting the church in the Holy Land. The Christian churches of the Middle East, Kozar said, face "great suffering because they find themselves in areas of deep tensions, of war and injustice, linked to a series of enormous problems. Many of these Christians have fled in recent years because of persecution, instability and political developments."

Kozar attributed the lukewarm Western response to the risks facing Christianity in the Middle East in part to ignorance. "Most people in the West are familiar only with the Latin Church," he said during a press conference in Rome on January 18, 2013. "They know little of the rich patrimony of the traditions of the Oriental churches. In many cases, these are the most historic and antique churches that make up the Catholic church."

WHY CHRISTIANS?

German scholar Thomas Schirrmacher is a spokesperson on human rights for the World Evangelical Alliance, as well as chair of its theological commission. He's also a longtime observer of religious freedom issues and contributed a chapter to the 2012 book *Sorrow and Blood: Christian Mission in Contexts of Suffering, Persecution, and Martyrdom* (William Carey Library Publishers). In a 2008 essay, Schirrmacher attempted to explain why Christians are the most persecuted religious group on the planet. He began by conceding that motives for victimizing someone are almost always complex, and often hostility against Christians is mixed in with racial, ethnic, cultural, linguistic, economic, and other factors.

That said, these are the ten forces that, according to Schirrmacher, explain why Christians today suffer persecution at such an astronomical rate.

1. Christianity is the largest religion in the world, with 2.2 billion adherents, so its raw numbers on any index are likely to be larger than everyone else's.

2. Christianity is experiencing phenomenal growth around the world, especially its evangelical and Pentecostal forms, and much of that growth is coming in dangerous neighborhoods such as parts of the Asian subcontinent, sub-Saharan Africa, and even regions of the Middle East. In some places, this growth threatens the traditionally dominant position of other religious groups or the state.

3. Aside from Islam, most non-Christian religions are not experiencing the same missionary success or don't have the same missionary ambitions. As a result, they don't tend to attract the same attention and resentment.

4. Some countries with a colonial past are now looking to regain their identity by recovering their precolonial, and hence

pre-Christian, religious traditions. In so doing, these nations often rely upon legal means to suppress "foreign" religions, especially those identified with Western colonialism—that is, Christianity.

5. Many countries are witnessing an increasingly strong connection between nationalism and religion, with Christianity, or some forms of Christianity, perceived as a threat to national identity. India and the rise of Hindu nationalism is a classic example.

6. Christians in some places have become outspoken advocates for human rights and democracy, which means they're seen as threats to authoritarian regimes—especially since Christians often can plug into international networks of support that most other religious groups don't have.

7. Christians in other places challenge well-established connections between religion and industry, or even between religion and crime. As Schirrmacher puts it, "Drug bosses in Latin America behind the killing of Catholic priests or Baptist pastors surely do not do this because they are furthering the cause of an opposing religion. Rather, it is because the church leaders are often the only ones who stand up for native farmers or indigenous groups, or standing in the way of Mafia bosses."

8. In some cases, the basic peacefulness of Christian churches—the fact that most forms of Christianity explicitly reject violence committed in the name of religion—may actually invite persecution, because the perpetrators do not have to worry about retribution.

9. Christians at the local level are often identified with the West, even though that's almost always inaccurate. For one thing, Christianity's origins are in the Middle East, not the West. For another, today's Christians in Africa, Asia, or Latin America are almost entirely indigenous and autonomous, meaning they have no real ties to Christianity in the global North.

10. The international dimension of Christianity is seen as a

danger in totalitarian states where allegiance to the nation is the highest value. China, for instance, is willing to tolerate churches that are subservient to state regulatory agencies, but not a form of Christianity that posits a higher authority than the nation.

The sixth point, about the role of Christians in pro-democracy and human rights movements, has become an established observation of political science. Samuel Huntington coined the term "third-wave democracy" to describe a broad trend toward democratic government that began to crest in the 1970s, and he attributed the movement in large part to the influence of Catholic social teaching and activism in the Philippines and parts of Latin America. Today, some of the most engaged activists in the Middle East pressing for democratic and pluralistic states are drawn from the region's Christian minority. In most African societies, the most outspoken critics of corruption and partisans of good government are drawn from the ranks of Christian activists. Naturally, those positions arouse opposition, and sometimes they lead to violent blowback.

GEOGRAPHY OF THE GLOBAL WAR

Given the Pew Forum's estimate that Christians have suffered harassment in a robust total of 139 nations, the truth is that the global war on Christians can break out anywhere. In 2011, a devout Mexican Catholic named Maria Elizabeth Macías Castro, who had been a leader in the Scalabrinian lay movement and a popular blogger, was beheaded for exposing the activities of a drug cartel. She ran the risk of death on the basis of her deeply held religious conviction that God was calling her to make a stand. Mexico is the second-largest Catholic country on earth, yet believers are every bit as vulnerable there, when they challenge entrenched interests or take stands in defense of the Gospel, as they might be in North Korea or Sudan.

Nevertheless, there are some corners of the globe where simply being a Christian on a routine level—owning a Bible, going to church, having religious symbols in one's home, and so on—is, all by itself, dangerous. Based on the Open Doors World Watch List in January 2013, the following are considered to be the most hazardous nations on earth in which to be a Christian.

1. North Korea
2. Afghanistan
3. Saudi Arabia
4. Somalia
5. Iran
6. Maldives
7. Uzbekistan
8. Yemen
9. Iraq
10. Pakistan
11. Eritrea
12. Laos
13. Nigeria
14. Mauritania
15. Egypt
16. Sudan
17. Bhutan
18. Turkmenistan
19. Vietnam
20. Chechnya
21. China
22. Qatar
23. Algeria
24. Comoros
25. Azerbaijan

Eighteen of the twenty-five countries are majority-Muslim nations, and the threats facing Christian minorities in those societies are real. As chapter 9 will show, however, it would be a mistake to conclude that Islam and its discontents are the lone force in the global war on Christians. Six of these nations are in Asia, seven in Africa, eight in the Middle East (broadly defined to include places such as Egypt and Algeria), and four in Eastern Europe and the former Soviet sphere. That distribution underscores that this is truly a global war, and these locales are far from the only places where it's being waged.

THE BODY COUNT

Perhaps the single most bone-chilling statistic regarding the global war on Christians is its estimated annual body count. Depending on which Internet site or advocacy group one trips across, different numbers may be floated, generally hovering in the range of 100,000 to 150,000 new Christian martyrs every year. These estimates are sometimes attributed to various sources, such as the Catholic relief agency Aid to the Church in Need or Italian sociologist of religion Massimo Introvigne, and they're also frequently cited without any attribution.

Drilling down, however, all these estimates have a common origin: the annual "Status of Global Mission" report produced by the Center for the Study of Global Christianity at Gordon-Conwell Theological Seminary, a Protestant institution with its main campus in Hamilton, Massachusetts. Each January, the center publishes in the *International Bulletin for Missionary Research* an estimate of the number of Christian martyrs per year over the previous decade. From there the figure usually takes on a life of its own, cited all over the place, and often without explaining where it comes from or how it's calculated.

The disparity in the numbers given, from as low as 100,000 Christians killed each year to as high as 150,000 or more, is explained by the fact that what the center provides is not actually a total of Christian martyrs in any given year, but rather an average number per year for the last full decade (e.g., 2000–2009, 2001–2010, etc.). The center's estimate in 2010 was 178,000 Christian casualties per year for the previous decade, while by 2011 it had dropped to 100,000—not because the killing of Christians trended downward in 2011, but rather because the peak periods of violence in both Sudan and Rwanda in the late 1990s were no longer part of the decade under consideration. (Notably, the violence in Rwanda was largely Christian on Christian, a point to which we'll return.)

In January 2013, the center published its estimate for the period 2003–2013, which once again came out at 100,000. According to Johnson, the major contributor to that average was the carnage in the Democratic Republic of Congo. All told, the thrust of the latest estimate is that in the period 2003–2013, there were 1 million new Christian martyrs and a grand total of 1.3 million martyrs in the opening years of the twenty-first century.

To be clear, no one actually moves around the world every year and conducts a physical body count of Christians who have been killed. Among other things, doing so would be essentially impossible in some of the most high-intensity killing fields, such as North Korea or Somalia, where no external human rights monitoring is permitted. As a result, the estimate put out by the center at Gordon-Conwell is based on statistical modeling and the analysis of various global conflicts to determine what share of their casualties may have been Christian—and to what extent those people died as a result of being Christian, as opposed to other ethnic, political, geographical, and sociocultural factors.

Todd Johnson, one of the researchers at Gordon-Conwell, says they use the following standard to establish when a particular death merits being included: "Believers in Christ who have lost their lives prematurely, in a situation of witness, and as a result of human hostility." That excludes deaths due to forces such as accidents, crashes, earthquakes, and other acts of God, but it doesn't require that someone be killed explicitly on the basis of hatred for some specific aspect of the Christian faith at the moment of death. Instead, as Johnson puts it, the standard is a death that's the result of "an entire way of life, whether or not the believer is actively proclaiming his or her faith at the time of death."

Though most people credit the "Status of Global Mission" report for providing a statistical baseline for contemporary realities, some experts believe it has an overly elastic conception of "martyrdom," which, in turn, results in an inflated body count. Critics charge that the estimates are being generated at least as much for political reasons, meaning to shock world opinion and to motivate people to action, as in the interests of strict accuracy. Even some scholars highly sympathetic to the case for defending Christians question the estimate of 100,000 deaths every year, on the basis that in the long run it won't serve the cause to float claims that seem shaky or overheated. During a September 2012 conference on anti-Christian persecution at the University of Notre Dame, Allen Hertzke of the University of Oklahoma called for a more rigorous examination of purported Christian casualties, based on "intercoder reliability" and "decision rules in advance," so that the final tally would be more empirically unassailable.

Hertzke says that field advocates have stressed the need for resources to help local people document the persecution.

"Because the term 'martyr' is, at least in part, theological, an organization like the Pew Forum would never touch it," Hertzke told me in early January 2013. "But I continue to believe that a major foundation-supported effort is necessary to assemble a high-level research team that would refine definitions, criteria, and decision rules, and then would support local groups and advocates across the globe to provide documentation."

In August 2011, Schmirrmacher of the World Evangelical Alliance argued that for a death to count as part of a war on Christians, the test should be the following: "Christians who are killed, and who would not have been killed had they not been Christians." He granted that it's an expansive standard, making no distinction, for instance, among children, lapsed believers, and people who just happened to be in the wrong place at the wrong time. Even by that fairly elastic rule of thumb, however, Schirrmacher was dubious that one could arrive at a count of 100,000 martyrs every year. He considered a tally of perhaps 20 such Christian fatalities per day, which adds up to 7,300 a year, more realistic. In any event, Schirrmacher concludes: "We are far from having a reliable report of the number of martyrs annually."

To be clear, Schirrmacher did not mean to suggest that anti-Christian persecution isn't that big a deal. On the contrary, he believes that at least 90 percent of all people killed on the basis of their religious beliefs in the world today are Christians, and that doing something about it deserves to be the premier human rights and religious freedom campaign of the early twenty-first century.

For his part, Johnson concedes that it sometimes takes years to sort out how many deaths in a given conflict situation can actually be considered instances of martyrdom or of anti-Christian oppression. Still, he argues that the broad view reflected in the center's estimate is consistent with recent trends in Christian theology in thinking about martyrdom, toward emphasizing not only deaths as a result of hatred of the faith but also those that result from hatred of the virtues and works of charity inspired by the Christian faith. Scores of men, women, and children who went to their deaths in Congo, Johnson argues, may not have been killed explicitly for their religious faith, but they neverthe-less died in "a situation of witness." By that test, Johnson believes the estimate of 100,000 martyrs per year in the last decade is justified.

THE FUTURE OF MARTYRDOM

Looking forward, Johnson believes that five factors may determine whether the annual body count of Christian victims goes up or down in the near-term future.

1. *Belief versus unbelief.* The world is less religious in 2010 than it was in 1910, Johnson says, but it's more religious in 2010, following the collapse of Communism and the global rise of both Christianity and Islam, than it was in 1970. This could augur increasing collisions between believers and nonbeliev-ers, which might put more people at risk of becoming the victims of oppression and violence.

2. *Migration.* There are 214 million people on the move in the early twenty-first century, 80 percent of whom are Christians and Muslims. How these migrants and refugees interact—whether they perceive a sense of common cause based on the similarity of their circumstances, or whether they fracture along confessional lines—will have enormous consequences.

3. *Fragmentation of Christianity.* Not only are the long-standing denominational divisions in the Christian family proving surprisingly enduring, but in the early twenty-first century the most rapidly growing forms of Christianity are fissipa-rous and essentially independent versions of Pentecostal and

evangelical spirituality. It's not yet clear whether these new centrifugal energies in Christian life will make it more difficult for Christians to mount a unified effort on behalf of their persecuted coreligionists.

4. *Uncertainty of the relationship between Christians and Muslims.* Johnson notes that in the year 1800, just one-third of the world's population was made up of Muslims and Christians. Today it's one-half, and the projection is that by 2100, two-thirds of humanity will be composed of Christians and Muslims. By definition, how this relationship sorts itself out will have massive implications across the board, including for Christian martyrdom.

5. *Relationship gap.* According to Johnson's data, 86 percent of all Muslims, Buddhists, and Hindus in the world do not personally know a Christian. That lack of familiarity, he said, creates a relationship gap that makes it easier to fall back on negative stereotypes in assessing the Christian "other." The extent to which Christians around the world are able to forge personal friendships with members of other religious traditions may, therefore, also have some impact on whether anti-Christian persecution trends up or down.

However these five factors unfold, Johnson said, there's no reason to believe that a famous insight from a Jesuit priest named Rutilio Grande, who was assassinated in El Salvador in 1977 for his advocacy on behalf of the poor, won't continue to apply.

"It's a dangerous thing," Grande said, "to be a Christian in this world."

2

AFRICA

As Rwandan troops poured into the eastern part of what was then Zaire in the fall of 1996, Roman Catholic archbishop Christophe Munzihirwa issued a final, fervent plea for help. "We hope that God will not abandon us and that from some part of the world will rise for us a small flare of hope," he said in an October 28 radio message, broadcast to anyone, anywhere, who might have been listening.

As it turned out, no one was.

The civil and military leaders of the region, representing the last shreds of the crumbling autocratic regime of Mobutu Sese Seko, had fled weeks before, knowing that Mobutu was doomed and the Rwandans were unstoppable. Those Rwandan soldiers were largely members of the country's Tutsi minority, who blamed Mobutu for harboring Hutu militants, and as their armed bands moved east they were killing anyone who got in their way.

Munzihirwa, bishop of the Diocese of Bukavu in eastern Zaire since 1993, had long criticized all parties to the region's violence. His last hope, shared with the handful of missionaries and diocesan personnel who stayed behind with him to shelter the refugees, was for rapid intervention by the international community.

It was not to be. Less than twenty-four hours later, in the afternoon of October 29, death came for the archbishop.

Munzihirwa, a Jesuit who called himself a "sentinel of the people," was shot and killed by a group of Rwandan soldiers, his body left to decay in the deserted streets. It took more than a day before a small group of Saverian seminarians was able to recover the body and prepare it for burial. Munzihirwa had surrendered himself in the hope that two companions might be able to get away in his car; they too, however, had been caught and executed.

Born in Lukambo in 1926, Munzihirwa was ordained a priest in 1958 and joined the Jesuits in 1963. He studied social science and economics in Belgium but returned to his country in 1969 to become the formation director for Jesuits in Kinshasa province. His prophetic streak surfaced in 1971, when Seko's CIA-backed government responded to a youth protest movement by forcibly enrolling university-age people, including seminarians, in the military. Munzihirwa insisted on being enlisted alongside his novices, much to the embarrassment of the regime.

Munzihirwa became the Jesuit provincial superior for Central Africa in 1980. In 1986 he was made a coadjutor bishop in Kasongo, and in 1993 he became archbishop of Bukavu. He quickly earned fame for his refusal to accept patronage from Mobutu. That occasionally created headaches, as in 1995 when a Catholic missionary and members of an international solidarity movement were arrested in Kasongo. When Munzihirwa demanded their release, military officials taunted him for not being a "friend" of Mobutu. Munzihirwa solved the problem by saying that until the group was let go, he would sleep outside their cell. They were freed that evening.

Munzihirwa was unafraid to denounce what he considered military misconduct. During a mid-1990s Mass to install a new bishop in Kasongo, in a time in which Mobutu had ordered the city sacked because he believed it was harboring dissenters, Munzihirwa said: "Here before me I see these soldiers. I see the colonel. Stop troubling the people! I ask you, I order you: Stop it!"

The commander wanted Munzihirwa taken into custody, and he

replied: "I am ready. Arrest me." Other bishops present, however, intervened and prevented the arrest.

After the genocide began in Rwanda in 1994, Munzihirwa became an outspoken protector of the Hutu refugees who flooded his diocese. His martyrdom was not unexpected, at least not to him. Munzihirwa had written in an Easter meditation: "Despite anguish and suffering, the Christian who is persecuted for the cause of justice finds spiritual peace in total and profound assent to God, in accord with a vocation that can lead even to death."

At his November 29 funeral, someone recalled Munzihirwa's favorite saying: "There are things that can be seen only with eyes that have cried."

AFRICA: OVERVIEW

According to the Center for the Study of Global Christianity, the current statistical center of gravity for the world's Christian population is somewhere near Timbuktu, in the African nation of Mali. That location reflects the massive shift to the south in the global distribution of Christians during the twentieth century, and Africa is the clear pacesetter. In 1919, just 9 percent of Africa was Christian. As of early 2013 it was 63 percent, for a grand total of 380 million Christians on the continent. Those folks are scattered across a stunning 552,000 congregations and 11,500 denominations, most of which are indigenous to Africa and essentially unknown in the West. Most of this growth has occurred since the last quarter of the twentieth century and is the result of indigenous African evangelizing efforts rather than Western missionaries.

Just as Africa leads the pack in terms of Christian growth, it has also become one of the primary fronts in the global war on Christians. Western missionaries have found themselves in danger as shifting waves of African conflicts have lapped up against their schools, clinics, and convents. Native African Christians, without the same degree of backing from global religious communities and Western governments, generally are even more vulnerable to instability and violence whenever it erupts. In the two Congo wars from 1996 to 2007, an estimated

5.4 million people lost their lives, and inevitably, killing on such a vast scale creates scores of new martyrs such as Munzihirwa—people of faith who lose their lives because they refuse to turn away from danger.

In some cases, this new host of victims might not pass the most rigorous traditional Christian tests of what being a "martyr" signifies. For the most part, the faithful are not being asked to sacrifice to idols or sign off on a king's illicit divorce. In a large number of instances, they're just in the wrong place at the wrong time.

"I was once confronted by a guy in Liberia who wanted to steal our car," said Catholic bishop Kiernan O'Reilly of Ireland, a veteran missionary in Africa, in 2001. "I could have been stubborn and gotten myself killed. I suppose the folks back home in Ireland would have said, 'How wonderful! He died for the faith.' The truth is I would have been dead because I didn't want to give up the keys. This guy couldn't have cared less if I was an Anglican priest, or a Buddhist monk, or whatever."

Yet when pressed about what he was doing there in the first place, O'Reilly acknowledged that his choice to remain in a place where such confrontations are the stuff of daily life—and similar choices made by missionaries and native believers all across Africa—was a matter of faith. While the motives of his attacker may not have been religious, O'Reilly's reasons for exposing himself to that risk certainly were.

"Presence is the key point," O'Reilly said. "It's a gospel principle."

The following are among the zones in today's Africa where presence alone sometimes exposes people to the hazards of the global war on Christians.

DEMOCRATIC REPUBLIC OF CONGO

Encyclopedia entries and geopolitical commentary often talk as if the great Congo wars of the late twentieth and early twenty-first centuries had a formal ending, but the truth is that there never was any armistice or surrender. Today the fighting continues, periodically waxing and waning. In the fall of 2012, a new round of violence in eastern Congo produced another wave of refugees, with at least a hundred thousand people heading for the hills and forests, leaving behind refugee camps and host communities where they had previously sought safety. Most observers report that the violence is being carried out by numerous militia groups, both large and small, which operate with almost total impunity and are responsible for murder and systematic rape, generally as part of campaigns to loot the area's rich natural resources.

Whenever the violence spikes in Congo, so too do attacks on Christian targets, generally because Christian churches and their personnel are often the lone social institution that doesn't pull out. The Democratic Republic of Congo (DRC) is roughly 95 percent Christian, with the Catholic Church the largest single denomination, claiming thirty-five million of the country's seventy-one million people. Among other things, that means Christians are often the only ones in a position to give witness to the atrocities being perpetrated. That makes them equal-opportunity targets, at risk from government-sponsored armies, private militias, terrorist outfits, and criminal gangs, not to mention armed bands working on behalf of corporations and entrepreneurs with a financial interest in the region. The lion's share of the world's deposits of cobalt, for instance, an essential mineral in the manufacture of cell phone batteries, is found in eastern Congo.

During Christmastime 2008, as many as four hundred people lost their lives during attacks on villages in eastern Congo near the border with both Sudan and Uganda. The killings were carried out by the Lord's Resistance Army, the notorious Ugandan rebel movement, which made the decision to wait until Christmas Eve and Christmas Day to attack civilian populations in an effort to pound them into submission. The rebels targeted people at their churches, Protestant and Catholic alike, surrounding them and killing them by crushing their skulls with axes, machetes, and large wooden bats. The victims were hacked into pieces, decapitated, or burned alive in their homes, and several people reportedly had their lips cut off as a "warning not to speak ill of the rebels." A pair of three-year-old girls reportedly suffered serious neck injuries when rebels tried to twist their heads off. More than 20,000 people were reported to have been displaced by the attacks, with as many as 225 people, including 160 children, abducted and more than 80 women raped.

In December 2012, the evangelical group Barnabas Aid reported that Christians in Congo, Protestant and Catholic alike, are being targeted by the rebel movement M23, which is trying to overthrow Congolese leader Joseph Kabila. The report indicates that when M23 moves into an area, it typically subjects women to systematic rape, with one estimate holding that forty-eight Congolese women are raped every hour. Men are often killed or conscripted, as are the children of the region.

In some cases, the killing of Congolese Christians has seemed deliberately calculated to intimidate and muzzle any criticism of the militias. In December 2009, for instance, Fr. Daniel Cizimya Nakamaga, age fifty-one, was shot in the head at point-blank range when gunmen broke into his presbytery during the night in Kabare, outside the eastern Congolese city of Bukavu. Less than forty-eight hours later, attackers struck at a nearby Trappist monastery, murdering Sr. Denise Kahambu. The nun had been the monastery's guest mistress, and when she opened the door to these strangers, they chased her down a hallway, shot her to death, and left her in a pool of her own blood. Because they didn't steal anything and left the other sisters alone, the impression was that it had been an "intimidation" killing.

Many observers drew the same conclusion from the November 2010 murder of Fr. Christian Mbusa Bakulene, the pastor of St. John the Baptist Church in Kanyabayonga in the province of North Kivu. The priest and a parish worker were returning to the church when two men in military uniforms stopped them and asked, "Which one of you is the priest?" They shot Bakulene while leaving his companion unharmed, prompting most observers to conclude that the aim was to frighten priests into either silence or flight.

The scale of the slaughter in Congo is so vast that it's easy for the individual stories of its victims to get lost. It's from those stories, however, that the overall narrative of the global war on Christians emerges.

Victims include Pastor Mbumba Tusevo, assassinated in December 2011 amid a wave of postelection violence. He was a member of the Kimbanguist Church, an African-originated denomination founded by Simon Kimbangu in 1921 and composed of over ten million people who believe Kimbangu was a prophet. Mbumba was blamed by one political faction for harboring members of a rival group in his church and slain in a reprisal killing. There's also Sr. Jeanne Yemgane, a native Congolese physician and former superior of the St. Augustine congregation of Dungu, who was shot to death by rebel forces in 2011. There's Marie-Thérèse Nlandu, a Christian human rights activist and attorney who survived 160 days of torture and abuse in a Congolese prison in 2007 for defending the country's most vulnerable and abused people. While behind bars, Nlandu lost almost sixty pounds, suffered a heart attack, got a chest infection, and was ravaged by malaria. She was denied medical attention because guards had heard her singing and leading the other women in songs of praise, and said, "If you are well enough to sing, you don't need a doctor." Also among the victims is a Catholic nun named Sr. Liliane Mapalayi, who was stabbed to death on February 2, 2012, in Kananga, in western Kasai. Mapalayi worked in a high school run by her congregation and was attacked while in her office at school. On hearing the screams, the director of the school and a nun rushed into the office of Sr. Liliane, who died in their arms with a kitchen knife stabbed in her heart. Sources say that militants and criminal bands had threatened the school before, but Mapalayi refused to leave.

What's remarkable about Congolese Christians such as Mbumba, Yemgane, Nlandu, and Mapalayi is not the suffering they experienced, which is commonplace, but rather that we know their names. Most of Congo's victims die in anonymity or are recorded merely as one among hundreds of people killed in a given incident. Stitching together the personal stories we do have, however, is enough to make clear that the Democratic Republic of Congo is among the most intense front lines in the global war on Christians.

IVORY COAST

A nation of roughly twenty million, Ivory Coast in some ways is Africa in microcosm. Both Christianity and Islam have a strong footprint, with each representing a bit less than 40 percent of the population. Islam tends to be strongest in the north, Christianity in the south. An additional 25 percent of the country practices some form of indigenous religion. As is often the case in Africa, religion and politics tend to be easily blurred, so it's little surprise that a bloody 2011 civil war opened a new front in the global war on Christians.

In 2010, the country's incumbent president, Laurent Gbagbo, a Roman Catholic, declared victory in a disputed election against Alassane Ouattara, a Muslim. Most observers felt that Ouattara had actually won, and after months of unsuccessful negotiations, violence broke out. Fairly quickly, Ouattara's forces took control of most of the country, with Gbagbo and his loyalists concentrated in and around the country's commercial capital, Abidjan. International monitors reported serious human rights violations by both sides as the conflict escalated. Given the fact that Gbagbo is a Christian and Ouattara a Muslim, it was inevitable that many people in Ivory Coast would frame the conflict in religious terms, and Christians in particular often paid a steep price for popular resentments against Gbagbo and his regime.

During the peak of the fighting in mid-2011, the evangelical organization Open Doors reported that several churches had been burned to the ground by rebel forces and their sympathizers, with the pastors often harassed and beaten up and members of the congregation driven into refugee status. Likewise, the Catholic bishops' conference of Ivory Coast reported that forty churches and religious structures had been attacked and damaged during roughly the same period, including the bishop's house in the Diocese of San Pedro.

Few assaults were more gruesome than what happened in the central Ivory Coast village of Binkro on May 29, 2011. Rebel forces loyal to Ouattara, the Muslim challenger, entered the largely Christian village that day in search of weapons they believed had been secreted by Gbagbo loyalists. The rebels seized two peasant brothers who lived in Binkro and demanded they reveal the secret caches of weapons. When the brothers, both evangelical Christians, professed not to know anything about any weapons, the rebels gave them both severe beatings, and then decided to subject them to "the example of Christ" by crucifying them, nailing their hands and feet to cross-shaped planks with steel spikes. One of the brothers, Raphael Aka Kouame, died of his injuries, while the other, Privat Kouassi Kacou, survived the ordeal. In the end, the rebels did not find any weapons in Binkro, only a store of medical supplies, which they looted before abandoning the village.

All told, the estimate is that at least a thousand people died in deliberate assaults on Christian targets during the spiral of violence in Ivory Coast, with thousands more injured and rendered at least temporarily homeless. At one stage in April 2011, a Catholic mission run by the Salesian order in Duékoué, Ivory Coast, was struggling to accommodate more than thirty thousand people who had been displaced by the fighting, the vast majority of whom were local Christians who had been targeted by the rebel forces.

To be sure, Christians weren't the only ones to suffer. Yet most observers believe that the Christians were the only religious community to be specifically targeted during the insurrection, and many Christians in the country report a deep sense of insecurity about what the future may hold. That's perhaps especially the case in western Ivory Coast, where reports suggest that the traditionally Christian Guéré ethnic group is exposed to systematic harassment and persecution by criminal gangs, mercenaries, and undisciplined elements of the former rebel militias.

NIGERIA

Nigeria, the "Lion of Africa," is not only Africa's most populous nation but also the world's largest mixed Muslim/Christian society, with roughly eighty-five million Christians and the same number of Muslims. Imam Sani Isah of the Waff Road Mosque in Kaduna, the capital of the Muslim-dominated north in Nigeria, says that his country is "Saudi Arabia and the Vatican rolled into one." While there are many impressive examples of Muslim/Christian harmony, there are also multiple fronts in the global war on Christians. That's especially the case in the twelve northern states, which are majority-Muslim and where beginning in 1999 efforts to impose Islamic shariah law led to periodic outbreaks of violence that left thousands dead.

One of the nastiest by-products of those conflicts was the rise of what's now known as Boko Haram, a jihadist militant organization founded by Mohammed Yusuf in 2001. It's emerged as something of a "brand" for a loosely affiliated network of terrorist groups apparently bent on fomenting chaos, and in particular on attacking Christian targets such as churches, schools, social service centers, and Christian-owned businesses. In July 2009, around the town of Maiduguri in the northwest, Boko Haram attacked police stations, prisons, schools, and homes, burning pretty much everything in its path. Scores of Christians were abducted and forced, under threat of death, to renounce their faith. The riots continued for five days before police were able to stop them, and an estimated seven hundred people died in the chaos. As it turns out, that outburst was a preview of things to come, with Boko Haram now held responsible for at least three thousand deaths. The overall effect is to create a climate of terror.

In September 2011, extremists attacked a Christian village called Vwang in the predominantly Muslim north, leaving fourteen people dead from gunshot and machete wounds, including five children under the age of fourteen and a pregnant woman. In November, a series of Christian-owned businesses went up in flames across the northern state of Kaduna, with at least sixteen people killed, including members of local Catholic, Anglican, and Living Faith denominations. (Police originally tried to blame faulty commercial gas canisters for the blasts, though an investigation showed that none of the shops actually sold gas.) In early December 2011, a Christian settlement of 425 people, who reportedly worshipped at a local denomination called Evangelical Church Winning All, was attacked, resulting in the shooting death of one unarmed woman and injuries to several people. Just days later, yet another Christian community in the north was attacked, this time leaving five dead and six injured—including a three-year-old girl who had to be hospitalized for the injuries she received from a machete.

Perhaps the signature atrocity carried out by Boko Haram to date was a coordinated series of assaults on Christmas Day 2011, which left at least fifty people dead and hundreds injured. Most of the carnage came in Madalla, a satellite town on the outskirts of the national capital, Abuja, where a bomb went off outside St. Theresa's Catholic Church that killed forty-four and left an additional eighty people injured, including both Muslim bystanders and Catholics exiting the

Christmas Mass, which had just ended when the blast occurred. An additional explosion hit the Mountain of Fire and Miracles Church, an independent Pentecostal community in the northern city of Jos, resulting in at least one death when a policeman confronted the attackers and was shot to death. The situation would have been far worse had an additional two bombs not been discovered and disarmed before they could detonate.

Compounding the sense of tragedy, the vast majority of the dead at St. Theresa's were very young. They included four-year-old Emmanuel Dilke, who was killed alongside his father, his brother, and his sister. Also left dead was Chiemerie Nwachukwu, an eight-month-old baby killed alongside his mother. Their bishop, Martin Igwe Uzoukwu of Minna, later said: "Our people have suffered so much, but our response should not be one of anger. It should be one seeking peace and justice."

Both the body count and the symbolism of striking on Christmas Day galvanized attention around the world to the threat posed by Boko Haram, including its specific menace to Christians. The Simon Wiesenthal Center, among the world's leading Jewish human rights organizations, urged the United States and the European Union to do more to protect embattled Christians around the globe: "As Jews, we recognize all too well when those who want to beat down a group add humiliation and contempt to their murderous violence," it said in a December 28 statement. "Picking Christmas Day to murder women and children on the steps of their church was calculated to intimidate all other Nigerian Christians."

In the weeks that followed, rarely a week went by without Christians being targeted at Sunday services. Those responsible also targeted markets, banks, police, government buildings, and schools, but churches usually bore the brunt of the violence. At least nine people died and nineteen more were injured in a shooting at an evangelical church in Gombe, a city in the northeast, in early January 2012. Pastor Johnson Jauro told reporters that gunmen burst into his church, killing people including his wife. He said: "The attackers started shooting sporadically. They shot through the window of the church. Many members who attended the church service were also injured." At the same time, up to twenty people died in Mubi in Adamawa state when gunmen opened fire in a town hall where Christian traders were meeting and holding prayers.

Any hope that a state of emergency declared by President Goodluck Jonathan in January 2012 would restore law and order was left in tatters, as Boko Haram stepped up its campaign of terror. In March 2012, a Boko Haram spokesman declared that a campaign was under way to eradicate Christians from parts of the north. The spokesman declared: "We will create so much effort to have an Islamic state that Christians will not be able to stay." Although a deadline for all Christians to evacuate the north established by Boko Haram came and went, thousands of Christians did in fact flee, while others who remain report a constant state of anxiety about when the next Boko Haram attack might come, and whether the police and security forces will be able to protect them when it does. Some observers warned that Nigeria is at risk of a slow-motion form of "religious cleansing" if the state isn't able to bring Boko Haram under control.

In mid-April 2012, up to forty people died and at least thirty were injured after a suicide bomber detonated explosives in a busy part of the city of Kaduna after being refused entry to a nearby church where an Easter service was taking place. Security guards at the gates of the First Evangelical Church, on Gwari Road, denied access to a man driving a car packed with improvised explosives. The man then drove off and detonated the bomb at a nearby hotel, close to two other evangelical churches, where windows were smashed by the explosion. An estimated sixty buildings within a 1,600-foot radius of the blast were severely damaged, and eight cars and several commercial vehicles were burned. At the same time, at least twenty-one people were killed and more than twenty others injured in an attack on Christian students attending a Sunday service at Bayero University in Kano state.

In December 2012, Boko Haram launched another round of assaults on Christian churches timed to coincide with the Christmas holidays, prompting Paul Marshall to observe, "In some parts of the world, Christmas is prime time for attacks on Christians." In Nigeria's Borno state, a heavily Muslim region in the country's northeast, six Christians were killed in an attack on the First Baptist Church in Maiduguri. In Yobe state, suspected Boko Haram gunmen entered an evangelical church in Pieri, near Postiskum, and shot six Christians to death, including the church's pastor, before setting the church and twenty nearby Christian homes ablaze. Earlier in the month, in Kupwal village in the Chibok local government area, suspected Boko Haram militants slit the throats of at least ten people in Christian homes. For the record, 2012 marked the third consecutive year that Boko Haram launched a bloody wave of attacks on Christians during the Christmas season.

During previous cycles of ethnic and religious tension in Nigeria, Christians haven't been simply victims. They've also been perpetrators, organizing themselves into militias in order to defend churches, schools, and homes, but at times taking the fight to their perceived enemies. At the village level, Muslim homes and businesses have sometimes been attacked by Christians, usually ostensibly in reprisal for some previous assault on Christian targets. Though most Christian leaders in Nigeria have called on Christians not to strike back at Muslims in frustration over the Boko Haram assaults, many observers worry that a broader cycle of religious violence could grip the country.

SUDAN

An estimated 2.5 million people died in Sudan's 1983–2005 civil war, fought between the central Sudanese government under President Omar al-Bashir, committed to strong Islamist rule, and a separatist movement in the largely Christian and animist south. The country's Christian minority had long taken the brunt of the conflict, trapped between al-Bashir's Islamist forces and the Ugandan-based Lord's Resistance Army. The LRA is generally considered not merely an armed faction but almost a new religious movement blending African mysticism and indigenous tribal beliefs with elements borrowed from Christianity and Islam. Although it claims Christian inspiration, it's committed some of the most appalling acts of cruelty in the global war on Christians. In the late summer of 2009, for instance, visitors to Ezo in the extreme south of Sudan stumbled across the decaying remains of several Sudanese Christians who had been nailed to pieces of wood and left to die in what appeared to be a mock crucifixion scene. Locals reported that these murdered Christians had been abducted by the Lord's Resistance Army during a church service.

After a referendum led to the creation of the world's newest nation, South Sudan, in July 2011, prospects for the Christians who stayed behind in the north (usually because that is where their homes and jobs are located) seemed grim. Labeled "cockroaches" by loyalists to the regime, the Christians in Sudan, mostly concentrated in and around the capital city, Khartoum, are subject to a wide variety of both de jure and de facto discrimination, as well as persistent physical danger.

In June 2010, for instance, a Christian teenager named Hilba Abdelfadil Anglo was kidnapped by a gang of extremists and subjected to a series of physical and sexual assaults, including gang rape. Her attackers called her family "infidels" for being Christians, insisting that she needed to become a Muslim. The fifteen-year-old eventually played along and convinced her abductors to relax, allowing her to escape. When she went to the police to report her abduction and abuse, she was told she couldn't file a report unless she formally converted to Islam. Christian women in Sudan report constant harassment, charged with offenses such as "inappropriate clothing" because they don't wear a head covering, and often receive floggings by religious police. Christians are also subject to arbitrary arrest and indefinite detention for any behavior perceived by the regime's personnel as "evangelizing."

It's not just the ordinary Christian believer at risk. In October 2010, Cardinal Zubeir Wako, Sudan's most senior Catholic prelate, was the object of an assassination attempt while celebrating Mass at a church-owned playground in Khartoum. A Muslim man had smuggled a dagger into the Mass and tried to attack the cardinal, but one of the other clergy managed to wrest the knife away and restrain the attacker. Though Wako was unharmed, the fact that he could be targeted during a Mass allegedly under the protection of security services symbolized the vulnerability many Christians in the north feel.

In June 2011, a pro–al-Bashir militia attacked and looted at least three Christian churches in South Kordofan state, which straddles the border between north and south. The assaults prompted many of the Christians in the area to flee, and as they did so the militia randomly detained and killed some of them. One such victim was a Catholic seminarian named Nimeri Philip Kalo; an eyewitness later reported that gunmen forced them to watch as they shot Kalo, warning that if anyone cried they would be gunned down too. The same day gunmen also killed Adeeb Gismalla Aksam, a young Christian bus driver whose father was an elder in an evangelical church. Most observers believed the overall thrust of the violence was to intimidate Christians in the border zone and drive them into South Sudan. Those impressions seemed reinforced a month later, in July 2011, after a rash of attacks on both churches and Christian homes and businesses across South Kordofan.

In January 2012, Sudan's Ministry of Guidance and Religious Endowments publicly threatened to arrest Christian pastors who were caught praying in public, saying that doing so would be interpreted as an illicit act of "proselytism." At least one church leader, James Kat of the Church of Sudan, was beaten while in police custody. At the same time, another Christian pastor, Gabro Haile Selassie, was arrested after refusing to vacate his home in Khartoum, which government officials had decided to transfer to a Muslim businessman. In early February, two Catholic priests were abducted from a church compound outside Khartoum, apparently by a regime-affiliated armed group. The abductors demanded a ransom, but when they didn't get it they eventually let the priests go with minor injuries.

Throughout February and March 2012, attacks in South Kordofan and the Nuba mountains by the Sudanese army and allied militia groups appeared designed to suppress the Christian presence. Heiban Bible College in South Kordofan, for instance, was bombed on the first day it opened for classes. An aid worker put things this way: "The Islamic north sees Nuba Christians as infidels who need to be Islamized through *jihad* . . . This war is ethnic cleansing—a religious as well as a political war." Reports state that between June 2011 and March 2012, twenty Christians were killed and four churches destroyed.

In April 2012, an Islamist mob set fire to a Catholic church in

Khartoum frequented by Christians with roots in what is now South Sudan. Witnesses and several newspapers said a mob of several hundred torched the church, shouting insults at "southerners." Firefighters were unable to put out the blaze. The newspaper *Al-Sahafah* reported that the church was part of a complex that also included a school and dormitories. Many observers believe it may only be a question of time before the "religious cleansing" campaign succeeds and Sudan is essentially empty of Christians.

Profile: Bishop Umar Mulinde

A well-known preacher and revivalist in the Pentecostal Gospel Life Church International, Bishop Umar Mulinde is, quite literally, a compelling public face of the global war on Christians. He bears the scars on the right side of his face, where Muslim extremists threw acid at him on Christmas Eve 2011, leaving him blind in one eye and threatening his sight in the other. A convert from Islam to Christianity in 1993, he had been among the most outspoken critics in Uganda of a parliamentary proposal to give legal recognition to shariah courts, and it's widely believed the attack on Mulinde was in reprisal for that position.

The assault came just outside the Ugandan church where Mulinde serves as pastor, which is on the outskirts of Kampala, the national capital. Ironically, a police substation is immediately across the street. As Mulinde describes it, he was on his way back to the church site for a party with the congregation and hundreds of new converts to Christianity when two assailants approached him and threw an unidentified acid directly at his face.

"As I was opening the door of my car, one poured a bucket of acid on my head," Mulinde recalls. "I had fire from the head up to the toes, to the legs down."

As he doubled over, the second attacker poured acid over his back. The acid that missed Mulinde burned a hole through the metal of his car, demonstrating its potency. Mulinde's last recollection of the assault was hearing the words "Allahu akbar" ("God is great," the signature Muslim chant) echoed three times. Mulinde, who had just turned forty, traveled to Israel throughout 2012 to receive treatment, undergoing multiple surgeries and skin grafts at Sheba Hospital's burn unit in Tel Aviv. He says he's forgiven the people who put him in this situation.

"The people who did this to me, they thought they are serving God. But I feel sorry for them and I forgive them, because they didn't know what they were doing," he said during an August 2012 interview.

Married with six young children, Mulinde was a lightning rod for radical Islamic outrage, and not merely because of his opposition to the Muslim Personal Law Bill. He's considered Uganda's most infamous Muslim apostate, the grandson of an imam and a former sheikh himself who converted to Christianity on Easter Sunday in 1993. He says that when he announced his conversion, his own family drove him away with clubs and machetes, and his brothers refuse to greet him in the street. In 1995 and again in 1998, Mulinde said, extremists attacked prayer meetings he was leading in various parts of Uganda, accusing him of apostasy, and in 2000 during another such assault he was actually beaten into unconsciousness. In 2001, one Muslim extremist attacked Mulinde with a sword during a revival service.

When he led the push-back against the law recognizing Islamic tribunals throughout 2011, Mulinde said, a fatwa was issued against his life by local Islamic jurists, paving the way for the Christmas Eve assault.

Demographically, Christians make up just over 80 percent of Uganda's population, with Muslims accounting for somewhere between 12 and 15 percent. Over the years, Mulinde has become well known for taking part in debates with local Muslim figures, drawing on his background as a sheikh and his ability to quote the Qur'an to challenge Muslims about their religion. In May 2011, he narrowly escaped a kidnapping attempt when a group of armed men tried to block his car at a location roughly halfway between his home and the church site. They attempted to grab Mulinde, then shot at him as he fled. He reported the incident to local police, but no one was arrested.

Mulinde insists that he's not looking to lead a holy war. He says he continues to support several Muslim families personally and financially, including some who are his own relatives, and is only interested in a "peaceful evangelism campaign" intended to offer the message of

Christ. At the same time, he also insists he will continue to speak out against efforts to impose shariah law on non-Muslims, and to defend the rights and physical safety of former Muslims who have decided to covert to another faith.

As for his wounds, Mulinde said that he's proud "to bear the marks of Jesus" in his own body.

"I am not happy about getting hurt," he said. "But it's a price I'm happy to pay in order to be faithful to what I believe."

3

ASIA

Aasiya Noreen Bibi, better known to the world as "Asia Bibi," is almost certainly the most famous illiterate Punjabi farm worker and mother of five on the planet. She's the classic exception that proves the rule—the rare celebrity victim of the global war on Christians in a universe of folks whose suffering typically unfolds under the cover of neglect.

Forty-three years old at the time of this writing, Bibi first came onto the radar screen back in June 2009, when she was charged with the offense of "blasphemy" under Pakistani law. As she would later describe it, the dispute began when Bibi, a Catholic who regularly attended the Church of St. Teresa in the nearby town of Sheikhupura, was harvesting berries in scorching 100-degree heat to support her family. She became thirsty and drank from a well, thereby defiling the water source in the eyes of some local Muslim women. As things escalated, she and some of the Muslim women began trading barbs about Jesus and Muhammad. Although Bibi insisted she meant no disrespect, the women used her words as a pretext to have her arrested.

Bibi remained in jail while an investigation and trial unfolded, which ended with her being sentenced to death by hanging in November

2010. If the death sentence is carried out, she would become the first woman to be executed under Pakistan's blasphemy law. Illustrating the depth of feeling that blasphemy cases arouse, two prominent Pakistani politicians, one Christian and one Muslim, have already gone to their deaths for supporting Bibi and for opposing the law. To add insult to injury, Bibi was also fined 300,000 Pakistani rupees, the equivalent of about $3,000, a staggering sum by rural standards.

Against all odds, Bibi's fate went viral and has become a cause célèbre in Christian activist circles around the world. Documentaries have been made about Bibi, concerts organized in support of her, websites and Twitter campaigns mobilized, books published, and petitions with hundreds of thousands of signatures delivered to the Pakistani authorities.

Bibi comes from a peasant family in Ittan Wali, a tiny village in Punjab. As of this writing she remains in prison, in a windowless cell, while her appeals to the Lahore high court play out. Bibi is in solitary confinement, able to be seen only by her husband and her lawyer. Her family hopes an international pressure campaign will eventually see her freed, but in the meantime, one mullah in Pakistan has offered a reward of roughly $10,000 to anyone who kills her—enough to purchase a three-room house with all the modern conveniences. The mullah might well find a taker if Bibi doesn't make it out of the country first; according to one survey, at least ten million Pakistanis say they would be willing to kill Bibi with their bare hands, either out of religious conviction, for the money, or both.

"I was a good wife, a good mother and a good Christian," Bibi said. "Now it seems I'm only good to hang."

That comment came in a 2011 book titled *Blasphemy: The True, Heart-Breaking Story of the Woman Sentenced to Death over a Cup of Water*, which was written clandestinely with a French journalist who passed questions to Bibi's husband, Ashiq, and then waited for hours outside the prison gates to collect Bibi's answers, relying on the help of an Urdu-English interpreter.

According to an analysis by the Pew Research Center's Forum on Religion and Public Life, as of 2011 nearly half the countries in the world, 47 percent, have laws or policies that criminalize apostasy, blasphemy, or defamation of religion. Anti-apostasy and anti-blasphemy laws tend to be most common in the Middle East, North Africa, and the Asia-Pacific; in the eyes of critics, such laws usually penalize religious minorities at the expense of the socially dominant tradition. To be sure, Christians are not the only victims. In India, a man who describes himself as a religious skeptic found himself facing blasphemy charges in 2012 because he claimed that a statue of Jesus venerated by Mumbai's Catholic community for its miraculous qualities is a fake. In Greece around the same time, a man was arrested and charged with blasphemy after he posted satirical references to an Orthodox Christian monk on Facebook.

Another Pakistani case from late 2012 illustrates how the application of the blasphemy law is typically a thin disguise for religious prejudice. A fourteen-year-old Christian girl named Rimsha Masih, who comes from an impoverished family of sweepers, was charged with blasphemy after accusations that she had torn pages out of a Muslim textbook used to teach the Qur'an. Relatives and human rights workers claimed that the girl has Down syndrome and should therefore be exempt, and the charges were dismissed in November 2012. In the meantime, her family went into hiding out of fears for their physical safety.

Perhaps the global pressure campaign that has crested around Bibi will succeed and eventually shame the Pakistani authorities into cutting her loose. That would be an important symbolic breakthrough, but it would not mark any definitive armistice or truce in the global war on Christians. The victims of that conflict will continue to suffer the same fate as Asia Bibi, only without her notoriety.

ASIA: OVERVIEW

Although Christianity represents just around 10 percent of Asia's population, that's still an enormous pool of almost four hundred million people. In 2010, for the first time, the estimate is that Christians in Asia actually outnumbered Buddhists, a mind-bending reversal of popular stereotypes about the continent's preferred religion. Christianity is the dominant religion in two Asian societies, the Philippines and East Timor. In two other Asian countries, Vietnam and South Korea, Christianity is probably the largest and best-organized religious option, even though the majority in both countries does not profess a religious affiliation.

Christianity is growing rapidly in many parts of Asia, including Indonesia, South Korea, Malaysia, Cambodia, Vietnam, Laos, Bhutan, Bangladesh, Pakistan, and even Mongolia. Just twenty years ago, there were essentially no Christians in Mongolia, whereas today there are more than five hundred Protestant churches, mostly of the evangelical and Pentecostal sort, and an established Catholic presence. There are now more Pentecostals in Asia, according to scholar Paul Freston, than in North America and Europe. One estimate is that there are forty-seven million Pentecostals in China alone, despite the best efforts of the officially atheistic government to rein in their expansion. The largest single Christian congregation anywhere in the world is thought to be the Yoido Full Gospel Church, a Pentecostal church located on an island within the city limits of Seoul, South Korea. Every Sunday, something like 250,000 worshippers show up for nine services simultaneously translated into sixteen languages.

China is perhaps the most eye-popping instance of Christian expansion. At the time of the Communist takeover in 1949, there were roughly 900,000 Protestants in the country. Today, the Center for the Study of Global Christianity, which issues the much-consulted *World Christian Database*, says there are 111 million Christians in China, roughly 90 percent Protestant. That would make China the third-largest Christian country on earth, following only the United States and Brazil. The center projects that by 2050, there will be 218 million Christians in China, 16 percent of the population, enough to make China the world's second-largest Christian nation. According to the center, there are ten thousand conversions every day.

Not everyone accepts these estimates. In the 2006 update of his book *Jesus in Beijing*, former *Time* Beijing bureau chief David Aikman puts the number of Protestants at 70 million. Richard Madsen, a former Maryknoll missionary and author of *China's Catholics*, puts the number still lower, at 40 million. That's in line with the *CIA World*

Factbook. Even those conservative estimates, however, would mean that Protestantism in China experienced roughly 4,300 percent growth over the last half century, most of it since the Cultural Revolution in the late 1960s and 1970s. Notably, Protestantism took off after the expulsion of foreign missionaries, so most of this expansion has been home-grown.

Despite Asia's popular reputation for religious tolerance, it's also home to a wide range of fronts in the global war on Christians. It includes old-style police states, such as North Korea and Myanmar; one-party states struggling to foster economic liberalization without political reform, such as China and Vietnam; societies where Muslims or Christians form a majority vis-à-vis the other group, such as Indonesia and the Philippines; and cultures where other religious traditions define national identity, sometimes to the detriment of religious minorities, such as India and Sri Lanka. In each case, there are impressive stories of interreligious harmony and solidarity, but there are also horrific examples of the war on Christians.

One can make a compelling case that as Asia goes, so goes the overall fate of religious freedom and the global war on Christians in the early twenty-first century. Asia contains both of the world's major emerging new superpowers, China and India, and both have troubled track records. The ability of religious freedom advocates to intercede with these great Asian societies to promote greater protection for minorities, in particular for their beleaguered Christian populations, will have much to say about whether Christianity continues to generate new martyrs at the same rapid clip.

CHINA

Legally speaking, China recognizes only four forms of religious expression: Buddhism, Taoism, Protestantism, and Catholicism. Adherents of those religions are tolerated, but they are expected to worship under the auspices of a state-approved and state-controlled body that manages the affairs of those denominations. For Catholics, this means the Catholic Patriotic Association; for Protestants, it is the Three-Self Patriotic Movement. Many Chinese Christians, however, refuse to submit to these official structures, ending up in what are often regarded as "underground" or "catacomb" churches. In truth, the boundaries between the recognized structures and the unofficial church communities are sometimes fuzzy; an estimated 90 percent of Catholics belonging to the state-sponsored bodies are thought to be loyal to Rome, just as roughly 90 percent of the "official" clergy are actually in good standing with the pope. In recent years, the Vatican has promoted a policy of détente with the Chinese government and of healing the gap between the official and underground churches. Most experts say that policy has, so far, met with mixed results.

Unregistered communities and missionaries face severe difficulties. According to the NGO ChinaAid, in 2011 more than a thousand Protestants in the country were detained for unauthorized religious activity and given prison sentences in excess of a year. Government officials have also stepped up their demands for "theological reconstruction," meaning purging Christianity of elements that the ruling Communist Party regards as incompatible with its methods and priorities.

The Kafkaesque situation facing Christians is illustrated by the Shouwang house church in Beijing, a massive Protestant house church subject to constant surveillance and harassment by government officials. Founded in 1993, the church was estimated to have a following in excess of a thousand people in June 2011. Its members are drawn from the middle and upper classes of Chinese society, including doctors, lawyers, students, and even, ironically enough, government officials. In early 2011, the leaders of the Shouwang congregation made arrangements to purchase a building for a worship venue but were denied permission by the government. As a result, they began to meet outdoors, facing weekly arrests for "unauthorized" worship services. Congregants are typically forced to sign loyalty statements before being released, and at least six church leaders have been placed under house arrest. Experts say the idea isn't so much to drive the Shouwang church out of business as it is to cow the congregation into submission.

The same pattern of harassment is directed at the smaller but politically influential Catholic presence. As of this writing, there were four Catholic bishops in detention in China, while ten more were under surveillance by security agents and not able to travel or to speak freely. These include Bishop James Su Zhimin, seventy-seven, the ordinary of Baoding, who disappeared in 1996, and Bishop Cosmas Shi Enxiang, eighty-eight, of Yixian, who disappeared in 2001. Given the periods of imprisonment and house arrest they suffered prior to their disappearances—and presuming they are still alive—Bishop Zhimin will have spent forty years in captivity, and Bishop Enxiang will have endured at least fifty-one years.

The story of Catholic auxiliary bishop Thaddeus Ma Daqin of Shanghai illustrates the dynamics. Daqin was ordained as a new bishop in July 2012, with the consent of both the government and the Vatican. Government officials, however, insisted that an illegitimate bishop, meaning one not recognized by the Vatican, take part in the ceremony in order to underscore the requirement of deference to the state. When the time came for the illegitimate bishop to lay hands on Ma, Ma got up and embraced him, thereby preventing the bishop not recognized by Rome from taking part in the sacramental rite. At the end of the ceremony, Ma publicly announced that he wanted to be the bishop of all, including those Chinese Catholics fiercely loyal to Rome. As a result, Ma said, he would not join the Patriotic Association. It was the first time in memory, and perhaps ever, that a bishop of the "open" church had made such an audacious statement at his ordination. Government authorities at the ceremony were reportedly stunned, interpreting his words as a direct challenge to their sixty-four-year-old system of control of the church.

Ma was swiftly placed under house arrest in the Shanghai seminary, which has been closed down by the government and now functions as a kind of prison. The few local Catholics who have been able to visit him report that Ma has lost weight and is very pale. According to Fr. Gianni Criveller, an Italian who is a leading Catholic expert on China, his contacts in the country are "very concerned" about his fate.

Since his arrest, Ma's only way of communicating with the outside world has been through his blog. In November 2012, he published an entry called "The Faith of a Child." In it, he revealed that his father did not want him to become a priest, because, he wrote, "his father, his younger brother and he himself were all jailed because of their Catholic faith," and "he did not wish to see his beloved son suffering the same hardship."

But when Ma insisted on entering the seminary, his father said: "If you are determined to go, do not come back and do not give up when you are halfway through." Ma wrote, "I did not hesitate to answer, 'Of course!'"

Though Ma's situation is dramatic, Criveller said Chinese bureaucrats have learned over the years that whenever possible, it's smart to avoid creating new martyrs. Before they harass or arrest members of the clergy, he said, they first try to buy them off.

"They offer entertainment, travel, even access to a political career," Criveller said in September 2012. "Those who go along are rewarded with substantial payoffs."

Sometimes, he said, the carrot that is dangled for cooperation with the state, and thus defiance of Rome, is badly needed financial support for the construction of church buildings. In that situation, he said, "it's easy to give in for the 'good of church.'"

When those carrots don't work, Chinese authorities have repeatedly shown that they're willing to wield the stick. According to reports, at least twenty "underground" Catholic priests have been tortured to make them join the Patriotic Association over the past two decades. One of those priests, Fr. Peter Zhang Guangjun, was physically and verbally abused and denied sleep for five consecutive days.

The same pattern goes for Protestant leaders. In May 2011, Yang Caizhen, one of ten house church Christians sentenced to jail and a labor camp in Shanxi province, was set free on medical parole after she nearly died in detention. She had been transferred in February from a prison hospital to a local hospital with a high fever. A chest X-ray and blood test results revealed she was in poor health, with liver inflammation. The church leaders were arrested for organizing a prayer rally in September 2009, one day after four hundred police officers and others raided the unregistered church's site, seriously wounding thirty Christians and destroying church buildings. This was not an isolated incident. In March 2012, an unauthorized Protestant church was demolished by local authorities in Jiangsu province. Two church members were beaten in the process, and one of them had her back broken in the assault.

In early 2012, officials confirmed for the first time in twenty months that the Christian lawyer and human rights activist Gao Zhisheng was in prison; prior to that, officials had steadfastly denied any knowledge of his whereabouts. Arrested in February 2009, Gao had essentially vanished into thin air, part of a series of detentions he'd experienced since a 2006 conviction on the charge of subversion. In early January 2012, Gao's brother received a brief letter indicating that he was being held in a prison in the remote western province of Xinjiang, with no further details.

In February 2011, more than a hundred riot police officers, in tandem with some local hoodlums, raided a house where at least twenty Christians were meeting in Hubei province. Officers destroyed video cameras, audio recorders, mobile phones, and other equipment capable of capturing the raid. Officers smashed the door open and broke into the house without presenting any legal documents. They then used tear gas on the group before beating them and taking them to the local police station. Authorities later justified the crackdown by claiming that the Christians had established "a site for religious activities without approval."

In 2011, the Chinese writer, artist, and dissident Liao Yiwu published a gripping book called *God Is Red: The Secret Story of How Christianity Survived and Flourished in Communist China*, describing his journeys among China's largely underground Christian communities. Now living in exile in Berlin, Yiwu is a nonbeliever, but one who came to admire the tenacity of Chinese Christians in keeping their faith alive in the teeth of often violent pressure. Making his way among Christian villages in Yunnan province, Yiwu noted that the soil seemed red, and wrote that perhaps it's because "over many years it has been soaked with blood."

Yiwu was especially captivated by a feisty Catholic nun named Zhang Yinxian, who was 101 years old at the time they met, partially deaf and blind, and missing virtually all of her teeth. Her spirit, however, was undimmed. She recounted to Yiwu in vivid detail how during the Cultural Revolution, she and other Catholics were forced to publicly confess to the most absurd crimes—murdering orphans, for instance, or sheltering priests who were secretly vampires. For thirty-one years, authorities refused to allow her to live in her convent or perform religious activities, forcing her to work as a farmer in a collective. Today, she said, things have improved, but fear remains pervasive.

Yiwu asked Yinxian whether, in keeping with the precepts of Christianity, she was prepared to forgive her Communist oppressors.

"No, certainly not!" she fired back. "They still occupy our church property. I refuse to die . . . I will wait until they return everything back to the church!"

INDIA

The emergence of India as a primary battleground in the global war on Christians is especially tragic, given India's great national aspirations to both democracy and religious tolerance. Although Christians are a small minority in India, just 2.3 percent of the population, they enjoy an outsize degree of visibility and respect, in part because they operate many of the country's best-regarded schools, hospitals, and social service centers. When the iconic Catholic figure Mother Teresa died in 1997, she was awarded a full state funeral. The gun carriage that bore her body was the same as that used to carry India's founding father, Mohandas K. Gandhi, and Jawaharlal Nehru, the country's first prime minister, to their cremations.

Yet India is also home to a powerful revivalist current in Hinduism, which in some cases shades off into a virulent form of radical nationalism hostile to religious minorities, especially Islam and Christianity. Some of the most violent outbreaks of anti-Christian animus anywhere on the planet over the last decade have come in India, and acts of violence against churches and worshippers have become so frequent as to pass without fanfare. In 2011, for instance, at least three Christian leaders were killed, and none achieved anything like the notoriety that surrounds Asia Bibi. They were activist Rabindra Parichha, who bled to death in the town of Bhanjanagar after his throat was slit; pastor Saul Pradhan, who froze to death after being dumped outside by unknown assailants; and pastor Michael Digal, whose badly beaten and decomposing body was found near the village of Mdikia in the northeastern district of Kandhamal. Originally all these deaths were attributed to random violence or accidents, but most Christians in the country are skeptical. Digal, for instance, had testified against Hindu radicals in court proceedings about the anti-Christian pogroms in Orissa in 2008, and many observers believe his murder was payback.

According to reports from monitoring bodies, anti-Christian violence has become especially common in the states of Gujarat, Maharashtra, Uttar Pradesh, Madhya Pradesh, and New Delhi in north-central and northwestern India. One survey conducted by an Indian monitoring body reported that in the thirty-two years from 1964 to 1996, only 38 incidents of violence against Christians were recorded, meaning 1.18 attacks per year. By the year 2000, that total had jumped to 116 attacks per year, and it rose to 170 in the year 2011.

The Evangelical Fellowship of India issues an annual "Persecution Watch Yearly Report," cataloguing anti-Christian violence and intimidation. It focuses primarily on evangelicals and Pentecostals, and is thus not necessarily a comprehensive overview of the situation for all Christians. For 2012, the group recorded 131 acts of violence—one attack every 2.7 days. Incidents included intimidation, harassment, false accusation, arrests and detention, churches being vandalized and assaulted, and direct physical attacks on individual believers. The report notes that many acts of violence and intimidation go unreported, so 131 is probably not a complete total. It also asserts that in cases when local police step in, charges often are filed not against those who instigated the violence but rather against the Christians for allegedly engaging in proselytism.

Observers link this trend to the rise of Hindu nationalist organizations such as the Vishva Hindu Parishad (VHP), the Bajirang Dal, and the Rashtriya Swayamsevak Sangh (RSS) and their related political affiliates, especially the Bharatiya Janata Party (BJP), which have engaged in aggressive propaganda campaigns faulting Christians for their alleged "forced conversion" of Hindus and for being agents of the West hostile to Indian national interests. Suspicion of political cover for the violence isn't just a conspiracy theory. In 2011, an independent inquiry led by a judge found that anti-Christian assaults in Karnataka state had been planned and backed by the state's highest authorities, including the chief minister and the police.

In other parts of India, especially the disputed province of Kashmir, Christians face instability and occasional violence from Muslims. In late December 2011, for instance, an Anglican pastor named Rev. Khander Mani Khanna was arrested for having baptized seven young Muslims, an act that had touched off ferocious backlash among local Muslim leaders. The pastor spent weeks in prison on the charge of "forcible conversion" before being released on bail, his health badly compromised by untreated diabetes.

The first tremor of a looming anti-Christian earthquake came in January 1999, when an Australian Christian missionary named Graham Staines was burned to death along with his two sons, ages seven and nine, while sleeping in their station wagon in the state of Orissa. Staines, who had been responsible for the Evangelical Missionary Society of Mayurbhanj, had been accused by local Hindu radicals of distributing beef and desecrating Hindu deities as part of a "forced conversion" campaign. The killings were dismissed at the time as an isolated act by authorities, some of whom not-so-subtly suggested that Staines had it coming because of his missionary activity. By 2008, however, claims that outbreaks of anti-Christian sentiment are random or not part of a pattern dissolved amid the notorious 2008 anti-Christian pogrom in Orissa that spread to three hundred villages, resulting in almost five thousand burned homes, fifty thousand displaced people, eighteen thousand injuries, and more than one hundred deaths. At the time, Prime Minister Manmohan Singh described the rising tide of anti-Christian violence as a matter of great "national shame."

The following are snapshots of the threats Christians in parts of India face, on what has become virtually a daily basis.

In late December 2011, Hindu extremists burned down a Protestant church in Tamil Nadu state, threatening Pastor K. Solomon. Radicals also destroyed the Christu Sabha Church and beat and stabbed its pastor, Paul Chinnasawamy, who said they threatened to abduct and abuse his four daughters. Around the same time, police in Madhya

Pradesh arrested a group of Christians and charged them with "forc-ible conversions" after Hindu extremists attacked their church and beat Pastor Dilip Wadia and other members of the Light Giving Church.

In Karnataka, Hindu extremists disrupted a service at the Agape Bible Church and attacked pastors Reuben Sathyaraj and Perumal Fernandes. Nearly two hundred radicals assembled outside the church and shouted derogatory slogans before bursting in and hauling out the pastors and other congregants, assaulting them with fists and sticks. The sixty-year-old Sathyaraj was hospitalized for his injuries. Another Christian pastor in Andhra Pradesh was grabbed at a railroad station, put in a car, and driven to a Hindu temple, where radicals burned his Christian literature and subjected him to a beating. Also in Andhra Pradesh, extremists stormed into a Sunday service at the New Fellow-ship Gospel Church and started throwing stones at the pastor, leaving him bleeding heavily and requiring fourteen stitches.

In January 2012, a group of radicals armed with sticks and iron bars assaulted twenty Pentecostal Christians in a home near Bangalore, accusing them of proselytism and forced conversions. Pastor Shantha-kumar Srirangam of the Pentecostal Agape Church lost a finger on his left hand, while one of his female congregants suffered a head injury and permanent loss of nerve function in part of her right hand. That incident came just days after a similar assault on another church, the Blessing Youth Mission Church, in a nearby district. According to re-ports, when Christians attempted to file a complaint with the police, a member of the local Commission for Minorities told them: "If you really knew the teachings of Jesus, Christians shouldn't be complaining."

In June 2012, in a village called Deopani in the state of Assam, Hindu extremists demolished three houses belonging to evangelical Christians named Bhageswarn Rabha, Rana Rabha, and Motiram Rabha, as well as their place of worship. The attackers also looted their grain stores, cattle, and poultry.

In Tamil Nadu in July 2012, Hindu extremists launched a series of attacks on Christian targets that left fifteen people seriously injured and at least one person dead. According to reports, a mob of extremists moved into the area on June 21 and directed local Hindus to boycott Christian businesses and to impede the Christians from gathering for worship. That evening, armed extremists attacked Christian homes with swords and sticks, burning four homes to the ground and forcing the residents to flee. Three days later another round of attacks took place, leaving one Christian man dead and scores more wounded. At the same time, a mob charged into the Bethel Prayer House in Tamil Nadu, destroying furnishings and beating up the church leaders. Both the pastor and assistant pastor were hospitalized. According to reports, the same mob of about 150 extremists forced the local Christians to assemble at a Hindu temple and to worship tribal and Hindu deities. Observers said that despite the obvious persecution, the Christians opted not to make any complaint to the local police for fear of courting even greater hostility.

One month later, in July 2012, another round of anti-Christian attacks broke out in the states of Karnataka and Utter Pradesh. In one incident, a pastor of the Pentecostal Church Zion Prathana Mandira was leading a prayer service in his home when roughly twenty members of a Hindu ultranationalist group burst in, accusing him of proselytizing. Facing threats of a beating, the pastor agreed to discontinue the service. He went to the local police station to file a complaint, but no action was taken. In another episode, local police raided the home of a Pentecostal minister conducting a three-day revival and warned him that he'd be beaten and tossed into prison if he didn't leave the area. The pastor, named Ramgopal, was released only after signing a statement promising not to conduct any more services.

Sajan George, president of the Global Council of Indian Christians, which acts as a clearinghouse and advocacy body for Christians, said at the time, "More and more, Christians do not enjoy the constitutional freedom to profess and practice their religion in their places of worship." George also complained that in regions where the Hindu radicals dominate the local government and police forces, "our appeals for greater security are useless."

In November 2012, Hindu extremists attacked a Christian worship service in Karnataka, reportedly tearing up Bibles in the process and beating a pastor named Koshy. They subjected the congregation to verbal abuse and accused Koshy of proselytism, beating him badly enough that he had to be hospitalized. At the same time, another band of roughly one hundred extremists invaded a series of Christian prayer meetings in the state of Chhattisgarh, herding the Christians into a public square and accusing them of forcible conversion, insulting Hindu deities and disturbing the social peace. Believers were threatened with bodily harm if they continued any Christian activities, while the radicals confiscated their Bibles and tossed them into a nearby river. After the radicals accused three Christians in particular of both forcible conversion and witchcraft, local police arrested them and charged them with offenses under the Indian penal code, though they were later released on bail.

Religious radicals are not the only threat. Sr. Valsa John was hacked to death in November 2011 not by ardent Hindus but by henchmen working for a mining mafia in the Dumka region of Jharkhand state. The fifty-three-year-old Catholic nun was a social justice activist, dedicated to defending members of the tribal underclass displaced from their homelands and subjected to various forms of discrimination by local mining interests. A former high school economics teacher, Sr. John felt drawn to missionary work among India's tribals, in particular insisting on an equitable distribution of revenue. For her trouble, she was attacked and dismembered by thugs working for the mining concerns.

Here's a rundown of incidents contained in the Evangelical Fellowship of India report just for the month of November 2012, some of which were noted above. The report documents nine attacks in thirty days, right in line with the statistical average for the year of roughly one every three days.

- On November 1 in Pitlam, Nizamabad, Hindu extremists accused an evangelical Christian named Elish of forcible conversion while he was distributing Gospel tracts.
- On November 7 in Ujjain, police arrested Pastor R. K. Badodiya after Hindu extremists from the Bajrang Dal shouting anti-Christians slogans barged into a prayer meeting he was leading, beat up the Christians gathered in the church, and accused Badodiya of forcible conversion.
- On November 12, Hindu extremists beat up Pastor Abraham

Koshy from the Indian Pentecostal Church, burned up Bibles in the church, and damaged its door and windows.

- On November 20 in Chippagiri, Yellapura Taluk, extremists utterly demolished the Blessing Youth Mission Church.
- On November 23 in Kammadahalli, Hindu extremists accused Pastor Girish of forcible conversion, disrupted the dedication of a new prayer hall, and forcibly installed a Hindu idol inside the hall.
- On November 25 in Chindwada, extremists beat up Pastors Rajkumar and Nanaswor and accused them of forcible conversion.
- On November 27 in Huzurabad, police arrested an evangelical named Abraham after Hindu extremists shouted accusations of rape while he was distributing Gospel tracts.
- On November 30 in Machewa village, Mahasamund, Hindu extremists attacked four Christians, accusing them of forcible conversion and of arranging intercaste marriage for three newly converted girls from the Sahu community.
- Also on November 30 in Boothpada, Ratlam, extremists assaulted two pastors, Govind Meida and Sharad Pargi, seriously injuring the latter.

On December 30, 2012, extremists disrupted a New Year's Eve program for tribal Christians in the western state of Maharashtra. They beat up the believers, tore Bibles, and broke musical instruments. Thereafter, most of the Christian men fled the area in fear, leaving behind their wives and children. The remaining Christians were harassed—for instance, they were not allowed to fetch water from the public well or gather firewood. A January 13, 2013, service took place without incident under police protection, but the next day extremists beat up three Christian women and a twelve-year-old girl for listening to a gospel song on a mobile phone, saying that "such songs should not be played within our hearing range."

On January 10, 2013, in Chhattisgarh, a mob of about eighty anti-Christian agitators barged into the dedication service of a church called

Inlightening Prayer Tower and started accusing Pastor Ritesh Barsa and other church members of forcible conversion. The next day, extremists broke into the home of a local man who had donated the plot of land for the church and beat his family. Also in Chhattisgarh, government officials demolished one side of the boundary wall of Karkapal Christian Graveyard after Hindu extremists filed a complaint of constructing a boundary wall in an encroached area. Unsatisfied with that solution, a group of about a hundred extremists arrived and demolished the entire wall. They desecrated the old graves, shouted anti-Christian slogans, and hurled verbal abuse.

As of this writing, Christian leaders and other religious freedom advocates were trying to convince the national parliament to adopt the Communal Violence Bill, which would give the federal government the power to intervene directly when interreligious violence erupts, bypassing state authorities. Activists say the bill is required because some local authorities are allied with the Hindu radicals and are therefore disinclined to take aggressive measures to combat violence. To date the bill has been blocked, in part because critics style it as an unconstitutional usurpation of the authority of the states.

INDONESIA

In the world's largest Muslim nation, Protestants represent roughly 7 percent of the population of 242 million and Catholics around 3 percent. Indonesia has long prided itself on a climate of tolerance, and the country's constitution guarantees religious freedom. In some cases, the state backs up those promises. In April 2009, ten jihadist militants in Palembang, Indonesia, were sent to prison for the murder of a Christian teacher. Nevertheless, Indonesian Christians also report increasing harassment and occasional violence. One eruption came in 1999, around the time of East Timor's independence. Tens of thousands of people were driven from their homes, injured, or killed as radical Muslim gunmen targeted Christians who had supported independence.

Anti-Christian hostility has become routine in parts of western New Guinea, Maluku, and Sulawesi, regions where radical Islamic groups such as Jemaah Islamiah and Laskar Jihad have attempted to impose Islamic law. In 2006, three Christian girls were beheaded in Poso in retaliation for previous deaths that had come amid a bout of Muslim/Christian rioting. Less dramatically, many Christian leaders have reported episodes of intimidation. Luspida Simanjuntak, a thirty-eight-year-old Lutheran pastor, told Francesca Paci in 2011 that her small church of fifteen hundred believers had been repeatedly assaulted by Muslim radicals wearing white shirts and sporting Islamic head-dresses. The church was burned to the ground in 2004, she said, then relocated, only to be effectively zoned out of existence. When they were forced to move yet again in 2010, a crowd showed up at the new location brandishing signs that read THE PEOPLE OF THIS AREA REFUSE A CHURCH and shouting "*kuffar* [infidels]." Radicals continued to show up to menace the services, even spitting on Christians as they left, and today's shrunken community worships in a private home.

In December 2011, a Christian church in West Java was ordered to halt its activities by the local mayor on the grounds that it represented an alien presence. Despite an order from the Supreme Court of Indonesia, the local authorities refused to lift the ban on Christian activity. In the run-up to Christmas in 2011, Islamic fundamentalist groups in West Java issued warnings to local Christians that they would be attacked if they persisted in holding holiday services. In particular, they targeted the Catholic parish of St. John the Baptist in Parung, which at the time was attempting to construct a new church building. Members of the Islamist group organized public demonstrations against the church and shouted warnings about violent consequences if the construction should continue, even though the parish had held the necessary permit for six years. In the end, the faithful moved their celebrations to an undisclosed location.

In June 2013, the powerful Indonesian Ulema Council (known by its local acronym MUI) issued a fatwa declaring that Catholic schools in Central Java province, where an estimated 96 percent of the population is Muslim, are *haram*, in this case meaning "forbidden" or "morally unsound." The edict follows efforts both by clerical authorities and the local government in Central Java to compel the schools to teach Islam, given that the majority of students in these schools are Muslims. Although the schools typically score well in assessments of educational quality, and many Muslim parents actually came to their defense, local authorities have periodically threatened to shut them down.

LAOS

A landlocked nation of roughly 6.5 million, Laos remains an officially one-party socialist state in which only three Christian denominations are tolerated: Catholicism, the Laos Evangelical Church, and the Seventh-day Adventists. The activities of any other form of Christianity are considered illegal. Even officially registered churches, however, report routine harassment and persecution. The preferred religion of the state is Theravada Buddhism, and local sources say the government encourages Buddhist monks and village shamans to keep Christians under observation and make reports about their activities. Christian leaders say the faith is growing among poor tribal groups, which has increased the backlash from the state. Anti-Christian repression tends to be especially strong among members of the Katin and Hmong tribes, who are seen as challenging to the regime.

In late 2011, police entered Savannakhet province in force to disrupt Christmas celebrations in a village where some two hundred Christians had gathered for worship, apparently with at least the tacit permission of the local village chief. Eight Christian leaders were arrested and detained, placed in handcuffs and wooden stocks. Human rights groups say that wooden stocks are commonly used in Laotian prisons and are sometimes combined with exposure to red ants as a form of torture. The leaders were later informed they had been charged with violating *hilt*, the traditional spiritual cult of the village believed to be important for safety and prosperity.

Three days later, fifty Christians belonging to four extended families were threatened with eviction from another village in southern Laos if they didn't give up their faith. In yet another village, officials forced a Christian family to renounce their faith in order to secure permission to bury a relative, a woman who died on Christmas Day. (The village is located in a tropical location, where immediate burial is essential because of the heat.)

NORTH KOREA

North Korea is widely regarded as the world's leading persecutor of Christians. Indeed, some observers regard the isolated state as occupying a category all by itself, engaging in systematic barbarity against Christians and other perceived dissidents reminiscent of the world's most appalling human rights violations, such as Auschwitz, Treblinka, and the killing fields of Cambodia.

Open Doors has placed North Korea at the top of its World Watch List of the worst persecutors of Christians for eleven consecutive years. The organization estimates the total number of Christians in North Korea to range from 200,000 to half a million, with at least a quarter of those believers currently behind bars in prison camps.

Defectors say that any form of adherence to the Christian faith, even the mere possessing of a Bible, can be considered a reason for arrest or deportation. They recount atrocities that almost defy the imagination, reports generally confirmed by a few external observers who manage to poke around. In 2005, for instance, a respected human rights investigator interviewed a North Korean army member who described his unit being dispatched to bulldoze a Christian church whose members refused to take part in the cult around the national leader. According to this soldier, the unit rounded up the church's pastor, two assistant pastors, and two elders. The five bound men were placed in front of the bulldozer and given a final opportunity to renounce their Christian faith. When they refused, they were crushed to death in front of other members of the church.

Christian Solidarity Worldwide estimated in July 2013, on the sixtieth anniversary of the end of the Korean War, that at least 200,000 people are detained in camps for political prisoners and enemies of the regime, with a substantial number of those inmates being Christians. According to the report, as many as 70 percent of these prisoners are "severely malnourished," and "torture, rape, and public executions are common."

PAKISTAN

The world's second-largest Muslim nation after Indonesia, Pakistan contains both a massive Sunni majority and a sizable Shi'ite minority. It also has small pockets of both Hindus and Christians, each group representing less than 2 percent of the population of 180 million. With the rise of Islamic radicalism and anti-Western tensions, Pakistan has become one of the primary battle zones in the global war on Christians. Like Asia Bibi and her family, many Pakistani Christians are the descendants of poor Hindu tribals who converted to Christianity to escape the caste system, so they often carry a powerful double social stigma, consigned to menial jobs and denied public services.

A 2009 anti-Christian atrocity in the town of Gojra, in Punjab province, is emblematic of the exposure of the country's Christian population. Seven members of a Christian family, including two children and three women, were burned alive by a frenzied Muslim mob after rumors had circulated that pages from a Qur'an had been burned during a Christian wedding the week before. Clerics in local mosques reportedly laced their sermons that week with anti-Christian rhetoric, inspiring a mob estimated at twenty thousand people to storm Gojra's Christian colony. They met some resistance from the Christians, but eventually they picked a house more or less at random, shot dead a family elder, and then set the home ablaze when the rest of the members of the family barricaded themselves inside. Although a hundred other homes were also torched, there were no other reports of fatalities. An investigation did not result in any prosecutions.

Acts of anti-Christian violence in Pakistan have become depressingly commonplace. Here's an incomplete sampling of events over the last decade:

- In 1998, a Christian man named Ayub Masih was convicted under the country's blasphemy law for allegedly voicing support for author Salman Rushdie, though in court proceedings he insisted the charge had been brought by a Muslim neighbor to force his family off their land and seize control of their property. Masih was eventually released.

- In October 2001, a gunman on a motorcycle opened fire on a Protestant congregation in Punjab, killing eighteen people.
- In August 2002, masked gunmen stormed a Christian missionary school in Islamabad, leaving six people dead and three more injured.
- Also in August 2002, grenades were tossed at a church on the grounds of a Christian hospital in northwest Pakistan, killing three nurses.
- On September 25, 2002, two terrorists entered a Christian "peace and justice" institute in Karachi, where they proceeded to separate the Muslims from the Christians and then murdered seven of the Christians by shooting them in the head. The hands of the victims had been tied behind their backs and their mouths covered with tape.
- On Christmas Day 2002, radicals tossed a hand grenade into a church near Lahore, leaving three young girls dead.
- In November 2005, some three thousand Muslim radicals assaulted Catholic, Salvation Army, and United Presbyterian churches in Sangla Hill, supposedly in response to violation of the blasphemy laws by a young Christian man. Dozens of people were injured.
- In June 2006, a Pakistani Christian stonemason was working near Lahore when he reportedly drank water from a public facility and was assaulted by a group of Muslims who called him a "Christian dog."
- In August 2007, a Christian missionary couple, Rev. Arif and Kathleen Khan, were gunned down by Islamic radicals in Islamabad. Authorities said that Khan had been killed over accusations of sexual abuse lodged by a member of his congregation, but local Christians disputed that account.
- In November 2011, an eighteen-year-old Catholic girl named Amarish Masih was murdered in her small village near Faisalabad, allegedly because she refused the advances of a local Muslim man. No charges were filed, which is not uncommon in Pakistan, where rape victims are sometimes imprisoned

for unlawful sex and released only on the condition that they marry the rapist.

- On December 26, 2011, a young Christian man near Lahore was arrested and imprisoned over the charge of blasphemy, allegedly because he burned pages of the Qur'an to prepare tea. The man said the charge was actually a pretext, arising from a rent dispute with his Muslim landlord.

- Also in late December 2011, a pregnant Christian woman and her husband were arrested by police and charged with theft on the basis of complaints by local Muslims. The couple complained of being beaten while in police custody, and the woman, Salma Emmanuel, thirty, was hospitalized for life-threatening injuries both to herself and to her unborn child. Her husband, a TV repairman, said police told him the beating would stop if he agreed to convert to Islam.

SRI LANKA

An island nation of roughly twenty million people, Sri Lanka is 70 percent Buddhist but it also is home to sizable pockets of Hindus, Muslims, and Christians, with Christians (mostly Roman Catholics) accounting for around 8 percent of the country. A long-running civil war between the majority Sinhalese, who dominate the government, and the Tamil minority is the most chronic source of conflict in the country, but Sri Lanka has also seen a spike in anti-Christian violence in recent years.

Beginning in 2009, the National Christian Evangelical Alliance of Sri Lanka began reporting an uptick in attacks. In July 2009, an Assemblies of God church in the Puttlam district was burned to the ground, almost a year to the day after an earlier act of arson had destroyed the original structure. The pastor of a Foursquare Gospel church and his wife had to barricade themselves inside their home after a mob surrounded the house and shouted that they would not tolerate any further Christian activity in the village. In June 2010, a mob consisting of more than a hundred people, including angry Buddhist monks, surrounded the home of a female Foursquare Gospel pastor and then broke in, shouting insults, destroying furniture, and threatening the pastor's thirteen-year-old daughter if she didn't abandon the area. Later, in the presence of Buddhist monks, she was forced to sign a document promising not to host worship services for anyone not a family member.

In the Kurunegala district, Buddhist radicals wielding swords attacked the Vineyard Community Church in mid-July 2009, leaving several people hospitalized and the structure damaged. Other attacks followed, including one in which the interior of the church was desecrated with human feces. At around the same time, a mob of more than a hundred people, half of whom were estimated to be Buddhist monks, forcibly entered an Assemblies of God church and posted notices on the walls declaring that "any form of Christian worship in this place is completely prohibited." Another Pentecostal pastor was reportedly stopped by a group of men on motorcyles who attacked him with knives while shouting "This is your last day! If we let you live, you will convert the whole town!" The pastor sustained severe cuts to his arms.

As of November 2012, a group of some 212 Tamil Catholic families were still living in a refugee camp after having been driven from their native village in 2007 by incensed mobs, who blamed them not only for supporting the Tamil rebels but also for undercutting the Buddhist identity of the town. The Christian refugees had been living in ramshackle huts in the Marichchikattu jungle, fearing the next strong rain could once again wipe away their flimsy residences.

"If we could go home, we wouldn't have to wait for other people to bring us food and clothing," one of the refugees told a reporter. "We want to earn our living, feed our children, and get back to a normal life. Instead, we are stuck here to suffer."

VIETNAM

Historically Vietnam is an overwhelmingly Buddhist society, though polling suggests that today a strong majority of Vietnamese, some 81 percent, are atheists. Christians make up about 8 percent of the population, divided between some six million Catholics and a million Protestants. Although state law ostensibly recognizes religious freedom, authorities keep religious activities under tight control, often charging

Christian leaders with causing "social disturbances" and "subversion." Public religious activity is subject to surveillance, and religious leaders are routinely detained for interrogations. Members of minorities who are largely Christian, such as the Hmong, are frequent targets for harassment and occasional armed assaults by security forces.

In late December 2011, a campaign of arrests of young Christians broke out in northern Vietnam, apparently as part of a broad government effort to tighten the screws on potential sources of dissent. A young Catholic named Pierre Nguyen Dinh Cuong was abducted on Christmas Eve, one of at least sixteen cases of Christians disappearing during the period. Witnesses later reported that the young man had been taken to the provincial public security headquarters, though officials would not confirm that he was being held nor what charges had been filed against him. Local sources said that many of the kidnapping victims had been active in a local Catholic group that speaks out against violations of human rights and the repression of political dissent in Vietnam. Catholic sources in Vietnam saw the abductions as a clear way of sending a shot across the church's bow, warning believers what would happen if their activism continues to embarrass the regime.

In July 2012, a missionary chapel in Con Cuong, a rural area of the Nghe An province, was shut down by authorities, following raids on local worshippers by armed gangs. Dozens of Catholics were injured during a Mass. According to news reports, local Christians said they were the target of a "religious cleansing" campaign intended to wipe out any trace of the faith in the region. They also complained that local authorities had hired criminal thugs to intimidate and harass believers in the area. On Saturday, July 1, thugs and plainclothes police tried to prevent a priest from entering the chapel to say Mass, beating him when he refused. One of the laity who tried to come to the priest's rescue, Mrs. Maria Thi Than Ngho, suffered a fractured skull in the fracas and was hospitalized in critical condition, while several other parishioners were arrested. The mob also desecrated a statue of the Virgin Mary while shouting abuse at the congregation.

The priest injured during the assault vowed not to back down. "To die on the altar," said Fr. J. B. Nguyen Dinh Thuc, "would be such a blessing to me."

Profile: Shahbaz Bhatti

As a moral and spiritual matter, no one martyr's death surpasses the significance of another's. In terms of shock value, however, the assassination of Pakistani politician and human rights leader Shahbaz Bhatti on March 2, 2011, has an undeniable pride of place. Just forty-two when he was killed, Bhatti had been the lone Catholic in Pakistan's cabinet, serving as minister of minority affairs.

In death as in life, Bhatti stood with followers of other religions committed to defending human rights and the rule of law. Bhatti's assassination came just two months after a Muslim politician, Salmaan Taseer, was killed for opposing the blasphemy law and for supporting Asia Bibi. A bodyguard shot Taseer twenty-six times, and when the assassin was later brought to trial, supporters showered him with rose petals. The judge who sentenced the killer was forced to flee the country for fear of reprisals, and Taseer's own son was kidnapped by militants.

Immediately after Bhatti was killed, there was a short-lived attempt by some investigators to shift blame to "internal Christian squabbles," but most independent observers now agree the killing was carried out by a Pakistani offshoot of the Taliban. One such group took public credit for the murder.

Of Bhatti's Catholic piety, there can be no doubt. In an interview shortly before his death, he said, "I know Jesus Christ who sacrificed his life for others. I understand well the meaning of the cross. I am ready to give my life for my people." There's momentum in the Catholic world to have Bhatti declared a martyr and a saint of the church. On March 31, 2011, the Catholic bishops of Pakistan wrote to Benedict XVI to say they had unanimously approved a petition that Bhatti's name be enrolled "in the martyrology of the universal church."

Bhatti's brother, Paul, was a medical doctor who had been practicing in Italy at the time of the assassination. He has since returned to Pakistan to take up his brother's cabinet post as "minister of national harmony," and his cause of promoting religious tolerance. In an interview in the fall of 2012, Paul recounted cleaning out his brother's spartan apartment shortly after he was killed, where the only three items on a small bedside table were the Bible, a rosary, and a picture of the Virgin Mary.

Paul Bhatti said that he and his brother come from a deeply devout Catholic family in a village where the local church was staffed by Capuchin missionaries. As early as age fourteen, he said, his brother led a protest against a proposal to require Christians in Pakistan to carry special identity cards. Shahbaz led a hunger strike in front of the parliament building, he said, and eventually the proposed law was withdrawn.

"I saw how a strong faith could change things that seemed difficult, if not impossible, to change," Bhatti said.

Over the course of his political career, Paul Bhatti said, his brother was sometimes offered money by Islamist parties and politicians to back down, and was also faced with a growing series of death threats. At one stage, Bhatti said, he tried to talk his brother into living with him in Italy, but he wouldn't bite.

"It wasn't possible to convince him," Bhatti said. "He left his life in the hands of Jesus."

Nor can Shahbaz Bhatti be styled as a parochial patron for Christians alone, because he defended the rights of Hindus, Sikhs, and others, including Muslims. Paul Bhatti said that point was brought home at his brother's funeral: "I saw this sea of people, gripped by uncontrollable emotion," he said. "My brother was a symbol not just for Christians but for other minorities, and even for very many Muslims."

One of his brother's last projects, Bhatti said, was opening a free school in an earthquake-damaged zone of northern Pakistan for children left homeless. The student body of some 250 children, he said, is entirely Muslim, and the school is still open.

To be sure, Bhatti moved in the complex world of politics, and there's legitimate debate about his political line. Some Pakistani Christians felt he had been co-opted by the government and was not aggressive enough in defending their rights. Yet the Catholic Church has always insisted that beatifying someone does not mean endorsing every choice he or she ever made; instead, it means that despite human failures, the light of faith somehow shone through his or her life. If ever there were a case in which the evidence for that conclusion seems like a slam dunk, many observers would say it's Shahbaz Bhatti.

4

LATIN AMERICA

Dayton, Ohio, is a long way from Brazil, but it happens to be the birthplace of the most famous "martyr of the Amazon," a feisty American Catholic nun named Sr. Dorothy Stang. Her story illustrates another face of the global war on Christians. It's one formed not by religious intolerance or a "clash of civilizations" but rather by a more prosaic brutality associated with simple greed, as well as the sometimes lethal risks associated with a courageous Christian stand in defense of justice.

One of nine children in a strong Catholic family in Ohio, Dorothy Stang grew up during the Great Depression, with her blue-collar Catholic faith instilling a ferocious commitment to defending the needy. Early on, she dreamed of being a missionary. She joined the Sisters of Notre Dame de Namur when she was seventeen years old, and in 1966 she was shipped off with four other young nuns to the city of Coroata in Brazil. Her first assignment was to educate local farmers who had no formal schooling. In the early 1970s, the Brazilian government decided to encourage development of the Amazon forest, offering poor farmers 250 acres of land while wealthy ranchers received 3,000 acres. Many farmers from Sr. Dorothy's area moved to take up the offer, and she followed them, helping to build schools and to pioneer sustainable methods of agriculture. She ended up in the town of Anapu, described as the "Wild West" of the Brazilian Amazon.

Stang's biographer, Sr. Roseanne Murphy, set the scene this way: "The area is lawless. Ranchers pay off the police and very often the judges. If the ranchers want more land for cattle, they simply send thugs with guns and say [to the farmers], 'This is our land.'"

Observers say that thugs acting on orders from the ranchers routinely burned the houses and crops of local farmers in order to drive them off, with police and the courts generally doing nothing. Stang emerged as a great advocate for the farmers and local indigenous groups, becoming famous for moving through the free-fire zone clad in a T-shirt, shorts, and a baseball cap. One of her favorite T-shirts bore the slogan *A morte da floresta é o fim da nossa vida*, Portuguese for "The death of the forest is the end of our life." Stang would camp outside police stations and courthouses, demanding that the rights of her people be upheld. At one point, local ranchers reportedly put a $50,000 bounty on her head, and she was well aware of the threats.

"I don't want to flee, nor do I want to abandon the battle of these farmers who live without any protection in the forest," Stang said during the period when death threats were swirling around her. "They have the sacrosanct right to aspire to a better life on land where they can live and work with dignity while respecting the environment."

Among other causes, Stang was vocal about the urgency of preserving the Amazon from creeping deforestation. According to one analysis, more than 20 percent of the rain forest has been cut down since it was opened to development, more than in the previous 350 years since European colonization began. Stang insisted that in the Amazon, environmental conservation and the defense of human rights were inextricably intertwined. In December 2004, she was given the Humanitarian of the Year award by the Brazilian Bar Association.

In February 2005, a powerful local rancher ordered that the houses belonging to twelve stubborn local farmers be burned down near the town of Esperanza (the town's name, ironically enough, means "hope" in Portuguese). Stang organized a meeting of the farmers to encourage them to stay put on their land and to rebuild the bamboo huts they'd been living in which had been knocked down in a previous raid. She also invited a couple of gunmen, trying to persuade them not to engage in further violence. According to their later testimony, Stang walked with them to the meeting, at one point taking a map out of her bag to show them the land that belonged to the farmers. When they asked if she had a gun, she pulled out her Bible and told them it was the only weapon she had.

Stang read to them from the Beatitudes: "Blessed are the peacemakers," she said, "for they shall be called children of God."

At that point, one of the gunmen gave the signal, and they proceeded to shoot Stang six times, leaving her dead on the muddy forest road. At the time of her death, according to a Greenpeace analysis, more than eight hundred poor people, labor leaders, and environmentalists had been murdered in the Amazon, with only nine convictions for those killings. Only ten cases had actually even gone to trial, according to statistics maintained by the Catholic Church in Brazil. Stang was seventy-three at the time of her assassination, having served in Brazil for thirty-nine years.

Stang's brother, David, himself served as a priest and missionary in Africa before returning to the United States. He spoke to his sister by phone the night before her death, from his home in Palmer Lake, Colorado. She told him that the next day she was "going down the road," to confront some ranchers and loggers, adding, "I'm a little concerned." David would later visit Brazil five times to track the progress of the criminal charges against his sister's assassins, saying that each time he did so he felt like he was watching the eternal "dance between good and evil."

Stang's murder turned out to be something of a turning point for the cause of justice in the Amazon, as not only were the two gunmen and an intermediary arrested and convicted, but so too was the landowner, Vitalmiro Bastos Moura—the first time, according to experts, that one of the intellectual authors of a land-related murder had been criminally charged and convicted. Another rancher also suspected of ordering the killing, Regivaldo Pereira Galvão, was also convicted and sentenced to thirty years in prison, though the Brazilian Supreme Court ordered him released in April 2012 on the grounds that his legal appeals had not yet been exhausted.

Stang's story continues to inspire people around the world. In 2008, an American filmmaker named Daniel Junge released a documentary titled *They Killed Sister Dorothy*, with a voice-over by famed actor and political activist Martin Sheen. In 2009 composer Evan Mack produced an opera devoted to Stang's life titled *Angel of the Amazon*. The Dorothy Stang Center for Social Justice and Community Engagement keeps her memory alive at her alma mater, Notre Dame de Namur University in Belmont, California. She's widely considered a saint, even in secular circles that typically take little notice of religious figures. In 2006, for instance, *National Geographic* hailed Stang as a model of "dedication to the ideal of family farmers who extract their sustenance in harmony with the forest."

David, her brother, expressed her legacy this way: "Sometimes we think of nuns as gentle women with habits on, and we say, 'Aren't they nice servants?' She was not that. She wasn't that at all. She chose to be a servant, but she wasn't anybody's slave."

LATIN AMERICA: OVERVIEW

At first blush, Latin America seems an improbable setting for the global war on Christians. It's the most thoroughly Christian corner of the map, home to the two largest Roman Catholic nations on earth, Brazil and Mexico, and more than 40 percent of the world's 1.2 billion Catholics. Latin America also has a burgeoning evangelical and Pentecostal population. Belgian Passionist Fr. Franz Damen, a veteran staffer for the Bolivian bishops, concluded in the 1990s that conversions from Catholicism to Protestantism in Latin America during the twentieth century actually surpassed the Protestant Reformation in Europe in the sixteenth century. A study commissioned in the late 1990s by the Conference of Bishops of Latin America and the Caribbean (CELAM), found that eight thousand Latin Americans were deserting the Catholic Church every day, most ending up in a new Christian church of an evangelical or Pentecostal flavor.

There's such a deep undercurrent of popular religiosity in Latin America that, in most societies, even socialist political movements and criminal gangs feel compelled to drape themselves in religious symbolism in order to enjoy popular legitimacy. It's also the kind of place where Christian leaders often enjoy superstar status, and can parlay that standing into political muscle. Fernando Lugo was a celebrated Catholic bishop and friend of the poor in Paraguay who traded in his miter for the sash of political office, serving as his country's president from 2008 to 2012. (He was defrocked by the Vatican, but that didn't diminish his electoral prospects.) If there's any place on earth where Christians ought to be safe, in other words, one might think Latin America would be it.

Yet the bloody history of Latin America in the twentieth century and the early twenty-first suggests a very different lesson. This is the homeland of the great martyrs of the liberation theology movement of the 1960s, 1970s, and 1980s, such as Archbishop Oscar Romero of El Salvador, shot to death as he celebrated Mass in 1980, as well as the six Jesuits slain at the University of Central America along with their cook and her daughter in 1989, and the four American nuns abducted, raped, and murdered by members of the National Guard in El Salvador in 1980. Latin America is also home to the single most dangerous place on earth to be a church worker, according to official Vatican statistics, which is Colombia. Since 1984, seventy Catholic priests, two bishops, eight nuns, and three seminarians have been slaughtered there, most falling victim to the nation's notorious narcotics cartels. Scores of Pentecostal and evangelical pastors and faithful also have lost their lives.

In general, Latin America does not produce many new Christian martyrs to a "clash of civilizations" with Islam, or who fall victim to angry Hindu or Buddhist radicals. Yet in the early twenty-first century, Latin America has become the premier zone for three other fronts in the global war on Christians:

- Martyrs to social justice, humanitarian concerns, and the basic virtues of the faith. These are Christians killed for standing up to corrupt regimes, to ruthless corporations willing to kill to defend their economic privilege, and to criminal gangs, on the basis of their reading of the Gospel. Poverty has long been a special concern for Latin American Christianity, given that the continent is widely regarded as having the greatest income disparities between rich and poor in the world.

- "Wrong place at the wrong time" martyrs, meaning Christians killed in essentially random circumstances, often as the victims of a robbery gone wrong or simply as innocent bystanders. Their deaths too are part of the global war, because these Christians chose to remain in dangerous or lawless situations in order to express solidarity with the ordinary people left behind. For instance, in February 2011 a prominent Honduran evangelical pastor named Carlos Roberto Marroquín, forty-one, was shot to death by two assailants as he walked his two schnauzers in the Colonia Aurora neighborhood near his house. He was the second pastor to be murdered in 2011, after the January 30 killing of Raymundo Fuentes, forty-three, of the New Jerusalem Temple, slain as he was leaving the evening service with his wife. Two days prior the daughter of an evangelical pastor also had been killed. Observers believe the pastors were not targeted because they were Christian, but were victims of robberies. Their choice to remain accessible in that environment, however, reflected a determination to live the Gospel despite obvious risks.

- Victims of intra-Christian violence, especially tensions between Catholic traditionalists in some parts of Latin America and the continent's rapidly expanding evangelical and Pentecostal footprint. Latin America, in that sense, offers a reminder that the enemy in the global war on Christians isn't always external. Sometimes the threat arises from within the Christian family—the war on Christians, in other words, sometimes is a civil war.

COLOMBIA

Although Colombia is an economically and politically sophisticated society of forty-six million people, large areas of the country are lawless zones controlled by criminal organizations, drug cartels, revolutionaries, and paramilitary groups that often operate like medieval fiefdoms. In many cases these criminal organizations and armed groups are hostile to the presence of Christian missionaries, preachers, pastors, and activists because they're the only respected figures in the area willing to speak out against violations of human rights, abuses of power, and the exploitation of both people and natural resources.

In a 2010 report, the Christian NGO Justapaz, a ministry of the Mennonite Church in Colombia, counted ninety-five death threats or attempted murders against Christians in that year alone, as well as seventy-one forced displacements, seventeen homicides, two disappearances, and multiple cases of beatings, torture, kidnapping, and forced recruitment. According to the report, criminal organizations accounted for 90 percent of this violence. In some parts of rural Colombia, there are fuzzy alliances between tribal groups practicing indigenous pre-Christian forms of religion and various paramilitary factions, especially the principal rebel group, the Revolutionary Armed Forces of Colombia (FARC). Reports suggest that the rebels sometimes enlist these tribal groups in attacking Christian targets and leaders, taking advantage of their resentment of Christian proselytism. Under Colombian law, certain indigenous areas are autonomous and government security forces aren't allowed to enter, which makes them natural havens for both guerrilla groups and criminal outfits. Christian churches are often the lone institutions that operate in these regions not co-opted by the guerrillas and the gangs.

The following incidents reflect the sort of thing that has become routine in various parts of Colombia:

- In February 2011, an evangelical pastor and two of his relatives were killed in the town of Dibulla, located in the country's La Guajira region, by right-wing rebel groups. The murders came in apparent retaliation for the growing number of believers in the region, and to stop the spread of fasting and prayer meetings perceived as a potential focal point for organizing efforts to resist the hold of the rebels.

- In March 2011, Pastor George Ponton of the Evangelical Christian Church of Colombia was poisoned by indigenous leaders in the Cauca department, which is widely considered the epicenter of the country's armed conflict.

- In September 2011, two missionaries working for the World Missionary Movement Church were killed by illegal militias.

- On January 26, 2011, Catholic priests Fr. Rafael Reátiga Rojas and Fr. Richard Armando Piffano Laguado, both pastors of parishes in Bogotá, were shot to death on the southern outskirts of the capital. The assassin had been riding in the same car with the two priests. He shot one in the head and the other in the chest, then escaped with the help of someone waiting to drive him away. Many observers interpreted this as a warning intended to frighten and intimidate priests to refrain from political and human rights activism.

- On February 12, 2011, Fr. Luis Carlos Orozco Cardona, twenty-six at the time, was seriously wounded when he was shot by a young man outside his cathedral, and the priest died the next morning of complications during surgery. The motives for the slaying were unknown.

- On May 12, 2011, Fr. Gustavo García was assassinated by an individual who attacked him to steal his cell phone. The priest was talking on his phone while waiting for a bus so that he could go look after a sick member of his congregation. A bandit attacked him with a knife and left him to die. García had been a university chaplain and a well-known figure in the Catholic Charismatic Renewal.

- In September 2011, Fr. Jose Reinel Restrepo Idárraga was killed in western Colombia while riding his motorcycle from one pastoral assignment to another. The assailants stopped the priest, shot him to death, and stole the motorcycle.

- On September 12, 2011, Fr. Gualberto Oviedo Arrieta, a

Catholic pastor in the Diocese of Apartadó, was found dead in the parish rectory, his body covered with stab wounds and the signs of a beating. Nothing was stolen, and the murder took place just after the conclusion of a "Week of Peace" mobilizing local schools and other institutions to oppose the use of violence.

- On October 16, 2011, Catholic layman Luis Eduardo García was kidnapped by a group of guerrillas and later murdered. He had been working on a project to assist people hit by a wave of cold weather. García was also known for his dedication to local farmers and the victims of natural disasters, often criticizing the indifference of both the government and the rebel groups to the suffering of ordinary people.

- On September 19, 2012, a Protestant pastor named Henry Rodriguez of the United Pentecostal Church was shot to death in Bogotá. According to eyewitness reports, the murder was carried out by multiple gunmen riding on a moped, a common method for paid assassins in Colombia. Many observers believed the murder was retaliation for Rodriguez's unwillingness to go along with the demands of a local criminal gang.

According to the evangelical watch group Rescue Christians, intensifying violence throughout 2011 and 2012 marked a deteriorating national situation in Colombia. Their figures suggest the following:

1. Twenty-five to thirty Colombian pastors are murdered by armed groups every year.
2. More than three hundred Protestant pastors have been murdered since 2000.
3. More than two hundred churches are currently closed in areas controlled by armed groups.
4. Entire Christian communities have been targeted by armed groups and forced to leave their homes. These internally displaced Christians often end up living in refugee camps.

5. Sixty percent of the murders of human rights workers throughout the world took place in Colombia in 2011 and 2012, including scores of Christians who speak up for justice and against corruption and illegality.

CUBA

Following the Cuban Revolution of 1959, the officially atheistic Castro regime confiscated church property, closed church-run schools, and actively discouraged participation in religious life. Thousands of Catholic priests and nuns, along with leaders in Cuba's small Protestant community, were either forced to leave the country or thrown in jail, while church attendance plummeted. In the 1990s, however, following the collapse of Communism in Europe, the regime began to reverse its hard-line policies, triggering a slow and still uneven glasnost for Christianity. In 1992, the constitution was amended to outlaw religious discrimination and to remove references to atheism as the official state ideology. In 1996, Fidel Castro visited the Vatican, paving the way for trips to Cuba by Pope John Paul II in 1998 and by Pope Benedict XVI in 2012. During the last two decades, the regime has alternated between allowing greater expressions of religious belief and practice, while still suppressing individual Christians who oppose the regime and push for swifter political reform.

Violence is still sometimes directed against the so-called "Ladies in White," meaning spouses and relatives of arrested leaders in the Christian liberation movement famous for wearing white dresses while marching in their memory. Even after most of these prisoners have been released, the Ladies in White continue to demonstrate in favor of broad political reform. The Catholic Church successfully negotiated with the regime to allow for peaceful assembly by the Ladies in White in one section of Havana, but the women continue to be subject to various forms of harassment and intimidation. One day prior to Pope Benedict's visit in March 2012, seventy members of the Ladies in White were detained by security forces, in what was seen as a warning not to embarrass the government while the pope was in town. (The trip also illustrated the tightrope that visiting Christian leaders sometimes have to walk in trying to cajole Cuba toward reform, without making things worse for the believers left behind after they go home. Benedict did not meet with the Ladies in White in order not to provoke the Cuban authorities, but he called on Cuba to build a "renewed and open society" and said bluntly that Marxism "no longer corresponds to reality.")

The Catholic Church continues to be restricted from operating religious schools and from operating private religious schools. Observers continue to report that limitations on churches and other forms of civil society, including restrictions on freedom of speech, of the press, and of free assembly, continue to be routine. Lay faithful continue to face discrimination in the workplace based on their overt expressions of religious identity, and there is still no breakthrough on the return of church properties expropriated by the regime forty years ago.

Further, rapidly growing Protestant forms of Christianity have not benefitted from the gradual opening under Raul Castro to the same degree as the Catholic Church. According to Cuba's Council of Churches, the number of evangelicals in the country has grown from seventy thousand to eight hundred thousand in the last twenty years, and Afro-Cuban religious traditions are also attracting large numbers of new faithful. The government continues to arrest members of these house churches, subjecting them to lengthy detention without legal recourse and to heavy fines. All Christian communities in Cuba have also voiced alarm about an upsurge in monitoring by the national security services.

Christian Solidarity Worldwide issued a report in April 2010 indicating that the Cuban regime remains inflexible in certain key areas related to religious freedom. It cited increasingly frequent visits to churches by security staff and government officials, which the report described as a strategy of intimidation. The government's Office of Religious Affairs also continues to block many religious activities and has refused visas to clergy wishing to travel abroad. The report concluded: "Rather than moving towards a more open society, the government of Raul Castro still views religious organizations, and in particular their leaders, as potentially dangerous, and as a result continues to exert as much control as possible over their activities."

At times the harassment of religious figures in Cuba becomes overtly violent. In early February 2012, a Pentecostal pastor named Reutilio Columbie was beaten unconscious in eastern Cuba and left for dead, though he survived the attack. Two months later, Columbie, who led the Shalom Christian Center in the town of Moa, continued to suffer dizziness, intense nausea, and vomiting as a result of the assault. The report by Christian Solidarity Worldwide indicated that Columbie had been advised to seek treatment from a neurologist in Havana but was physically unable to make the trip. According to Columbie, he had been on his way to file a complaint with regional authorities about the arbitrary confiscation of a church vehicle when he was attacked by unidentified assailants. The only thing taken from him, he said, was a document proving his legal ownership of the vehicle. Columbie said that local police were reluctant to investigate the attack, and because his ownership papers had disappeared, he also never got back the confiscated car. Most observers saw the attack as part of a broad campaign by pro-Castro elements to intimidate Christian leaders into silence on human rights and religious freedom issues.

The story of Rev. Carlos Lamelas, an evangelical pastor once imprisoned by the regime, is emblematic of the current realities in Cuba. In July 2011, the fifty-year-old Lamelas, along with his wife and two daughters, arrived in Miami after having been granted political asylum in the United States. A prominent national evangelical leader in Cuba, Lamelas had been arrested in 2006 and charged with "human trafficking," the usual accusation for dissident leaders who help people escape the country. Lamelas had also been an outspoken critic of the Castro regime's record on religious freedom. He was released from prison four months later after an international campaign on his behalf, but he could no longer serve openly as a pastor, since his congregation had expelled him under pressure from the regime. Lamelas supported his family as a freelance photographer while continuing to engage in informal pastoral activity, constantly facing the threat of another arrest and long-term imprisonment. He first applied for asylum in the United States in 2010 and was denied, but a reapplication in 2011 succeeded.

It's still not entirely clear whether the death of famed Christian activist Oswaldo Payá in July 2012 was an accident or another chapter in the global war on Christians. Cuban officials have insisted that Payá lost control of his car and collided with a tree, while members of Payá's family have suggested that the sixty-year-old dissident was run off the road by government agents. What's clear, however, is that the harassment and intimidation Payá endured over the years illustrate the price of Christian resistance in Cuba. He founded the Christian Liberation Movement in 1987 to oppose the one-party rule of the Cuban Communist Party, and was internationally known for launching the Varela Project, a petition drive demanding that the Cuban government recognize freedom of speech and assembly. He was a devout Catholic and frequently suffered for it. As a young man, he was expelled from the University of Havana when officials discovered he was a practicing believer. He was sentenced to three years of hard labor when he refused to transport political prisoners during his mandatory military service.

Over the course of his life, Payá reported receiving multiple death threats and complained that he was subject to constant surveillance. Some fellow activists were arrested following a scuffle with police at his funeral, a further reminder that democratic reform in Cuba remains a work in progress.

MEXICO

Like Colombia, Mexico is a sophisticated democracy, regarded by many observers of the geopolitical situation as an emerging regional power in the twenty-first century. Yet also like Colombia, Mexico is also a society of contradictions. Criminal gangs and various paramilitary groups exercise essentially unchallenged authority over some neighborhoods and even entire regions. Especially in those combat zones, Christians may be the only voices speaking out on behalf of the interests of ordinary folks.

The story of Maria Elizabeth Macías Castro, a journalist, blogger, and leader in a Catholic lay movement, illustrates the sometimes harrowing realities facing dedicated Christians in today's Mexico. On September 24, 2011, her decapitated body was found on a road near her town of Nuevo Laredo in the eastern state of Tamaulipas. Her corpse was left naked in a small piazza, along with a note saying she had been killed for using her blog to expose the activities of a local drug cartel known as the Zetas. According to the Committee to Protect Journalists, it was the first murder ever documented for the use of social media. Thirty-nine at the time of her death, Macías had been the editor in chief of a local newspaper in addition to blogging about the cartels under the pen name "The Girl from Laredo." She was also a champion of the poor, especially migrants, volunteering regularly at the Casa del Migrante center in Nuevo Laredo.

By all accounts, Macías was a woman of deep courage. She called herself "Marisol" after a sister who died of leukemia in childhood. Later she suffered an accident in which she lost a leg, triggering her husband to abandon the family and leave Macías to raise two young children on her own. She persevered, regaining the ability to walk with a prosthetic leg, keeping her family intact, and building a career as a journalist and human rights activist. She was also a woman of deep religious faith, becoming the local leader of the Scalabrian lay movement and a strong devotee of Blessed John Baptist Scalabrini, the Italian bishop who had founded the community in 1887. Her Skype account featured a picture from her commitment ceremony as a lay member of the movement on June 1, 2009, along with a quote from Scalabrini: "We must do good, all the good possible, and do it in the best way possible."

Based on later reconstructions of what had happened, Macías apparently was abducted on September 21 and abused by her kidnappers for three days before she was killed. Her body was left near a monument at the main entrance to the city of Nuevo Laredo. A keyboard, a DVD, and a sarcastic sign were left next to her, and a pair of headphones was posed on her decapitated head. According to many Mexican observers, because established media outlets often censor themselves out of fear and under political pressure, bloggers such as Macías have become the leading edge of efforts to expose the drug gangs. Friends and colleagues reported that Macías had been determined not to bow to their intimidation, believing that her Christian faith required her to speak out.

Though chilling, Macías's fate was hardly unusual. In February 2011, a Mexican priest named Fr. Santos Sánchez Hernández, a pastor in Mecapalapa, Puebla, was murdered in his rectory. According to the local bishop, the assailants had probably entered the rectory in order to steal, and upon discovering the priest, they hacked him to death with a machete. Sánchez, who was forty-three at the time of his death, was known locally as a passionate friend of the poor.

On April 26, 2011, Fr. Francisco Sánchez Durán was beaten to death at dawn in the church of El Patrocinio in San José, in Coyoacán, south of Mexico City. Local observers attributed the murder to retaliation against the priest, who had been critical of local bands of thieves preying upon the area's families and businesses. One month later, the body of Fr. Salvador Ruiz Enciso was discovered in a Tijuana neighborhood, with his hands and feet tied, beaten so far beyond recognition that positive identification had to rest on DNA testing. "Father Chavita," as he was popularly known, was well liked in the area for promoting a "family Mass" in which he used hand puppets to explain Christian teaching to young people in an attractive way. Some locals suspected he had been targeted by criminals because of his success in persuading young people to stay away from the gangs.

In July 2011, Fr. Marco Antonio Durán Romero, a diocesan priest, was shot to death amid a gunfight between Mexican soldiers and an armed guerrilla group in the state of Tamaulipas, near the border with the United States. He was struck by a stray bullet and taken to a nearby hospital, where he died from the wound.

In July 2012, a Protestant youth camp was attacked by a criminal gang in the Colibri ecological park near the town of Ixtapaluca, about twenty-two miles outside Mexico City. Prosecutors said the gang subjected the campers to an ordeal lasting several hours. Seven girls were sexually assaulted, and several other youths were beaten. The attackers took cash, cameras, and mobile phones and escaped in two stolen vehicles. The attackers burst into the camp at around midnight on Thursday, firing shots into the air, the victims said. The campers were rounded up and held at gunpoint while their belongings were ransacked and some were assaulted. The park is located in a hilly region with no mobile phone coverage, so it was some time before the alarm was raised. There did not appear to be any religious motive for the assault. Nevertheless, the incident was a reminder that simply taking part in religious activity in public in some parts of Mexico is tantamount to wearing a bull's-eye.

Mexico is also home to a nasty, and reportedly growing, intra-Christian form of violence. It's often fueled by traditionalist groups of Catholics who see the mushrooming evangelical and Pentecostal footprint in the country as a threat to Mexico's Catholic identity. These traditionalist groups tend to be especially strong in rural areas.

In September 2011, a group of about seventy Protestant Christians living in the village of San Rafael Tlanalapan in Puebla state were issued a frightening ultimatum: leave immediately or be "crucified" or "lynched." Traditionalist Catholics in the village, located about sixty miles from Mexico City, threatened to burn down their homes and kill any Protestants who remained, styling them as a threat to the Catholic identity of the area. The threats were hardly shocking, as local Protestants had complained back in 2006 about the traditionalist Catholics cutting off their water supply. According to reports, the community continued to experience small growth despite the harassment, which led to the ultimatum in 2011. After the intervention of government authorities, the Protestants were eventually allowed to remain and to construct a small church far from the town center.

One evangelical organization claims that almost fifty thousand Protestants have been dislodged from their homes due to conflicts with Catholics over the past thirty years, while hundreds of people have been injured in violent altercations and possibly dozens killed. One such victim was Lorenzo López, a twenty-year-old evangelical in the state of Chiapas, who was killed in 2007 when he entered the village of Jomalhó in order to repay money he had borrowed for his wedding. Two relatives who were with López that day, and who escaped, reported that a band of thirty assailants shouting Catholic slogans tied a rope around López's neck and dragged him into a nearby hall for a "trial." After they sentenced López to death, he was forced to dig his own grave. The attackers strangled López until he collapsed, threw his body into the grave, and smashed his skull with rocks. López had been a member of a fellowship of evangelical churches called New Hope. At roughly the same time he died, other reports from Chiapas indicated that a group of traditionalist Catholics had kidnapped four evangelical women—ironically, to prevent them from attending a workshop on religious freedom sponsored by an evangelical human rights commission.

The 2001 murder of a forty-eight-year-old Mexican Pentecostal pastor named Gilberto Tomás Pizo may also fall into this category. Pizo was shot to death while on his way to attend a service at his small church in Villa Hidalgo Yalalog, located in the state of Oaxaca, leaving behind a wife and five children. A police investigation concluded that "religious reasons" were the motive for the slaying, meaning tensions between traditionalist Catholics and non-Catholics. Pizo had been born a Catholic and was active in the faith, even supporting the construction of his local Catholic parish. When he converted to Protestant Pentecostalism, he experienced strong blowback. When Pizo tried to build a Pentecostal church in his neighborhood, he was forced to move it to the outskirts of town following repeated threats from ultra-orthodox Catholics. An evangelical human rights group sent investigators to Oaxaca to look into the case, charging that local police seemed to have "little interest" in identifying and charging those responsible.

VENEZUELA

Christians and their churches have emerged as important centers of opposition to the government of the late president Hugo Chávez and his successor, Nicolás Maduro, particularly with regard to human rights abuses and the suppression of political dissent. Because the vast majority of Venezuelans are at least nominally Catholic, the Catholic Church has borne the brunt of the resulting anti-religious crackdowns. Some church-owned properties have been expropriated, church-affiliated media outlets have been muzzled or intimidated, and a new education law essentially eliminated instruction in religion from state-owned schools. The United States Commission on International Religious Freedom reported that in 2012, "the government began wire-tapping the telephones of some Catholic leaders; expropriated some Catholic schools and community centers; and prohibited church representatives from visiting prisoners for humanitarian or spiritual missions."

Chávez liked to quote from the Bible to suggest that Jesus was a proto-socialist, and he had supporters and advisors in the clerical ranks, such as Fr. Jesús Gazo, a Jesuit who says that Venezuela's ruler had "a strong theological formation." Despite that, Chávez also repeatedly lashed out against his Christian opposition. Hundreds of Christian missionaries have been expelled from the country, accused of contaminating the cultures of indigenous populations. The government's Ministry of Interior revoked their permission to serve in the Venezuelan jungles or run schools, clinics, and nutrition centers that had been in operation for decades. Chávez called the missionaries "imperialists" and proclaimed he felt "ashamed" at their presence. Spokespeople for the government routinely accuse Christian leaders in Venezuela of conspiring with the United States against the regime.

A Protestant group called New Tribes Ministries has been singled out for special harassment. One of Latin America's biggest missionary organizations, its leaders were forced to leave remote tribal areas after government officials warned that they would be expelled and banned from working with indigenous tribes. Chávez called them "part of a broader conspiracy in Washington to topple a president whose regional influence is growing thanks to massive oil revenues."

Occasionally the anti-religious backlash turns violent. In 2004, Joel Briceño, twenty-seven, a minister for an evangelical church in Cabudare, was shot to death by Venezuelan police, who claimed they had mistaken him and his companions for criminals. Local observers said the willingness of the police to open fire on a car carrying Briceño and a friend suggested a fairly open contempt for Christian leaders, especially those known to be critical of the regime's record on religious freedom.

In January 2009, members of the government-affiliated La Piedrita militia launched a tear-gas assault on the residence of the Apostolic Nuncio, the pope's ambassador in Venezuela, marking the sixth such attack in the previous two years. The attackers left behind pamphlets denouncing priests who had criticized the government. The 2009 attack was believed to have been motivated by a decision by the nuncio to grant temporary asylum to members of the political opposition, as well as an anti-Chávez student activist.

In late April 2010, an elderly American priest named Fr. Esteban Woods was found dead at his home in the state of Bolívar, where he had served for nearly half his life. The missionary priest had been gagged and stabbed multiple times. Although local officials attributed the killing to a robbery gone wrong, the bishop of Ciudad Guayana, Mariano Parra, said Woods's death was a "sign of the violence" being experienced throughout Venezuela.

In May 2010, a Catholic church in Caracas was assaulted by vandals who painted crude renderings of weapons of war on images of Jesus and the Virgin Mary, in an incident widely taken as a warning of violence against religious leaders who give aid and comfort to the political opposition. A leader of the Catholic bishops' conference in Venezuela described the acts "as a way of sowing hatred and death" among the people. Later that year, in July, Chávez went on national television to describe Cardinal Jorge Urosa Savino as a "Neanderthal" and the other Catholic bishops of the country as "a bunch of cavemen."

There's little sign these tensions are about to ebb. In early January 2013, after Chávez had been reelected to another six-year term but questions about his health were rampant, the Catholic bishops of Venezuela criticized the government for making shifting and incomplete statements about the president's health, saying that "the government hasn't told the nation all of the truth" and warning that "the nation's political and social stability is at serious risk." Several government officials responding by telling the bishops to stay out of politics and warning of possible reprisals should they continue attempting to "destabilize" the country.

Profile: Manuel Gutiérrez Reinoso

Catholics are not the only ones in Latin America who have their martyrs to social justice. Although not quite as celebrated as Sr. Dorothy Stang, a sixteen-year-old Pentecostal named Manuel Gutiérrez inadvertently gave his life to defend the poor during a tumultuous series of protests that gripped Chile from 2010 to 2012.

Popularly known as the "Chilean Winter," and also referred to as the "Chilean Education Conflict," these student-led protests began with demands for a new educational framework in the country, including more direct state support for secondary education and an end to subsidies for a for-profit model in higher education. More broadly, the uprisings reflected Chilean young people's deep discontent with the country's entrenched economic inequalities. Chile has the highest per capita income of any country in South America, but also the continent's widest income gap between rich and poor. As they developed, the student protests linked up with similar movements among the working classes, especially the country's all-important mining sector.

Manuel Gutiérrez was among those Chilean youth pressing for a more just future. He was an active member of the Methodist Pentecostal Church in the Villa Jaime Eyzaguirre neighborhood of Santiago, the national capital. (Pentecostalism in Chile was born within the Methodist Church and retains much of its heritage, although the Methodist powers that be, appalled by the shouting and speaking in tongues, kicked out the rowdy Pentecostals in 1910.) Manuel was described as a cheerful and deeply faithful member of the congregation; his dream was to enter the seminary and become a Pentecostal pastor. He told friends he hoped to mobilize the church to become an agent for change. Friends and relatives described him as a quiet teenager who was not part of a gang or any radical political groups, and who never had any difficulties with the law.

On August 25, 2011, Manuel took his brother Gersón, who is confined to a wheelchair, to take part in a two-day national strike that had been called by a union known as the Workers United Center of Chile. Four separate marches took place in Santiago over those two days, along with additional demonstrations in other parts of the country, reportedly involving six hundred thousand people. Hundreds of protestors were arrested and scores injured in conflicts with police, who used tear gas and water cannons in an effort to disperse the crowds. Eventually panicked police officers opened fire on one such crowd, discharging their weapons at least three times. One of those bullets struck Manuel Gutiérrez in the chest, leaving him dead on the spot.

The death inflamed an already tense situation, and outrage swept across the country. Five policemen were detained for questioning, and charges were eventually filed against Officer Miguel Millacura, who was found by an investigation to have fired the fatal shot. As pressure mounted, a total of eight officers were dismissed and the chief of Chile's national police force resigned. The scandal marked a turning point, as just days later the Education Committee of the Chilean Senate approved a reform package that included several of the protestors' key demands. The memory of the incident has not been lost. On the one-year anniversary of his death, a group called the Committee for Justice for Manuel Gutiérrez Reinoso continued its battle to reform the way charges against police are handled in Chilean courts.

By all accounts, Manuel Gutiérrez was not killed for religious motives, and he wasn't anyone's explicit target. The police officer charged with the shooting, Millacura, apologized to the family and insisted that he hadn't meant to kill anyone. At the same time, there's little reason to doubt that Gutiérrez chose to attend that August 25 protest for reasons rooted in his Christian faith. By that stage, it was already clear that things had turned violent, and Manuel knew that he and his wheelchair-bound brother could be caught up in the mayhem. He chose to go anyway, because he believed that's what an authentic Christian and a future pastor would do. We'll return to this point in chapter 10, but the death of Manuel Gutiérrez is a classic example of a broader point: in evaluating whether an act falls within the scope of the global war on Christians, it's not enough to focus on the motives of the perpetrator—one has to bring the motives of the victim into view as well.

Gutiérrez was buried in a Protestant cemetery called Road to Canaan on the outskirts of Santiago, in a service attended by hundreds of fellow Pentecostals as well as students, laborers, and other leaders in the protest movement. His disabled brother, Gersón, described Manuel as a "martyr."

5

THE MIDDLE EAST

Pastor Youcef Nadarkhani has become an international symbol of the press for human rights in Iran. Amnesty International and other NGOs have rallied to his cause, while heads of state and foreign ministers have warned Iran of serious consequences should a death sentence passed against the thirty-five-year-old Protestant pastor be carried out. Christian groups have made Nadarkhani into an emblem of the threats not only in Iran but across the Middle East. Vicissitudes in Nadarkhani's case make international headlines, and in the ultimate proof of celebrity status in the twenty-first century, he's got his own Wikipedia page.

In part, this visibility is due to the fact that, like Asia Bibi, Nadarkhani seems to be experiencing a slow-motion form of martyrdom. He's been arrested, sentenced to death, allowed to stew in prison, released, then rearrested and released anew. In part too, Nadarkhani's fate is intertwined with Western ferment over Iran itself. His situation is reported not only in terms of anti-Christian oppression but also as a politics story about tensions with a potential nuclear power. Furthermore, the Iranians have helped make Nadarkhani a star by handling his case in a deliberately provocative fashion—releasing him in September

2012, only to take him back into custody three months later on Christmas Day, a choice calculated to elicit outrage. He was released again in early January 2013, though in a grotesque hint of how precarious his situation continues to be, false rumors of his execution swept the blogosphere in March 2013.

Born in Rasht, in Gilan province in northern Iran, Nadarkhani grew up in a Shi'ite Muslim family, though he says he never practiced the faith. Court documents say that Nadarkhani converted to Christianity when he was nineteen, and he exuded the typical zeal of the convert, becoming an active member of his church and moving into a position of leadership. Although he's described as a member of the Protestant Evangelical Church of Iran, his particular brand of Christianity is more akin to Pentecostalism than what most Americans think of as evangelical Protestantism. His church upholds a "oneness" doctrine of God, meaning they reject the Trinity, and they emphasize speaking in tongues and other "fruits of the Spirit." Nadarkhani is married with two sons, aged eleven and nine.

Although Iranian law does not include a crime of "apostasy," judges may still find people guilty of the offense based on religious fatwas, recognized by Iranian courts as legitimate sources of case law. That custom reflects popular sentiment, confirmed by a June 2013 Pew Forum survey that found 83 percent of Iranians favor the use of shariah and only 37 percent believe that the country adheres closely enough to Islamic law.

Nadarkhani was first arrested in December 2006 and charged with both apostasy and proselytizing. (Iran recognizes several Christian churches, but that means that only Iranians born into these churches are permitted to practice their faith. The country does not tolerate missionary activity.) Nadarkhani was released two weeks later, receiving a warning about engaging in evangelism. He got in hot water again in 2009, when Iran revised its educational policies to require all students to take courses in the Qur'an. Nadarkhani went to a school to protest on the grounds that the law violated constitutional protections of freedom of religion, an action that led to his being rearrested in October 2009. His wife, Fatemeh Pasandideh, was also charged with apostasy and sentenced to life in prison. She was later released in October 2010, after serving four months in the Lakan prison near their hometown of Rasht.

As furor over the treatment of Nadarkhani began to build, government officials briefly said that he had been accused of rape and extortion, but those charges never figured in any official proceedings and most observers regard them as a smokescreen. He eventually came to trial in September 2010, facing charges of apostasy and proselytism. Although his attorney claims there were numerous procedural errors, Nadarkhani was found guilty on all charges and sentenced to death by hanging.

After the verdict, Nadarkhani was placed in a jail for political prisoners and denied access to his family and his attorney. Officials repeatedly delayed the death sentence, apparently wanting to give the pastor an opportunity to save himself by reconverting to Islam. Meanwhile, his attorneys pursued an appeal to the Iranian Supreme Court, which upheld the death sentence in July 2011 but offered Nadarkhani a reprieve should he embrace Islam. In September 2012, another court retried Nadarkhani and acquitted him on the charge of apostasy. He was still found guilty of proselytizing and sentenced to three years in jail, but was released on the basis of time already served.

That seemed to be the end of Nadarkhani's ordeal, but it was not to be so. Officials rearrested Nadarkhani on Christmas Day in 2012, insisting that the paperwork for his release had been improperly filled out and that he actually had another forty days left on his sentence. Most people saw the decision to jail him during Christmas as a fairly blatant reminder that Christians who evangelize are not welcome. Nadarkhani was eventually released the following month.

Nadarkhani, to be sure, is hardly the only pastor in Iran to land in jail. There's also Saeed Abedini, a Christian convert who once aspired to be a Shi'ite suicide bomber. He and his wife moved to America in 2005 but continued to support Christian missions in Iran, and during a missionary trip in July 2012 he was arrested by Iranian authorities and shipped off to Evin prison in the country's northwest, where activists claim he has been beaten and abused. His wife remains in Boise,

Idaho, while he awaits trial on unspecified charges. During Christmas 2012, activists in the West urged Christians to leave an honorary place at their Christmas tables for Abedini. There's also Vruir Avanessian, an Iranian Armenian Christian minister who was interrogated at the notorious Evin prison after being placed under arrest along with several other Christians for gathering at a home in northern Tehran for a prayer service. Avanessian was released after spending fifteen days in prison, and he was required to post bail of roughly $60,000.

Even if geopolitical reasons temporarily induce officials to grant a reprieve, Christians in Iran face a constant sword of Damocles in the risk of being rearrested. In essence, they either have to abandon the country or live in a state of perpetual fear. To date, Nadarkhani is the only Christian figure formally designated for capital punishment. Metaphorically, however, any Christian in the country who insists on the right to normal pastoral life, including the ability to share the faith, is at least potentially facing a death sentence.

THE MIDDLE EAST: OVERVIEW

The term "Middle East" can include as few as sixteen states and as many as thirty-eight, depending on how expansive a notion one adopts. Here, we'll use it to designate the Islamic-dominated stretch of the globe that extends from North Africa and the Fertile Crescent all the way into portions of Central Asia. For our purposes, places such as Egypt, Somalia, Algeria, and Afghanistan will count as part of the Middle East, as well as the usual countries such as Syria, Iran, Iraq, and Saudi Arabia.

Across the board, Christianity in the region faces steep challenges. In the early twentieth century, Arab Christians represented 20 percent of the population. They had an outsize social footprint, running the lion's share of the area's schools, hospitals, and social service centers. Christians were overrepresented among the professional and educated classes, and they played significant roles in both the Arab Renaissance and the pan-Arab nationalist movement. Leading lights included George Habash, founder of the Popular Front for the Liberation of Palestine, and Syrian intellectual Constantin Zureiq, among the first to popularize Arab nationalism. Both came from Greek Orthodox families.

Today, however, that vibrant Arab Christianity feels like a dying species. Christianity now represents just 5 percent of the population, no more than twelve million people, and current projections show that number dropping to six million by the middle of the century. The Christian population began to drop in the early twentieth century, due to factors such as lower birth rates and immigration. In the last three decades, the decline has accelerated due to armed conflict, political and economic stagnation, and a rising tide of religious persecution.

At the same time, things aren't entirely gloom and doom. In the Gulf States there's a burgeoning Christian presence, formed mostly by guest workers from countries such as the Philippines, Korea, India, Lebanon, Vietnam, and Nigeria. Looking just at Catholics, there are now believed to be 350,000 Catholics in Kuwait, 300,000 in Qatar, 150,000 in Bahrain, and 1.5 million in Saudi Arabia, which includes 1.2 million Filipinos in the Saudi kingdom. For the most part they work in either the petroleum or domestic services industries, and most will be in their host countries only temporarily. These workers face a wide range of difficulties, from abusive working conditions and a lack of legal protection to a fairly complete absence of religious freedom. Some Western embassies allow them to gather for prayer, as do compounds operated by the oil companies. Apart from those protected spaces, Christians are at risk, and even "house church" services are routinely raided and harassed. As these migrant workers continue to make their way in the region, they represent tempting new targets in the global war on Christians.

AFGHANISTAN

Open Doors rates Afghanistan among the top two or three countries in the world in terms of dangers to Christians. Ten years after the Taliban was swept from power by U.S.-led forces, the situation remains chaotic for minority groups, including the small Christian community, estimated at perhaps no more than twenty-five hundred out of a national population of twenty-nine million. Although the Afghan government has signed agreements promising to respect religious freedom, its ability to project control is limited.

Most Afghan Christians come from a Muslim background, which means they are often seen as apostates. Converts and their families face severe social, political, and economic discrimination. There isn't a single Christian church or school in the country left standing, and even gatherings for prayer and worship in private homes are fraught with danger. In the summer of 2010, a group of former Afghan Muslims who had been sentenced to death for converting to Christianity managed to escape to India and told their stories, pleading for greater international protection for religious minorities.

In October 2011, local Taliban authorities issued a statement on a website vowing to purge all Christians from Afghanistan, whether local or foreign. They also promised to target foreign relief organizations, especially those of Christian inspiration, accusing them of being agents of the West and of proselytizing Afghan Muslims. These Taliban spokespeople claimed to have a "hit list" of two hundred foreign organizations and vowed to go after them one by one. That this wasn't an idle threat was confirmed in August 2011, when two German development workers were kidnapped in the Parwan province, north of Kabul, and shot to death. Their bodies were discovered in early September. As international forces continue withdrawal, the situation for minority groups, and Christians in particular, is expected to become even more perilous.

The following episodes illustrate the realities for Christians in Afghanistan.

In February 2006, an Afghani citizen named Abdul Rahman was arrested by police and charged with apostasy after he revealed to friends and family that he had decided to convert to Christianity. After a brief criminal trial, Rahman was sentenced to death. Under heavy international pressure, Afghani officials announced that Rahman was suffering from what they described as a "mental disorder." After being temporarily released on the basis of medical reasons, Rahman left Afghanistan and took refuge in Italy.

In July 2007, twenty-three South Korean missionaries were kidnapped by the Taliban, and two of the hostages were executed before a deal to secure the release of the group could be worked out. The group, composed of sixteen women and seven men, was captured while traveling from Kandahar to Kabul by bus on a mission sponsored by the Saemmul Presbyterian Church. Two men, Bae Hyeong-gyu, a forty-two-year-old South Korean pastor of the church, and Shim Seong-min, twenty-nine, were executed on July 25 and July 30. The release of the remaining hostages was secured with a South Korean promise to withdraw its two hundred troops by the end of 2007.

In September 2008, Islamic experts in the district of Jaghori arrested a religion teacher, Amin Mousavi, who was allegedly promoting Christianity. They sentenced the teacher to death, but later he was released and fled the country. One month later, a foreign aid worker named Gayle Williams, of joint British and South African nationality, was shot to death on her way to work in Kabul by two men on a motorbike. A Taliban spokesman later claimed Williams had been assassinated "because she was working for an organization which was preaching Christianity in Afghanistan."

In May 2010, news reports from Afghanistan indicated that a forty-five-year-old Christian named Saeid Mousa, who was physically disabled and wearing an artificial leg, had been arrested and sentenced to death. He was released in February 2011 and left the country. Later that same year, in October, another Afghan Christian named Shoaib Assadullah was imprisoned after he handed a Bible to someone who later reported him to authorities. Assadullah was able to obtain a passport in 2011 and also fled Afghanistan.

In May 2010, a local Afghan TV station broadcast a documentary titled *Afghan Christian Converts*, with footage and photographs claiming to document a secret Christian offensive to proselytize the country. Riots and demonstrations followed, in which dozens of Christians were beaten and Christian-owned businesses and homes burned. One Afghan lawmaker publicly stated that it is "not a crime" to kill a Muslim who converts to Christianity. In June 2010, more than twenty Christians were arrested after political leaders called for the detention and execution of converts. Many remain behind bars.

In August 2010, the Christian relief organization Assistance Mission suffered the greatest tragedy in its forty-four-year history when ten members of a medical team were massacred in a mountainous northern region. The team included seven men and three women—six Americans, one German, one Briton, and two Afghans—who had been on a mission offering free eye care. The Taliban claimed responsibility, asserting that the medical volunteers were foreign spies involved in a plot to convert Muslims to Christianity. According to an investigation by Afghan officials, Taliban gunmen with their beards dyed red marched the doctors, nurses, and technicians into a nearby forest, stood them in a line, and shot them one by one. According to the relief agency, the team had intended to found infant health and dental clinics in the area.

A spokesperson for the organization insisted the medical volunteers were not covert Christian proselytizers. "That would be against the laws of this country and the rules of our organization," said Dirk Frans, the group's executive director. "Although we are a Christian-supported charity, we absolutely would not proselytize."

Frans also said the group would not abandon Afghanistan. "We have worked here under the king, under the Russians, under the Communists, and under the warlords and the Taliban," he said. "Is it time to quit now?"

EGYPT

Egypt is the crucible of the Arab Spring, which many observers believe is fast turning into a Christian winter. By the middle of 2012, it seemed clear that the political initiative had been seized by a variety of hardline Islamist groups, with many Christians forecasting a grim future. A spokesperson for the Catholic Church in Egypt said: "The Salafists look at Christians and even moderate Muslims as *kuffars* and say they want to implement *shariah* rigorously. . . . Their attitude to Christians is to say that they can get their passport to go to the USA, France, the U.K., or somewhere else in the West."

During the Mubarak years, Christians were tolerated as a permanent body of second-class citizens, facing social and economic discrimination and frozen out of the most prestigious positions in political life and in the military. They were subject to occasional bouts of violence, usually without any legal consequences. According to statistics maintained by the Coptic Church, eighteen hundred Christians were murdered in Egypt during Mubarak's rule and two hundred acts of vandalism were perpetrated, with few arrests and convictions.

Well before the Arab Spring, the rising influence of the Muslim Brotherhood and various Salafist factions spelled trouble. In April and May 2009, at the height of the swine flu pandemic, the Mubarak government ordered the slaughter of all of the country's roughly three hundred thousand pigs. The decision was condemned by the World Health Organization, which said that the virus was spread exclusively through humans, and in any event there had not been a single documented case of the pandemic inside Egypt. Because of Muslim sensitivities, the vast majority of pig farmers in Egypt are Christians, and most observers felt the pandemic was a pretext for Mubarak to placate critics by taking a shot at Christians.

In June 2009, radical Muslims attacked Coptic residents in the village of Ezbet Bouchra-East, destroying their homes and harvests. According to reports, the attack was motivated by the arrival of twenty-five Christians from Cairo in the area to visit a local priest. Local Muslims interpreted the visit as a prelude to proselytism. Nineteen Christians were arrested, although they were released. In September 2009, a Coptic man was beheaded in the village of Bagour, part of a spurt of anti-Christian violence that left two other Christians dead in neighboring villages.

In January 2010, extremists disrupted an Orthodox Coptic Christmas midnight Mass outside Mar Girgis (St. George) Church in Nag Hammadi, in a shooting spree that left nine people dead. Another dozen people were seriously wounded, including two Muslim bystanders. Observers interpreted the attack as a form of retaliation for the alleged rape of a Muslim girl by a Coptic man in a nearby village in November 2009. When those charges first circulated, local Muslims looted and set fire to Christian shops, with about 80 percent being destroyed, and also abducted seven Christian women.

In March 2010, a court in Assiut acquitted four Muslims accused of killing a Christian in October 2009. The decision set off shock waves, as there had been multiple witnesses to the slaying. The victim, Atallas Farouk, was shot in the head multiple times before being beheaded, after which his assailants reportedly dragged his body through the streets shouting "Victory!" A lawyer acting on behalf of the victim's family told reporters, "This verdict sends out a message that a Copt's blood is extremely cheap."

In March 2010, twenty-five Christians were wounded when a mob estimated in excess of three thousand people disrupted a Coptic service in Mersa Matrouh, a coastal town west of Alexandria. More than four hundred Copts had gathered at the site of a proposed nursing home when a group of Salafists started hurling stones at both the building and the worshippers. One Christian said he had been seized and asked to convert to Islam, and when he refused, he was stabbed in the leg. According to reports, the mob had formed after a local imam called on Muslims to fight against their "enemies," saying, "We do not tolerate the Christian presence in our area."

In November 2010, two Copts were killed and roughly fifty injured when security forces surrounded a new church that was being erected with government permission near the pyramids, demanding that construction come to a halt. Thousands of Copts turned out to protest the interference, and violence followed when security agents began beating the Coptic demonstrators. A local human rights organizer said the security agents had given in to the demands of Muslim fundamentalists, generating excuses to prevent the completion of the church. Naguib Ghobrial, president of the Egyptian Union of Human Rights, said: "By this behavior, the chief of the local authority is encouraging Islamists to fight with Christians."

In retrospect, those pre–Arab Spring episodes now seem like tremors of a looming anti-Christian earthquake.

Open Doors reports a substantial increase in the numbers of Christians killed and injured since the transition in Egypt, as well as in the number of assaults on churches, schools, and Christian-owned shops and homes. Salafi Muslims have made a habit out of blocking the entrances to churches, demanding that the churches be moved to other locations, and refusing to allow repairs to be made. There are also increasing reports of Coptic girls being abducted and forced into Islamic marriages. In rural areas, Christians say, police and security forces turn a blind eye. Although national law guarantees religious freedom, courts enforce the rulings of religious authorities, and conversion from Islam is de facto treated as a crime.

In January 2011, more than twenty Christians were killed and at least seventy wounded when a car bomb went off outside the Orthodox Church of All Saints in the Sidi Bechr district of Alexandria. Almost a thousand people had turned out to celebrate a Mass marking the Orthodox New Year. The violence had a pretext, in this case rumors that local Copts were holding two women against their will who had converted to Islam. The charges were widely dismissed as false, but they continued to stir anger. Not long after the attack on the church, an off-duty policeman shot dead a seventy-one-year-old Christian, his wife, and four other Christians during a train ride to Cairo.

The infamous "Maspero Massacre" in October 2011 seemed to mark a turning of the waters, a transition toward an even more volatile and lethal situation. A peaceful protest led mostly by Copts in the Cairo neighborhood of Maspero, and designed to promote secular democracy, turned into a riot when Islamist thugs attacked. The army then opened fire, leaving twenty-seven people dead and more than three hundred injured, most of the victims Copts. The carnage was perceived by many Christians as their Kristallnacht, heralding the beginning of the end. Estimates are that ninety-three thousand Coptic Christians fled the country in the aftermath of the massacre.

In January 2013, a mob estimated at roughly five thousand Muslims shouting "Allahu Akbar" armed with hammers and other instruments destroyed a Christian social service center in the village of Fanous, located in the Tamia district eighty miles southwest of Cairo. The facility housed a welcome center and a kindergarten, but rumors in local mosques apparently held that the Copts were planning to turn it into a church. According to media reports, loudspeakers outside mosques in surrounding villages called upon Muslims to help their brothers in Fanous beat back the effort to build a church. Nader Shukry, who leads a group called the Maspero Coptic Youth Organization, named for the anti-Christian massacre, charged that local security forces were aware of the violence but arrived only after the facility had been utterly destroyed. Shukry also said that no one was immediately arrested, not even the local imam, although according to Shukry he should have been charged under Egyptian laws banning "incitement to violence."

Also in January 2013, a criminal court in the central Egyptian city of Beni Suef sentenced a woman and her seven children to fifteen years in prison for converting to Christianity. Nadia Mohamed Ali, raised a Christian, had converted to Islam when she married Mohamed Abdel-Wahhab Mustafa, a Muslim, twenty-three years ago. When he died, Nadia planned to convert her family back to Christianity in order to obtain an inheritance from her family. She sought the help of others in the registration office to process new identity cards between 2004 and 2006. When the conversion came to light, Nadia, her children, and even the clerks who processed the identity cards were all arrested and tried for criminal offenses.

Samuel Tadros, a research fellow at the Hudson Institute's Center for Religious Freedom, has described Egypt's new shariah-based constitution as "a real disaster in terms of religious freedom." On January 25, 2013, representatives of Coptic Orthodox, Catholic, and evangelical churches announced their withdrawal from a "national dialogue" convened by then president Mohamed Morsi to discuss objections to the constitution. Spokespeople for the churches described the initiative as a sham, given statements by senior officials to the effect that its decisions are nonbinding. It remains to be seen whether the deposition of Morsi by the army in early July 2013 will result in a legal order that respects minority rights, though most Christian leaders in the country backed the military intervention.

ISRAEL AND THE PALESTINIAN TERRITORIES

In Christian argot, Israel, the Palestinian Territories, and Jordan are known as the "Holy Land," meaning the territory where Christ lived, died, and rose again, and where early Christianity took shape. By now, the threat facing Christianity in its birthplace has become depressingly clear. Christians represented 30 percent of British Mandate Palestine in 1948, while today their share is estimated at 1.25 percent. The risk, as the Catholic Patriarch of Jerusalem, Fouad Twal, put it in July 2011, is that the Holy Land could become a "spiritual Disneyland"—full of glittering attractions, but empty of its indigenous Christian population.

By all accounts, Christians in the Holy Land face difficulties on both sides of the Israeli/Palestinian divide. In Israel, the headaches are often related to state security policies and a generalized impression of second-class citizenship for non-Jewish minorities. In Palestine, the rising influence of militant Islamic currents poses an obvious menace, coupled with the general climate of political and economic chaos. In both settings, Christians are often perceived as suspect. Israelis often see them primarily as Arabs and thus pro-Palestinian; Palestinians sometimes see them as Christians and thus potentially not Arab enough, perhaps too close to the West.

On the Israeli side, officials like to say that theirs is the region's only democracy, and point to a growing Christian population as proof that Israel does a creditable job of protecting minority rights. Some fifty thousand Christians have recently settled in Israel from the former territories of the Soviet Union, and adding to those numbers are other émigrés from the Balkans and from Asia, especially the Philippines. There's certainly truth to the argument that Christians enjoy greater physical safety and freedom of action in Israel than most other places in the Middle East. For instance, the northern region of Galilee is home to a relatively stable Christian presence. In Nazareth, the three-term mayor is a Greek Orthodox Christian even though the city is about two-thirds Muslim.

Yet most Arab Christians living in Israel do not describe their situation in glowing terms. Samer Makhlouf, a Catholic and executive director of One Voice, a grassroots movement in Palestine that brings together young Palestinians and Israelis to promote peace, says that of the four problems facing Christians in the Holy Land, the first three are "occupation, occupation, occupation." Makhlouf described Israeli military and security policy as "the father of all the problems in the region." That perception seems widespread. A 2006 poll by Zogby

International found that in the city of Bethlehem, 78 percent of Christians said that Christians were leaving the city because of Israeli occupation, while only 3.2 percent attributed the Christian exodus to the rise of Islamic movements.

One frequently cited difficulty involves access to Christian holy sites. Palestinians living in the West Bank and in East Jerusalem hold different residency cards, and they cannot move from one place to the other without special permits. It can be virtually impossible for a Christian in Bethlehem to travel to Jerusalem to worship in the Church of the Holy Sepulchre. That's true even if a permit is granted, since Easter coincides with the Jewish festival of Pesach, when a security lockdown is imposed.

As Raphaela Fischer Mourra, born and raised in Bethlehem as the daughter of a German father and a Palestinian mother, put it, "It's easier for a camel to pass through the eye of a needle than for a Palestinian to go to Jerusalem."

Residency policies also can have a devastating impact on families. Reportedly, there are some two hundred Christian families in the area living apart today, their members split between the West Bank and Jerusalem. Some villages in the region are under military control, which also makes it challenging for family members to move back and forth. Other difficulties include Christians whose income traditionally derives from agriculture but who have lost a portion of their lands to the construction of Israel's security barrier, as well as Christians who have lost land to the expansion of Jewish settlements. In 2012, for instance, three thousand acres were reportedly confiscated from fifty-nine Christian families in Beit Jala to continue expansion of the Gilo settlement and the separation wall.

Hana Bendcowsky, a Jewish Israeli affiliated with the Jerusalem Centre for Christian Jewish Relations, warns of hardening Israeli attitudes toward Christianity. A 2009 survey, she said, found that Israelis between the ages of eighteen and twenty-nine hold more negative views of Christians than older generations. At root, she said, Jews in Israel have a hard time thinking of themselves as a majority. They tend to see the Christians in their midst not as an embattled minority, she said, but as a "doubly threatening majority"—part of both the Arab world and the Christian West.

Among Catholics in the Holy Land, there's frustration about negotiations that have lingered since 1993 over the Fundamental Agreement between Israel and the Vatican, which among other things was supposed to regulate the tax and legal status of church properties in Israel. The terms of the agreement have never been implemented by the Israeli Knesset, and in the meantime, Israel has declared certain important Christian sites, such as Mount Tabor and Capernaum, to be national parks, overriding Christian control.

Bernard Sabellah, a Palestinian Christian academic and a member of the Palestinian Legislative Council, also argues that claims of a growing Christian community inside Israel are misleading. He says that there were roughly 35,000 Christians in the territory of Israel in 1948, while today the number is 110,000. Given the natural rate of demographic increase over a half century, he said, the Christian population today should be 150,000, which means that there are a "missing" 40,000 Christians in Israel. He also said that a recent survey of young Christians in Israel found that 26 percent want to leave—the same percentage as in the Palestinian Territories.

Christian churches and other sites have also become targets for "price tag" attacks in Israel, a term for assaults carried out by Israeli settlers and their sympathizers intended to exact a price on groups perceived to oppose settlement activity. In December 2012, vandals spray-painted obscenities at the Monastery of the Cross, which is a Greek Orthodox church in Jerusalem. The offensive slogans included "Jesus is a son of a bitch" and "Jesus is an ape." The vandals also defaced three cars belonging to the monastery, spray-painting "Victory of the Maccabees" and, ironically, "Happy holidays." A similar attack had occurred ten months earlier at the same church.

Life is hardly idyllic for Christians inside the Palestinian Territories either. In 2007, the only Christian bookstore operating in the Gaza Strip was firebombed and its owner, Rami Ayyad, kidnapped and murdered. The store had previously been bombed two other times, in February 2006 and April 2007, with the second attack doing substantial damage. Witnesses said that Ayyad was publicly beaten before being killed by Muslim radicals who accused him of attempting to spread Christianity in Gaza. Called the Teacher's Bookshop, the store had been established by the Palestinian Bible Society, a branch of the Gaza Baptist Church, in 1998, serving the approximately 3,000 Christians living amid a Muslim population of 1.5 million.

After the assault that left Ayyad dead, Sheik Abu Saqer, leader of an Islamist group known as Jihadia Salafiya, a group suspected of masterminding the April 2007 bookstore bombing, denied any involvement in Ayyad's killing but accused Gaza's Christian leadership of "proselytizing and trying to convert Muslims with funding from American evangelicals." Although Hamas officials condemned the attack and pledged to protect the Christian minority, the bookshop is no longer an ongoing concern.

In June 2013, the five Christian schools operating in the Gaza Strip, two Catholic and three Protestant, faced closure after the Hamas government issued an order banning coeducational institutions, part of a broad trend toward application of a strict Islamic moral code. Although the order did not single out the Christian schools, they were the only coeducational schools in the Gaza Strip. The order also specified that teachers could not teach classes of the opposite sex, which would force the already impoverished schools to hire additional faculty. For the record, the five schools serve a largely Muslim population.

Fr. Faysal Hijazin, the Catholic director general of Latin Patriarchate Schools in Palestine and Israel, said the order threatens the Christian presence in the Gaza Strip. "It is a concern that in education things are getting more conservative," he said. "It reflects the whole society. This is of concern to both Christians and moderate Muslims. It is not easy to be there."

Neither is the West Bank free of risks, despite the repeated efforts of the Fatah government to tout their Christian minority as evidence of their openness and worthiness for statehood. Paci, for instance, reported in 2011 that rapidly growing social pressure on the West Bank against mixed Muslim/Christian marriage has meant that unwed couples who have children are increasingly likely to abandon them. She also says that Christian owners of vineyards, who have been producing wine for generations, face mounting pressure to shift to the more morally acceptable but less profitable business of cultivating olives. In 2010, the lone Christian orphanage on the West Bank was shut down under pressure from the Social Affairs Ministry of the Palestinian Authority. In 2003, a seventeen-year-old Christian girl named Rawan William Mansour was raped on the West Bank, allegedly by two members of Fatah who were never prosecuted, while Mansour was forced to flee to Jordan out of fear of being the victim of an honor killing. In 2005, two more Christian teenage girls, in this case sisters, were raped and murdered, and in September 2006, seven Christian churches on the West Bank and Gaza were firebombed amid protests over controversial remarks by Pope Benedict XVI about Islam.

According to Open Doors, reports indicate that pressure against Christians is increasing in the Palestinian Territories, especially with regard to incidents against Muslim-background believers. Converts to Christianity are frequently discriminated against by the larger community, and often by their own families, if their faith becomes known. According to the Open Doors 2012 report, there was an "honor killing" of a Christian convert from Islam in 2011, though for security reasons they did not publish any details about the assault. In February 2011, a Christian surgeon named Maher Ayyad was attacked when a bomb was hurled at the car in which he was riding. Though Ayyad was unhurt, the car sustained serious damage. Ayyad said that after the attack he began receiving text messages warning him to stop any proselytizing activity, though he denied engaging in any missionary work. Majed El Shafie, president of One Free World International, said at the time that such assaults have become increasingly common. "The Christians in the Palestinian Authority [are] facing persecutions," he said. "Their homes, their churches—they get attacked almost every day."

IRAN

Iran officially tolerates religious minorities, but in practice minority groups such as Christians, Baha'is and Sufi Muslims often face severe political, legal, economic, and social discrimination. As anti-Western attitudes have hardened, reports suggest that physical attacks, harassment, detention, and imprisonment of religious minorities have intensified.

Christians are legally prohibited from worshipping in Farsi, the national language. The idea is that the recognized branches of Christianity serve ethnically distinct populations, Armenians and Assyrians, and should restrict their activities to those languages. Conducting religious activity in Farsi, according to authorities, would be tantamount to proselytism. Christian leaders have been required to sign "loyalty agreements" promising not to engage in any missionary activity directed at Muslims, and religious leaders are subject to tight surveillance by security agents, including when traveling outside the country.

Members of unrecognized Christian communities are subject to arrest. According to the United States Commission on International Religious Freedom, between June 2010 and February 2012 approximately three hundred Christians from various churches and communities were arbitrarily arrested. Human rights groups believe the real number is much higher. Often these Christians are arrested, imprisoned for a brief period, released, and then rearrested. Observers say these detainees face bleak conditions, including sleep deprivation, solitary confinement, and the denial of medical care. Reports also say that violence and psychological coercion are used on religious prisoners to compel them to make confessions and to offer information about fellow believers. Sanctions for "apostasy," meaning conversion from Islam to another religion, are firmly enforced both by the judicial system and by Iranian society. In September 2008, the Iranian parliament approved a new penal code that included the death penalty for apostasy. A committee removed this provision in 2009, but in many cases Iranian judges are willing to base their rulings on religious edicts.

Despite these pressures, according to some reports Christianity in Iran is growing, especially in a clandestine network of evangelical and Pentecostal "house churches" spread across the country. The Open Doors organization claims that forty years ago, the number of Islamic converts to Christianity living in Iran was just 200, while by 2012 the total had risen to 370,000. The group asserted that there is a "Christian revival" taking shape, especially among youth in Iranian cities.

Perhaps because of that growth, pressure on Christians seems to be intensifying. In January 2009, three members of the Church of the Assemblies of God were arrested in Tehran, the national capital. They included a husband and wife who had converted to Christianity from Islam. They were charged with leading unauthorized Bible studies in their home and eventually released on bail.

In March 2009, two female converts from Islam, Maryam Rostampour and Marzieh Amirizadeh Esmaeilabad, were arrested and charged with acting against the security of the state on the basis of attending illegal religious activities and distributing Bibles. Both were denied medical care, despite suffering from infections and fever. Both were warned they would face lengthy prison sentences if they didn't embrace Islam. They were eventually released under international pressure, and both women subsequently left the country.

In December 2009, security agents raided the home of a Christian woman named Hamideh Najafi in the city of Mashhad. She was sentenced to three months of house arrest, and her daughter, who suffers from a kidney condition, was placed in foster care. Najafi and her husband were informed by police officials that their daughter would be returned to their care provided they abandoned the Christian faith and refrained from speaking publicly about their situation.

In February 2010, a Protestant minister named Rev. Wilson Issavi, a leader in the Assyrian Evangelical Church, was arrested by state security. His church had been shut down in January. Issavi remained behind bars for three months before being released, and his wife reported that he appeared to have been tortured while in custody.

In October 2010, Ayatollah Ali Khamenei gave a speech in which he warned of a growing Christian presence in the county, blaming "the enemies of Islam for establishing and encouraging the expansion of Christianity in Iran." In the same month, Iran's intelligence minister announced that his agents had discovered hundreds of illegal underground churches and were preparing a crackdown. In January 2011, another government official referred to Christian evangelism as a "corrupt and deviant movement" threatening Iran's national interests.

In late December 2010 and early January 2011, Iran's security services launched a wave of arrests of Christians for participating in prohibited "house church" services. According to human rights monitors, roughly seventy people were arrested in the raids and spent varying periods of time in prison. Observers believed the arrests were timed to discourage Christians from using the Christmas holidays as a springboard for missionary activity.

In January 2011, an Iranian pastor named Behnam Irani, from the city of Karaj, was convicted of crimes against national security and sentenced to a year in prison. He began serving his sentence in May when the forty-one-year-old was informed by authorities that he would actually have to spend five years behind bars due to a previous conviction.

In March 2011, a Muslim convert to Christianity named Masoud Delijani was arrested during a house church service, along with his wife and nine other Christians, by plainclothes security agents. Delijani was later charged with "having faith in Christianity," "holding illegal house church gatherings," "evangelizing Muslims," and an unspecified action against Iran's national security. He spent 114 days in custody, mostly in solitary confinement, before being released after his family put up $100,000 in bail. Delijani was arrested again two weeks later, and in February 2012 a Revolutionary Court in the province sentenced him to three years in prison.

In April 2011, a pastor in the Church of Iran named Behrouz Sadegh-Khanjani and five other church members were sentenced to a year in prison for "propaganda against the regime" by the First Branch of the Revolutionary Court in the southern city of Shiraz. The accused were acquitted of the more serious charge of crimes against national security.

In May 2011, a Revolutionary Court in the northern Iranian city of Bandar Anzali put eleven members of the Church of Iran on trial on charges of crimes against national security. In this case, the eleven Christians indicted by the regime included a sixty-two-year-old grandmother. As of this writing, the eleven Christians had not yet received a verdict.

In June 2011, human rights and religious freedom monitors reported an uptick in anti-Christian propaganda delivered through the official state-sponsored media outlets. One such article published on a website directed at Iranian youth claimed that young Christian women were entering stores as a pretext for talking to staff and customers, proposing sexual relations and insulting Islam as means of luring people into conversion. In August 2011, Iranian police seized sixty-five hundred pocket Bibles as they were being transported from one town in northwestern Iran to another. A parliamentary official announced the seizure, claiming that it was a blow against a well-funded campaign to proselytize Iranians, especially young people.

In December 2011, security agents raided an Assemblies of God church service in Ahvaz, in southwestern Iran, taking worshippers into custody. Most were released after just a few days, but the pastor, named Farhad Sabokroh, and another church member were forced to serve two months behind bars before being released on bail. Media reports indicated that a wave of arrests gathered steam in the first part of 2012, with Christians detained in Tehran, Ahwaz, Shiraz, Isfahan, and Kermanshah. One agency reported that in Isfahan alone, more than a dozen Christians were arrested in less than a month beginning in late February.

A new round of harassment broke out in June 2013 in the run-up to presidential elections. An Assemblies of God church in Tehran was closed after its pastor, Robert Asserian, was placed under arrest. Not long afterward, three Iranian converts to Christianity were detained following a raid on a worship service of a house church in Isfahan, a city a little over two hundred miles south of Tehran, known in the West as the site of one of Iran's nuclear technology centers. Reports also surfaced that an evangelical pastor named Behnam Irani, a 1992 convert to Christianity who had been arrested in 2011 for allegedly acting against national security, was facing death in prison because officials had denied him adequate medical care to treat severe ulcers. Activists charged that the neglect amounted to a de facto death sentence for Irani, without the need for a potentially embarrassing formal verdict.

Firouz Khandjani, a spokesperson for the Church of Iran house church movement, charged that authorities had exploited the distraction created by the presidential campaign to tighten the screws.

"In the West people often seem more interested in the elections than in individual cases of persecution," Khandjani said. "Authorities . . . used the electoral calendar in order to suppress Christians."

It remains to be seen if the victory of the moderate Hassan Rowhani will materially change the situation. Khandjani said that Rowhani had been the only presidential candidate who explicitly vowed to protect religious minorities but also noted that under Iran's complex distribution of power, the president's authority is carefully circumscribed vis-à-vis the Supreme Leader, currently Ayatollah Ali Khamenei. It's the Supreme Leader rather than the president, for instance, who controls the Interior and Intelligence ministries that tend to be most feared by Iranian Christians. In the immediate wake of the election, Khandjani said that Christians had prayed for a Rowhani victory but did not expect "magical solutions."

IRAQ

To be sure, life for Iraq's Christian minority was no picnic under Saddam Hussein. Christians were consigned to a permanent underclass and reminded of their subjugation in myriad ways. To take one example, Iraqi law required that at least 25 percent of the student population of a public school had to be Christian in order to permit a course in Christianity to be offered, but all it took was one Muslim in order for study of the Qur'an to be obligatory. In addition, Christian families were strongly encouraged to give their newborns traditional Arab Muslim names, as opposed to names associated either with Christianity or the minority Assyrian community.

Despite the hardships of the Hussein regime, nothing prepared Iraqi Christians for the apocalypse that followed its fall.

During a Vatican meeting on the Middle East in October 2010, Cardinal Emmanuel III Delly, who at the time was still serving as the Chaldean Patriarch of Iraq, described life after the fall of Saddam as "a Calvary" in his "tortured and bloodied country." Among other things, Delly said, sixteen priests and two bishops had been kidnapped and released only after the church had paid a steep ransom, and other Christians in Iraq had been killed, joining "a line of new martyrs that today pray for us from the Heavens." Across the Middle East, Iraq has become the leading symbol of the war on Christians, a chilling confirmation that the choice facing Christians in the Middle East is often not between a police state and a vibrant democracy but rather between a police state and annihilation.

According to numbers from the U.S. Department of State, there were 1.4 million Christians in Iraq at the time of the first U.S.-led Gulf War in 1991. By 2010, the United Nations pegged the number at 700,000, and today the high-end estimate for the number of Christians left is around 450,000. Some observers believe the real tally may be lower still, in the neighborhood of 200,000. The Christian presence in Iraq stretches all the way back to the era of the Apostles, which means that a church that took two millennia to construct has essentially been gutted in the arc of just two decades.

According to reports from multiple sources, the situation began to deteriorate most seriously in 2006. Attacks on Christian targets at the time included:

- A Catholic church and a Syrian Orthodox church in Kirkuk, as well as an Anglican church and the Apostolic Nuncio's residence in Baghdad, were bombed in January 2006, killing three people.
- In September 2006, two other churches were attacked in Kirkuk and Baghdad, killing two people, one a child.
- Also in September 2006, Fr. Boulos Iskandar Behnam was kidnapped and murdered. His head had been sliced from his body and placed upon his lifeless chest, apparently in retaliation for controversial comments by Pope Benedict XVI about Islam.
- In November 2006, Isoh Majeed Hedaya, president of the Syriac Independent Unified Movement and an advocate for the formation of an Assyrian-Chaldean-Syriac administrative area in the Nineveh Plains, was murdered on his front doorstep.
- In December 2006, a high-ranking member of the Presbyterian Church in Mosul was murdered.

- In June 2007, a Catholic priest and three deacons were murdered outside of their church after saying Mass in Mosul.

Around the same time, radical groups adapted the tactic of demanding payment of *jizya*, or protection money, from Christian families and churches. A seeming point of no return arrived in March 2008 with the murder of Archbishop Mar Paulos Faraj Rahho, the Chaldean Catholic prelate of Mosul. In late February, Rahho had been kidnapped from his car in the Al-Nur district of Mosul, while his bodyguards and driver were all killed. Church officials would later report that immediately before Rahho was pulled from the car by his abductors, he called the church and said that no ransom should be paid for his release, because the limited funds of the church would be better used for good works. His kidnappers demanded $3 million, and when they didn't get it, they killed Rahho, leaving his body buried in a shallow grave.

More recently, in the period from 2010 to late 2012, life has become even more perilous. Bombers targeted churches and homes, priests and faithful were kidnapped, and there were arson attacks on Christian-owned shops and other businesses, forced religious conversions, anti-Christian discrimination in the workplace, and attacks in the media. Reports released in spring 2012 showed that over the past eight years seventy-one churches were attacked, most of them bombed, with forty-four assaults on churches in Baghdad and nineteen in Mosul, a northern city with ancient Christian links. Leading church sources reported that nearly six hundred Christians had been killed in religious and politically motivated attacks—almost 60 percent of them in Baghdad, the rest mostly in the north. The dead included seventeen priests and one bishop who died in captivity.

In most cases, those responsible for the crimes said they wanted to rid the country of its Christians. Reports document the grotesque killing of very young Christians, including a seven-month-old baby and a pair of fourteen-year-old boys, one reportedly decapitated for being "a dirty Christian sinner" and another crucified in his village on the edge of Mosul. In May 2010, bomb attacks on a group of Christian students traveling on buses to Mosul University left at least one person dead and eighty wounded. Eyewitnesses say that shrapnel and shattered glass left many students dazed and bloodied, while a nearby shop owner died from the force of the blast.

Christians in Baghdad had fled in vast numbers following the October 31, 2010, siege of the Syrian Catholic cathedral of Our Lady of Salvation, which left fifty-eight dead. Within six weeks of the atrocity in the cathedral, sources indicate that more than thirty-two hundred Christians had fled their homes, and by the start of 2011 nearly six thousand had arrived in the north. Many of these displaced people were desperate for safe passage, ultimately to the West.

During the spring of 2012, the respected Catholic humanitarian agency Aid to the Church in Need carried out a fact-finding mission in Iraq. In key parts of the north, the mission concluded, extremism was becoming a problem, meaning that Christians were now unsafe in the very part of the country where they had sought sanctuary. An attack on Christians and their businesses in the ancient Christian city of Zakho in late 2011 showed the extent of the problem. In addition to the threat of physical violence, Christian leaders also reported that lower-level harassment and discrimination were gathering steam. A requirement that identity cards state the holder's religion was reportedly making it easier for employers to discriminate against Christians in hiring practices and in salaries.

In January 2011, a senior priest from the Assyrian Church of the East, Archdeacon Emanuel Youkhana, told Aid to the Church in Need that Christians in Iraq were being systematically attacked in a coordinated effort to drive them out of the country. Youkhana described growing pressures for Islamization, including the fact that the music department at Baghdad University had recently been closed because music is incompatible with shariah law. He said that Christian women face growing pressure to wear the Islamic veil in public and are often subject to verbal abuse or physical attack for refusing to do so. Youkhana also denounced the state-controlled media for denying that Christians were subject to specifically religious persecution in Iraq.

In April 2011, a bomb exploded on Easter outside Sacred Heart Church in Baghdad's Karrada district, leaving two policemen and at least two passers-by injured. In a second attack, obviously coordinated to occur at the same time, four police officers were wounded in a firefight with gunmen outside St. Mary the Virgin Catholic Church while people attending Easter Mass huddled inside.

In May 2011, the decapitated body of a twenty-nine-year-old Christian man named Ashur Yacob Issa was discovered in Kirkuk, a few days after he had been kidnapped. His family had been unable to pay the $100,000 ransom that Issa's abductors had demanded. In August 2011, at least thirteen people were injured when a bomb exploded at Holy Family Church in Kirkuk. Another bomb planted near an evangelical church in the city reportedly failed to explode. These two attacks followed a bombing ten days earlier at St. Ephraim's Syrian Orthodox Church, close to the Chaldean cathedral, in the center of the city. That bomb detonated at 1:30 a.m., so no one was injured in the attack, but it did extensive physical damage to the church.

In October 2011, two Christians were shot dead in Kirkuk. One of the victims, thirty-year-old Bassam Isho, was executed by an armed group, while the other, sixty-year-old Emmanuel Polos Hanna, was found dead by the side of a road leading to Baghdad. The Asia News agency quoted a source in Kirkuk as saying, "The attacks on Christians continue and the world remains totally silent. It's as if we've been swallowed up by the night."

In December 2011, Muslim extremists launched a campaign to force the closure of a beauty parlor in the Kurdish city of Zakho, triggering a series of riots in which Christians suffered the most serious fallout. Reportedly thirty people were injured, scores of Christians received death threats, and twenty Christian-owned businesses were set ablaze. The property damage was estimated at $5 million. As part of the mob violence, enraged youths threw stones at churches and homes belonging to Christians, and leaflets were distributed threatening the shop owners with death if they reopened their businesses.

In January 2012, gunmen opened fire on the residence of the Catholic archbishop in Kirkuk. Security agents and police returned fire, leaving two of the attackers dead and a third in custody. Officials did not release any motive for the assault, though many observers suspect it was related to a nearby incident three days before in which a member of the Iraqi parliament was attacked.

In March 2012, extremist Muslim groups assaulted St. Matthew's

Syrian Orthodox Church in Baghdad, where bomb attacks left two guards dead and five others wounded. The assault came on March 20, the anniversary of the beginning of the U.S.-led invasion, as part of a coordinated series of bomb attacks across the country that killed at least fifty-two people. Officials at the time said it was unclear if the militants had specifically intended to target the church, though most observers felt the choice was deliberate.

SAUDI ARABIA

As counterintuitive as it may seem, Saudi Arabia is home to a mushrooming Christian community, numbering perhaps as many as three million, amid a total national population of twenty-eight million. There are believed to be eight million guest workers, with at least a third, and perhaps as much as half, being Christians drawn from the Philippines, India, Pakistan, Bangladesh, Sri Lanka, Indonesia, Malaysia, Thailand, Ethiopia, Lebanon, Syria, Jordan, Nigeria, Kenya, and other sub-Saharan African nations.

Guest workers who are not Sunni Muslims face severe restrictions on the practice of their faith. The Qur'an is considered the constitution of Saudi Arabia, and no provision is made for freedom of religion. Apostasy is considered a crime, and the accused can be put to death if he or she does not recant. There are persistent reports of "honor killings" in Muslim families when a conversion is discovered. In theory, the state tolerates private expressions of alternative religious belief, though in practice the religious police in Saudi Arabia, the Muttawa, sometimes harass and detain Christians even for private "house church" observances. Worshippers who defy the ban on public religious expression risk arrest, imprisonment, lashing, deportation, and sometimes torture. Reports suggest that migrant women often face the greatest difficulties, including sexual abuse and rape, which sometimes overlaps with religious discrimination. Some female guest workers allege that they have been threatened with rape if they do not convert to Islam.

According to Open Doors, a number of Christians have fled the county, in some cases believing that their lives are at risk. Even white-collar elites are not exempt. Speaking on background for fear of being identified, a senior Western executive with Aramco, the Saudi oil giant, said in 2012 that although he's well paid and lives in luxury accommodations, he's experienced harassment for his Christian faith both overtly and subtly. He called the situation akin to living in a "gilded catacomb."

In India, a Catholic group called Christ Army for Saudi Arabia has organized fasts, protests, and other events to promote the religious freedom of Indian Catholics in Saudi Arabia. The group's founder is an Indian priest named Fr. George Joshua, who spent four days in a Saudi prison in 2006 for celebrating Mass in a private home. Joshua was later expelled from the country by the Muttawa.

Sensitivities in the kingdom about protecting the country's Islamic identity can sometimes be taken to almost self-parodying extremes. When an Italian soccer team came to play a match in Saudi Arabia, it had to blot out part of the cross on the team's jerseys, turning their logo into a stroke instead. Even secular symbols associated with Christmas are banned; one year, in an American school, a Santa Claus barely dodged the religious police by escaping through a window.

Often, however, the climate of restriction on religious freedom is no laughing matter. In January 2009, an Eritrean Protestant pastor named Yemane Gebriel was forced to leave Saudi Arabia after receiving numerous threats from the Muttawa that he would be arrested and potentially harmed while in prison if he didn't leave. According to reports, Gebriel had led an underground Christian community in the country composed of more than three hundred believers, most of them fellow Eritrean nationals working in the country.

Also in January 2009, the religious police arrested and imprisoned a Saudi national named Hamoud Bin Saleh for describing his conversion to Christianity on a blog titled *Christ for Saudis*. Bin Saleh was released in March 2009 but placed under a ban on travel and prohibited from blogging.

In March 2009, three Indian Christians were found praying together and arrested by the religious police in Saudi Arabia's eastern province. The authorities also seized religious material from their apartment. The Christians were released after a few days in prison and instructed not to engage in any further religious activity.

In December 2009, a Filipino national named Norma Caldera returned to her country and described her experiences while in Saudi Arabia as similar to being in a prison. She had worked as a household aide, and said she had been harassed so consistently on the basis of her Christian faith that she was compelled to leave five months ahead of the end of her contract. Caldera said that when she informed her employers that she was a Catholic, the first thing they did was to lower her salary. She was forbidden to leave her place of work and was denied a bed, forced to sleep either on the kitchen floor or in a tent outside the house. She was also forbidden to attend Mass and was forced to fast during Ramadan.

In August 2010, a man claiming to be a leader in Al-Qaeda ordered Muslims in the Saudi military to topple the monarchy for supporting U.S.-led conflicts with fellow Muslims in Afghanistan, Iraq, and elsewhere, and he also called for Christians in Saudi Arabia to be killed. Though no immediate anti-Christian violence ensued, the well-publicized threats generated deep fears among the country's underground Christian communities.

In September 2010, a Filipino nurse employed at Kharja Hospital in Riyadh, the national capital, died in the hospital after being raped and left dying in the desert by her rapists. Many local Christians suspected she had been attacked because she refused to renounce her Catholic faith. Two weeks later, again in Riyadh, three nurses in the National Guard Hospital were abducted and raped while returning from work and were left in serious condition.

In October 2010, twelve Filipinos and a French Catholic priest were arrested and charged with proselytizing after attending a Mass staged in a hotel in Riyadh. The liturgy, which was attended by approximately 150 Filipinos, had been raided by members of the Saudi Commission for the Promotion of Virtue and Prevention of Vice, according to reports from Asia News. The thirteen people arrested were charged with organizing and leading the group. The priest was released when the French embassy in Saudi Arabia provided a legal note called a *kafala*, a guarantee that an arrested person will appear if and when requested by Saudi authorities. The other Filipino detainees were also eventually released after their embassy provided similar assurances.

In January 2011, two Indian nationals, Yohan Nese, thirty-one, and Vasantha Sekhar Vara, twenty-eight, were arrested by the Mut-tawa for attending a private prayer service and accused of converting Muslims to Christianity. They later testified that they had been beaten while in prison and subjected to revolting conditions. Sekhar Vara was released in May and Nese in July, and both left the country to return to India. In February 2011, according to Open Doors, an unnamed foreign worker was arrested in Jeddah for discussing his Christian faith with Muslim friends, at their invitation, in the vicinity of a mosque. Initially Saudi authorities threatened him with the death penalty for the crime of attempting to proselytize Muslims, but it was eventually decided to deport the worker back to his home country.

SYRIA

Christians have long been an important minority in Syria, compos-ing roughly 10 percent of the population of 22.5 million. The major-ity is Greek Orthodox, followed by Catholics, the Assyrian Church of the East, and various kinds of Protestants. Today there's tremendous fear among Christian leaders that Syria will be the next Iraq, meaning the next Middle Eastern nation where a police state falls and Chris-tians become the primary victims of the ensuing chaos. That prospect is ironic, given that Syria had been seen as a relatively safe haven for Christians and a destination of choice for Iraqi Christian refugees.

Politically, Christians are sometimes seen as sympathetic to the re-gime of President Bashar al-Assad, largely because the Assad family has positioned itself as a bulwark against the spread of Islamic radical-ism. They've become targets of choice for Islamist elements in the rebel alliance, who want Syria to be an Islamic state governed by shariah law. Reports from various parts of the country indicate that Christian meeting places have been raided, individual Christians kidnapped and held for ransom, and Christian women raped. Killings of Christians are also on the rise. One news report suggests that fundamentalist taxi drivers have made a vow that they will murder any unveiled female cli-ent, meaning women who tend to be Christians.

Yet because Christians are also usually seen as having good ties to the West, they're also seen with suspicion by some Assad loyalists.

In March 2013, former Italian foreign minister Franco Frattini told a Rome conference that he had recently met with a group of young Christian pro-democracy activists from Syria who said they feared militias allied with the Assad regime far more than the rebels.

Compounding their peril, Syria's Christians are not concentrated in a single defensible enclave. According to a 2012 analysis prepared by the Catholic Near East Welfare Association, the Greek Orthodox, who form the country's largest Christian community, are concentrated in and around the national capital of Damascus, which means they're largely located on territory still controlled by Assad's forces. Syriac Christians are concentrated in a largely autonomous region east of the Euphrates River that is mainly Kurdish, bordering Kurdish-controlled regions in Turkey and Iraq. Catholics and Armenians tend to live in Sunni-dominated middle Syria, including the cities of Aleppo and Homs. It's an area where the Free Syrian Army is strong, and where the fighting has been the most intense.

As of October 2012, the United Nations estimated that 300,000 Syrians had fled the country, while at least 1.5 million were internally displaced. A disproportionate share of those refugees and displaced people were believed to be Christians. What's distinct about the Christian exiles, according to the CNEWA report, is that they generally haven't headed for major refugee camps in Turkey or Jordan under the auspices of either the UN or international NGOs, fearing further exposure to rebel forces and to Islamic radicals. Instead the Christians have headed for southern Syria and Lebanon, relying on extended family and friends. As a result, these Christian refugees are not being reached by major international relief efforts, and are expected to be most at risk of hunger and disease.

The CNEWA report cites several waves of displacement among Syria's Christians since the anti-Assad uprising erupted in March 2011:

- In Homs, anti-government militants have expelled 90 percent of the city's Christians and confiscated their residences by force, according to the Fides news agency. Sources say the militants went door-to-door in the neighborhoods of

Hamidiya and Bustan al-Diwan, "forcing Christians to flee, without giving them the chance to take their belongings." At least fifty thousand Christians sought refuge in the Wadi al-Nasara area (the name means "Valley of the Christians"), in western Syria near Lebanon, as well as in Damascus and Tartous.

- In Qusayr, nine miles from Homs, a Christian population estimated at ten thousand was compelled to flee following an ultimatum from the military chief of the armed opposition. Some mosques relaunched his message, announcing: "Christians must leave Qusayr within six days, which expires this Friday." The ultimatum expired June 8, and sources say the vast majority of Christians left the area.

- Rableh is a Christian village around fifteen miles to the north of Homs, near Qusayr. Half of its seven thousand people were Greek Catholic, and the rest were Maronite. It became a refuge for five thousand of the Christians displaced from Qusayr, and following their arrival, the village was placed under siege by the rebels. Government forces then imposed a siege on the rebels, and the village turned into a battlefield. Hundreds of Christians are believed to have died.

- In Deir el Zor, around five hundred Christian families left their homes following acts of violence and threats against them by the opposition militants. Many found refuge in a nearby town called Al Hassake, which has a Kurdish majority.

- In Aleppo, the second-largest city in Syria, the situation of the large Christian population is increasingly imperiled as fighting spreads from one neighborhood to another. In November 2012, a Catholic missionary in Aleppo described the situation in one Christian neighborhood this way: "It's one of the poorest parts of Aleppo, and one of the most devastated by the fighting. . . . Many of these Christians now don't have a home, they don't have any work, they're penniless, and on top of all that, most of the refugee centers are for Muslims. Although in general co-existence is good, that doesn't lessen the risk posed by fundamentalist Muslims taking advantage of the situation. They're a threat to minorities, and many Christians don't go to the refugee centers out of fear."

In January 2012, the Catholic relief group Aid to the Church in Need said that a secret report out of Syria, whose author could not be identified for security reasons, charged that Christians were being murdered and kidnapped as part of the violence spreading across the country. The report said that the anti-Christian attacks had intensified in the three weeks following Christmas 2012. Accounts provided in the report included the story of two Christian men, one age twenty-eight and the other a thirty-seven-year-old father with a pregnant wife, who were allegedly kidnapped by rebels in separate incidents and later found dead. The first was found hanged, and the other was reportedly cut to pieces and thrown in a river. Four more Christians were kidnapped and abducted, with their captors threatening to kill them too if they didn't convert or leave the area.

In March 2012, a deadly car bomb exploded in the heavily Christian Suleimaniyeh neighborhood of Aleppo, leaving at least two people dead and thirty more wounded. Mar Gregorios Yohanna Ibrahim, the Orthodox archbishop of Aleppo, said at the time that his people were terrified and many were planning to leave the city.

In April 2012, there were no Easter services in the churches of Homs for the first time in centuries. The three principal Christian churches in the city were deserted, while smaller churches and places of worship had already been destroyed. Priests and worshippers gathered in private homes, in secret, for fear of reprisals.

In July 2012, the German magazine *Spiegel* interviewed a group of Christian refugees from Qusayr. Rim Khouri, a young Christian woman who fled the town with her family, said: "Last summer Salafists came to Qusayr, foreigners. They stirred the local rebels against us. . . . They sermonized on Fridays in the mosques that it was a sacred duty to drive us away. We were constantly accused of working for the regime, and Christians had to pay bribes to the jihadists repeatedly in order to avoid getting killed."

Khouri said that her own husband had fallen victim to anti-Christian animosity. "He was stopped at a rebel checkpoint near the state-run bakery," she said. "The rebels knew he was a Christian. They took him and then threw his dead body in front of the door of his parents' house four or five hours later."

In October 2012, a car bomb went off in the Christian heart of Damascus, in the Bab Touma ("Thomas Gate") square, killing at least ten people and leaving fifteen others seriously injured. Some observers believed the attack was a response to a Vatican announcement that a delegation of five senior bishops from around the world would lead a peace mission to Syria, while others saw it more broadly as an attempt to strike fear in the Christian population of Damascus. Because of the violence, as well as logistical difficulties, the Vatican delegation never materialized.

In November 2012, a car bomb exploded in front of the Orthodox Church of the Annunciation in the city of Raqqah, in northeastern Syria, causing two deaths and injuring a woman, all civilians. According to sources cited in a report by the Fides news agency, the Christians of the area had almost entirely fled. The attack came on the heels of two other church bombings in October, one directed at the Evangelical Church of Damascus and another in front of the Syrian Orthodox Church in Deir Ezzor.

Also in November 2012, a Syrian Catholic nun named Agnes-Mariam de la Croix reported that a Christian taxi driver named Andrei Arbashe had been pulled from his vehicle by rebel forces in western Syria and beheaded, with his body scattered in parts on the ground as food for stray dogs. Sr. de la Croix told reporters at the time, "The uprising has been hijacked by Islamist mercenaries who are more interested in fighting a holy war than in changing the government," and she added that "Christians are paying a high price."

The kidnapping of two prominent Orthodox bishops in April 2013 further underscored the dangers. The Syriac Orthodox bishop of Aleppo, Msgr. Youhanna Ibrahim, and the Greek Orthodox Metropolitan of Aleppo and Iskenderun, Msgr. Boulos al-Yaziji, were taken from their car by a group of armed men on the road to Aleppo, while their driver, a Syriac Orthodox deacon, was shot to death. Kidnapping Christians reportedly has become a growth industry among armed factions seeking revenue streams. In late February 2013, the website Ora Pro Siria, operated by Italian missionaries in Syria, launched an emergency fund-raising appeal it called "Ransom a Christian." The website said the going price for a kidnapped priest was in the neighborhood of $200,000.

In June 2013, the Franciscan Custody of the Holy Land, a Catholic group representing the Franciscan order that has a centuries-long presence in the Middle East, reported that a cluster of Christian villages along Syria's Orontes River had been almost totally destroyed in the fighting.

"Of the 4,000 inhabitants of the village of Ghassanieh, as just one example, the local pastor reports that no more than 10 people remain," said Fr. Pierbattista Pizzaballa, director of the Custody, adding that bombs had also seriously damaged a Franciscan monastery in Knayeh near the border with Lebanon. "There is no longer any glass in the windows, the roofs have been damaged, water is leaking everywhere and people are in terror as the bombs continue to fall," he said.

The Custody issued an emergency appeal for food and medicine to aid Syria's Christian population.

In August 2013, a well-known Italian Jesuit priest and pro-democracy activist named Fr. Paolo Dall'Oglio disappeared under mysterious circumstances in Syria. The Vatican issued a communique lamenting the uncertainty about Dall'Oglio's situation, as well as "the absolute silence that weighs on the fate of the two [Orthodox] bishops and priests kidnapped months ago, as well as so many others, Syrians and foreigners, in the same painful situation."

TURKEY

Turkey may be an officially secular state, but sociologically it's an Islamic society, with a population of seventy-five million that's 97 percent Muslim. There are just 150,000 Christians in the country, mostly Greek Orthodox. Only the Greek Orthodox and Armenian communities are officially recognized, so other forms of Christianity are forced to operate in a juridical gray zone—not quite illegal, but not quite fully legitimate either. In general, the greatest threat facing Christians comes not from the most religiously zealous forms of Islam but from ultranationalists who see Christians as agents of the West, often accusing them of being in league with Kurdish separatists.

Christians report various forms of harassment, including difficulties in obtaining permits to build or repair churches, surveillance by security agencies, unfair judicial treatment, and discrimination in housing and employment. The Greek Orthodox Halki Seminary is an emblematic case. Founded in 1844 as the principal school of theology for the Ecumenical Patriarchate of Constantinople, it was considered one of the premier centers of learning in the Orthodox world. It was forced to shut down in 1971, after Turkey adopted a law prohibiting the operation of private universities. Today the buildings and grounds are maintained by monks, while a global campaign to reopen the facility has been under way for more than forty years. Many Orthodox believers see the closure as a way of gradually suffocating the Patriarchate of Constantinople.

Toward the end of 2009, Bartholomew I, the normally reserved and diplomatic Ecumenical Orthodox Patriarch of Constantinople, appeared on CBS's *60 Minutes*. He shocked Turkey's political establishment by arguing that Turkey's Christians are second-class citizens and said that he felt "crucified" by a state that wants to see his church simply die out.

Christian converts from Islam experience strong opposition, frequently being disinherited by their families and losing their employment. Foreign missionaries are often denied residency permits if they identify themselves as religious workers. Christian worship is officially permitted, but congregations report they experience various forms of harassment and verbal abuse. When Turkey was negotiating membership in the European Union, it adopted a series of reforms intended to protect religious minorities in keeping with the Copenhagen criteria on human rights, but local sources say the implementation of those guarantees is inconsistent. As a result of these pressures, Turkey's already small Christian community is today in further decline.

During the past decade, physical attacks on Christians have become increasingly common. In January 2006, a Protestant church leader named Kamil Kiroglu, a Muslim convert to Christianity, was beaten unconscious by five young men. The attack followed church services on January 8, and Kiroglu later reported that one of the young men, wielding a knife, had shouted, "Deny Jesus or I will kill you now!" Another reportedly shouted, "We don't want Christians in this country!" As the attackers left, they told a friend of Kiroglu's that they had left a gift for him. It turned out to be a three-foot-long curved knife, left behind as a further warning against Christian activity.

In February 2006, a well-known Italian Catholic missionary priest named Fr. Andrea Santoro was gunned down by a sixteen-year-old Muslim in the small city of Trabzon. The teen reportedly shouted "Allahu Akbar!" as he fired. The young man told police that he had been angered by Danish cartoons insulting Muhammad. Other observers floated different theories about the motive. Some suggested the teenager had been put up to the killing by the mafia, angry at Santoro for his opposition to the thriving local trade in prostitutes. (In a letter to the pope published after his death by *L'Osservatore Romano*, Santoro had quoted from three Georgian victims of the prostitution trade asking the pope to visit Turkey to speak out on their behalf.) Others believed the teenager had heard rumors that Catholic priests would give money to Muslims to convert to Christianity, and became angry when Santoro declined. For his part, the boy's father said he had a history of mental illness, and styled the attack as a senseless act of madness.

Santoro's bishop at the time, Luigi Padovese, insisted that a virulent climate of anti-Christian propaganda was part of the backdrop. (Padovese would later be killed himself.) As one example, Padovese cited a rural Turkish newspaper that in 2006 carried an article titled "A Priest Sighted." It reported that local children had seen a priest in the vicinity of their town but chased him away, to great applause. The article quoted a local politician: "Priests who arrive in our area want to reestablish the Christian Greek Orthodox state that was here before. There are spies among these priests, working for the West."

Three other Catholic priests were attacked shortly after the murder

of Santoro. Fr. Martin Kmetec, a Slovenian, was threatened by nationalists in the city of Izmir, while a mob reportedly chanted, "We will
kill you all!" A French priest named Fr. Pierre Brunissen was stabbed
with a knife in Samsun, while a French Capuchin priest named Fr.
Henri Leylek was attacked in the Mediterranean city of Mersin. A
forty-seven-year-old man was arrested for the assault on Brunissen, but
police denied any religious motive, saying the perpetrator suffered from
mental illness. Witnesses, however, said the man had complained that
the seventy-four-year-old priest was attempting to convert Muslims.
No arrests were made in the other cases.

In January 2007, a Turkish journalist of Armenian descent named
Hrant Dink was assassinated in Istanbul. A prominent Protestant,
Dink was known as an advocate for human and minority rights, including criticizing Turkey for its denial of the Armenian genocide. He
had been prosecuted three times for "denigrating Turkishness," and
he frequently received death threats. He was shot to death by Ogün
Samast, a seventeen-year-old Turkish nationalist, shortly after the premier of a documentary on the Armenian genocide. Dink was a member
of both the Armenian Apostolic Church, a branch of Orthodoxy, and
an Armenian evangelical fellowship. Though he was killed primarily
for his pro-Armenian politics, most observers said Dink's Christian
beliefs also provided a pretext. Observers also said that the Dink assassination illustrated the increasing militancy of the Turkish nationalist
underground.

In April 2007, a particularly gruesome murder took place in the
central Anatolian city of Malatya, where three Protestant Christian
missionaries, two Turks and one German, were tortured, stabbed, and
strangled. The five young assassins, armed with knives and covered in
blood, were arrested at the scene of the crime. All five turned out to
have links to Turkish nationalist groups. The victims were:

- Necati Aydin, a Turkish convert to Christianity from Izmir,
  who operated a small Christian publishing house in Malatya
  called Zirve (the name is Turkish for "peak"). Since 2005, he
  had served as the minister of the small Protestant community
  in Malatya.

- Tilmann Geske, a German missionary and pastor of a Protestant Free Church in Germany. He had moved to Turkey in 1997 along with his wife and three children to teach English, and he also preached in the local community.
- Ugur Yuskel, who came from an Alevi family in Elazig, a province of Turkey east of Malatya. He had studied in Izmit, where he came into contact with a local Protestant community and converted to Christianity. He had worked for the Zirve publishing house since 2005.

A crescendo to the violence came in June 2010, when Luigi Padovese, the Catholic Apostolic Vicar for Anatolia and president of the country's Catholic bishops' conference, was killed by his driver and longtime aide, Murat Altun. The murder took place at the bishop's residence in Iskenderun. An autopsy showed that Padovese had received multiple stab wounds to the chest and was then beheaded. Although both Turkish and Vatican officials played down any religious motive, suggesting the driver suffered from mental illness, some experts believe the pattern of wounds reflected an Islamic ritual killing. Witnesses reported that Altun had shouted, "Allahu Akbar, I have killed the greatest Satan!" A fellow Catholic bishop in Turkey, Ruggero Franceschini, claimed that the killing was the work of "religious fanatics and ultra-nationalists."

In December 2011, a journalist writing for the Turkish daily *Zaman* complained that "the Vatican is not doing anything" to ensure that the investigation of Padovese's death "is handled in a serious manner." Columnist Orhan Kemal Cengïz wrote that if the Vatican would take a more aggressive stance, it would "really contribute to the well-being of all non-Muslims" and offer "a huge contribution to the promotion of human rights and freedom of religion in Turkey."

Profile: The Martyrs of Algeria

Perhaps the most compelling martyrology of the last two decades belongs to seven Catholic monks in Algeria who went to their deaths in 1996 amid that country's bloody civil war, after having been kidnapped and held by militants for two months. They belonged to the legendary

Trappist order and lived in an Algerian monastery called Notre-Dame de l'Atlas de Tibhirine, developing deep friendships with their Muslim neighbors. The story of the Tibhirine monks has been told in books, in sermons, and even in an award-winning 2010 French film titled *Of Gods and Men*.

During the era of French colonial occupation, when Algeria was incorporated as a territory of France, the country had a flourishing Christian presence largely due to the more than one million *pieds-noirs*, or European settlers. The vast majority left after Algerian independence in 1962. Life became precarious for the country's tiny remaining Christian community in 1992, when the militant Islamic Salvation Front won Algeria's first democratic elections, only to have the results annulled and military rule imposed. Several waves of violence ensued, leading to a civil war that resulted in a hundred thousand deaths and more than a million people injured or left homeless.

In their own quiet way, the monks of Tibhirine had been pioneers in Muslim/Christian relations. They gave their Muslim neighbors part of the monastery to use for daily prayer, taught them French, delivered their babies, and watched over their health. Algerians said the monks were regarded not just as Catholic brothers but also as "true Muslims."

The monks were well aware of the risks of staying. In 1993, a band of militants showed up at the monastery demanding money and logistical help. Told they were interfering with preparations for Christmas Mass, the soldiers departed, apologizing for interrupting the religious observances. As things turned out, however, it was a temporary retreat.

Fr. Christian de Cherge, prior of the monastery, wrote the following words on Pentecost Sunday in 1996, a matter of weeks before his death at the age of fifty-nine:

> If it should happen one day—and it could be today—that I become a victim of the terrorism that now seems ready to encompass all the foreigners in Algeria, I would like my community, my church, my family, to remember that my life was given to God and to this country.
>
> I would like them to be able to associate this death with so

many other equally violent ones allowed to fall into the indifference of anonymity. My life has no more value than any other. Nor
any less.

I don't see how I could rejoice if the people I love were indiscriminately accused of my murder. . . . I know the contempt in
which Algerians taken as a whole can be engulfed.

This is what I shall be able to do, if God wills: immerse my
gaze in that of the Father, to contemplate with him his children of
Islam as he sees them, all shining with the glory of Christ, fruit of
His Passion, filled with the Gift of the Spirit whose secret joy will
always be to establish communion and to refashion the likeness,
playing with the differences.

De Cherge and six other monks were kidnapped by elements of
the Armed Islamic Group on March 27, 1996, and initially offered
for ransom. Two months later, their severed heads were found. Three
heads were hanging from a tree near a gas station; the other four had
been tossed onto the grass. Besides de Cherge, the other victims were
Celestin Ringeard, sixty-two; Christophe Lebreton, forty-five; Bruno
Lemarchand, sixty-six, who was visiting from a monastery in Morocco;
and Brs. Paul Favre Miville, fifty-seven, Michel Fleury, fifty-two, and
Luc Dochier, eighty-two.

The monks of Tibhirine offer an antidote to facile theories about
the relationship between Christianity and Islam. Their complex lives
and deaths debunk both overly romantic notions of tolerance and co-
existence as well as any hawkish insistence on an inevitable "clash of
civilizations." These Algerian martyrs were artisans of the patient and
often painful work of building relationships, overcoming stereotypes,
and confronting hard truths with both honesty and hope.

6

EASTERN EUROPE

Pastor Dritan Prroj, a thirty-four-year-old father of two, knew full well that leaving his exile in the United Kingdom in 2010 and returning to his native Albania would make him a marked man. Five years earlier in the city of Shkodra, where the family lived and where Prroj pastored a thriving evangelical church, his uncle had shot and killed a twenty-eight-year-old man who came into his place of business after hours. The man had been tossed out the night before, because he had been obnoxious and was bothering other customers, and the uncle suspected he was back to cause trouble—which seemed especially likely given that the man was armed and had brought a bodyguard. The uncle pulled out a gun and, in what he insisted was self-defense, killed the intruder.

In Albania, that's rarely the end of things. The incident triggered a blood feud rooted in the *kanun*, a centuries-old set of traditional Albanian laws. According to the *kanun*, the uncle's entire extended family was now subject to vengeance. Because the intruder had been shot in the face, which is considered a special form of disgrace, the *kanun* specified that two relatives of the shooter should pay for his offense with their own blood. Most members of the family immediately went into hiding.

For a time Dritan Prroj tried to maintain life as normal, but he repeatedly discovered people with guns sitting in cars outside his house hoping to get a shot at him. Friends went to the family of the killed man on his behalf, hoping to secure forgiveness, but they were always rebuffed. (The *kanun* specify that priests are off-limits, but the family of the killed man apparently didn't think that applied to an evangelical pastor.) Eventually Prroj and his wife, Elona, decided to move to England, where Prroj ministered in another church. Albania, however, continued to gnaw at him. Friends say he felt God was calling him to return to the country and to continue building the church in Shkodra.

When Prroj came back, his routine was to take his children to school in the morning, go to the church for study, leave the church at 1:00 p.m., and then go pick up his children, Gabriel and Sarah (ages nine and seven at the time of his death). On October 8, 2010, as he was leaving the church to round up his kids, the twenty-one-year-old brother of the man shot by Prroj's uncle fired six bullets into his body, including three in the head. Prroj died a short time later in a local hospital. An off-duty policeman chased the shooter and caught him. As he wrestled him to the ground, the shooter reportedly asked the policeman, "Did I kill him? Is he dead? Tell me he is dead!"

Prroj was well aware that one day the blood feud might claim his life. Friends and family members reportedly begged him to stay out of public view, but Prroj insisted he had to continue serving the community. He led his congregation in worship at regular times and predictable places, despite the risks. In the weeks prior to his death, he led the distribution of humanitarian aid provided when floods swallowed nearby villages, causing hundreds of Albanians to be without homes, food, or clothes. A week before his death, he and his wife had dinner with friends, who recalled him saying that he felt God had told him his life was in God's hands. His brother later revealed that he and Dritan had agreed that if one of them was killed, the other would forswear vengeance, in a deliberate imitation of Christ. Prroj reportedly told friends that he suspected God might use his life to bring an end to the plague of the blood oath.

At the time he was shot, Prroj had two items in his hands. One was a Bible and the other was a briefcase containing notes for an essay he planned to write trying to convince Albanians to abandon blood feuds, which, according to a national reconciliation committee, have been responsible for as many as ninety-five hundred deaths since 1991. In a sign of the respect Prroj enjoyed, the local Catholic parish agreed to host his funeral, because his own small church could not contain the overflow crowd. His widow has started a foundation to fight the cultural tolerance of blood feuds in Albania and to minister to those affected by it, while she and Prroj's brother continue to lead the congregation he pastored.

During the funeral, Elona summed up her husband's view this way: "True revenge . . . is in forgiving." During a massive rally in Tirana, the Albanian capital, two weeks after Prroj died, participants carried signs that read TO FORGIVE IS MANLY—an inversion of traditional cultural understandings, and a hint that Prroj's witness had made a difference.

It might be tempting to conclude that Prroj did not die in the global war on Christians, given that he was slain for his blood ties, not his religious beliefs. Yet the manner in which he accepted that risk and the use he hoped that God would make of his death make clear that it's impossible to understand the death of Pastor Dritan Prroj without also grasping the reasons for which he lived.

EASTERN EUROPE: OVERVIEW

The term "Eastern Europe" can mean different things depending on who's using the term. Some use it to mean everything east of Germany; some think it refers only to former members of the Warsaw Pact; others think it basically designates the majority-Orthodox states of the European continent. Without getting sucked into a geopolitical debate, we'll use the term here to designate twenty-one states that, in one way or another, were once part of the Soviet sphere of influence: Albania, Armenia, Azerbaijan, Belarus, Bosnia and Herzegovina, Bulgaria, Croatia, Czech Republic, Georgia, Hungary, Kosovo, Macedonia, Moldova, Montenegro, Poland, Romania, Russia, Serbia, Slovakia, Slovenia, and Ukraine.

In terms of religion, this definition of "Eastern Europe" includes five states where Catholicism is the dominant tradition (Croatia, Hungary, Poland, Slovakia, and Slovenia), one country that's overwhelmingly Muslim (Azerbaijan), and two others with mixed Muslim/Christian populations (Bosnia and Herzegovina and Kosovo), which leaves thirteen where Orthodoxy sets the cultural tone. That includes Ukraine, though the country is also home to the largest Eastern Catholic church in the world, the Greek Catholic Church, which plays an important role in national affairs. The Czech Republic was historically home to both a large Catholic population and the Bohemian Reformation, though today it's one of the least religious societies on earth, with only 16 percent of the population professing belief in God. (Social scientists often say the Czech Republic and the former East Germany are societies in which atheism is the "state church.")

For much of the twentieth century, Eastern Europe was ground zero for the global war on Christians. The Soviet era unleashed several massive waves of anti-Christian persecution, generating millions of new martyrs. Prayer and activism for the church behind the Iron Curtain, often referred to as the "Church of Silence," became a staple of Cold War Christian activism. Though conditions have improved dramatically with the collapse of Communism, there are still victims of the global war on Christians across Eastern Europe as a result of a variety of forces. In some cases, the protagonists are Muslim radicals; in others, authoritarian states or criminal gangs; in others the violence is Christian-on-Christian; and in still other instances, Christians fall prey to ancient cultural viruses, as the example of Dritan Prroj illustrates.

BELARUS

Sometimes considered the last surviving dictatorship in Europe, Belarus is dominated by fifty-eight-year-old President Alexander Lukashenko, who has ruled the country since 1994. Human rights observers routinely rank Belarus under Lukashenko among the world's worst offenders, charging that his regime provides almost no space for political opposition and represses any potential centers of dissent, including religious groups. The campaign of intimidation reportedly intensified following a disputed 2010 presidential election.

In theory, the constitution of Belarus provides for religious freedom and the equality of the different denominations. Yet the Orthodox Church remains the state church, some 85 percent of the population is Orthodox, and most other forms of Christianity are seen as a nuisance by the state. The Catholic and Lutheran churches are tolerated but not recognized, while other Christian denominations are often harassed and discouraged. Observers say that obtaining registration of a church in Belarus is often difficult, if not practically impossible. In practice, they say, it is impossible to carry on unauthorized religious activity without running the risk of severe sanctions. A 2002 Freedom of Conscience and Religious Organizations law makes unauthorized religious activity a crime subject to two years in prison and/or heavy fines. Among other complaints, church leaders routinely report difficulty in obtaining visas for clergy, even after remedial action is promised by government officials.

According to Open Doors, even officially registered religious organizations do not have the right to develop their own media, to establish educational institutions, to train personnel, or to invite foreign clergy to minister to their membership. Adherents do not have the right to share their convictions or to carry out religious activity beyond the borders of the location where the community is registered. Tolerated traditions, such as Catholicism and Lutheranism, are subject to surveillance by the state security agencies, and unsanctioned forms of Christianity such as evangelical and Pentecostal churches face arrest and punishment. In August 2009, a coalition of fifty Protestant pastors, many of whom had been punished for religious activity, wrote Lukashenko to complain about the lack of religious freedom.

Pro-democracy Christian activists are often special targets. Several leaders of the Christian Democratic Party in Belarus have been sentenced to long stretches in prison, with two party leaders dispatched to a labor camp. A youth leader in the party, Dzmitry Dashkevich, suffered inhumane conditions in prison and was subjected to forms of torture including sleep deprivation, denial of food, and constant psychological assault.

Church property also remains a contentious issue. An estimated

95 percent of the Orthodox churches that had been seized by the state during the Soviet era have been returned, but the Catholics and Lutherans have not had similar success. Officials have announced plans to turn several historic Catholic and Lutheran churches into museums or hotels, including a famed seventeenth-century monastery in Minsk. Church leaders also report steep difficulties in obtaining permits for the construction of new facilities, and say that stringent quality control checks imposed by the state typically cause costs to soar.

In May 2007, a legally registered Pentecostal congregation was raided and its pastor was arrested by police during a service attended by a hundred people. Pastor Antoni Bokun of John the Baptist Pentecostal Church was detained overnight at Minsk's Central District Police Station, according to the human rights group Forum 18. Bokun was heavily fined, an amount roughly twenty times the minimum monthly wage, for holding an "unsanctioned mass meeting."

In January 2009, a Catholic priest named Fr. Zbigniew Grygorcewicz, of Polish origins, was told that he was being expelled from Belarus for organizing a Christian music festival. In the same month, the New Life Church, a charismatic Christian group in Minsk, lost its appeal against the seizure of its church building. Prosecutors charged that the facility had begun life as a cowshed and was being used illegally for religious purposes, while church leaders complained they had repeatedly sought registration and been denied. In the same month, a Baptist pastor named Alexaander Yermalitsky was fined for hosting a religious event at which the Bible was read in his home.

In February 2009, two Danish visitors in Belarus were deported for "expressing ideas of a religious nature." They had been filmed participating in a service at the Living Faith Church, a Pentecostal congregation located in the city of Gomel. One month later, a Christian rehabilitation program for alcohol and drug addicts was twice raided by police, on the grounds that residents had been overheard singing Christian hymns. Later in 2009, two Polish priests were informed by security agents that they had to cease all religious activity or face deportation.

In March 2010, an evangelical pastor in Belarus was twice fined more than a typical month's wage for leading an unregistered church, following a police raid on his church's worship service. In July 2010, another evangelical pastor named Viktor Novik was fined three times in one day for sharing his faith in a local village. Novik asserted that he had repeatedly applied for permission, although that was disputed by local officials.

In December 2012, the New Life Pentecostal Church on the outskirts of Minsk was once again under fire from government officials, who had established a December 5 deadline to evict the church from its premises, only to belay that order temporarily. Leaders of the church organized a thanksgiving service to celebrate their temporary victory but acknowledged that because the land and the building technically belong to the state, they have little leverage to compel a happy ending. At one stage in 2006, church members had organized a hunger strike to stave off an earlier attempt to evict the church and bulldoze the structure. Church leaders claimed they were the victims of "the hostility of the dictatorial government of Alexander Lukashenko."

BOSNIA AND HERZEGOVINA

Bosnia and Herzegovina is officially made up of what it calls three "constituent peoples": Bosniaks, the term for the Muslim ethnic group; Serbs, who are overwhelmingly Orthodox; and the Catholic Croats. Functionally, the country is divided into two essentially autonomous states: the Federation of Bosnia and the Republic of Srpska, with Catholics and Muslims living in the former and Serbian Orthodox in the latter. All that makes the country a cauldron for interreligious and intra-Christian tensions, and thus it's little surprise that Bosnia and Herzegovina is among the combat zones in the global war on Christians. Ethnic, political, and social discrimination are serious problems against non-Serbs in the predominantly Serbian region, against non-Croats in western Herzegovina, and against non-Muslims in central Bosnia. Quite often, these forms of conflict easily give way to, and augment, religious violence.

Leaders of religious minorities routinely complain about discrimination in the regions of the country where they live, both by government officials and at the grass roots. Christians often face difficulties in using their own properties for religious purposes. The Alliance of Protestant-Evangelical Churches in Bosnia and Herzegovina, for instance, has run into problems while seeking registration with the state, allegedly because bureaucrats didn't know what to make of the term "alliance" in a religious context.

Many Christian leaders have also expressed concern about what they see as increasingly radical forms of Islam. Some reports suggest that Bosnia and Herzegovina is a training ground for Muslim terrorists, charging that more than a hundred thousand Bosnian Muslim youth have been exposed to an extremist Wahhabi vision of Islam through a variety of organizations active in the country, many of them enjoying foreign financial support. Some media accounts say that young Bosnian men who attend officially registered Islamic youth camps receive training in marksmanship and explosives.

In January 2009, on the eve of Orthodox Christmas, an Orthodox cathedral in the city of Tuzla was attacked by arsonists. Two months later, St. Luke's Catholic Cathedral in Novi Grad, part of the greater Sarajevo area, suffered its sixteenth attack since 2005. Windows of the church were shattered three different times. Police eventually arrested a suspect who admitted responsibility, but they never filed charges.

In August 2009, shots were fired at an Orthodox church in the Reljevo neighborhood of Sarajevo. The priest who served in the church said it was the fifth such attack in the past year. Bosnian police arrested a man who confessed to firing the shots, claiming he was drunk at the time, but officials did not pursue the question of whether there was an underlying political or religious motive. A month later, Catholics attending a service at the Londza cemetery in the Bosnian Federation were assaulted with rocks by unidentified attackers. A woman suffered minor injuries, and police dismissed the incident as the work of rowdy youths.

In October 2010, a former inmate in the Bosnian Federation charged that Islamic groups inside the prisons were targeting Christians, both Croats and Serbs, and also alleged that prison officials engage in religious discrimination. Among other things, he charged that a notorious Muslim inmate charged with murdering several Croats during their Christmas celebrations received "superb" treatment.

In February 2013, the Catholic auxiliary bishop of Sarajevo, Pero Sudar, charged that the 1995 Dayton Peace Accords and their aftermath put the survival of Bosnia's Catholic community at risk. By splitting the country into two republics, one dominated by Muslims and the other by Serbian Orthodox, Sudar said the message was that "there's room in the country only for two peoples, not for three."

The impact, Sudar said, has been dramatic. In 1992, there were almost a million Catholics in Bosnia and Herzegovina, the vast majority ethnic Croatians, representing almost 20 percent of the country's population. Today Sudar says there are only 460,000 left, meaning the Catholic presence has been cut in half, and most of those who remain are considering exit strategies. Sudar predicted that Croatia's entry into the European Union will further exacerbate the exodus.

Sudar, now in his early sixties, was born during the Communist era in a small Bosnian village that was roughly half Catholic and half Muslim, and he says there were few religious tensions because Muslims and Catholics found themselves in the same boat vis-à-vis an oppressive regime. Up until the war, he said, that spirit still prevailed, with Muslim and Catholic seminaries exchanging faculty to teach courses in one another's creeds. Today, however, he charged that religious and ethnic tensions are if anything "more intense than immediately after the war"—a result, he charged of the "unjust" situation imposed by Dayton, along with a dysfunctional economy and general stagnation.

RUSSIA

The climate for religious freedom in Russia has improved dramatically since the Soviet era, when Russia set the all-time mark for Christian martyrdom. According to the Center for the Study of Global Christianity, the peak periods for martyrdom in more than two thousand years of Christian history occurred in Soviet prison camps from 1921 to 1950 and again from 1950 to 1980. Statistically speaking, the Russian Orthodox Church is by far the most martyred church among the various branches of Christianity, with its total number of victims under both the Nazis and the Soviets estimated at twenty-five million. When

Mikhail Gorbachev repealed a 1960 ban on the ringing of church bells in Russia as part of his glasnost reforms in the late 1980s, it marked the end of a long winter and the beginning of a period of rebirth.

Not only has the post-Soviet opening benefitted the Russian Orthodox Church, but it's created something of a boom market for religion generally. Sociologist of religion Nikolai Mitrokhin, who directs the Institute of the Study of Religion in the CIS and Baltic Countries, believes there are now at least one million practicing Protestants in Russia, and he calls their growth "the most important religious trend" in the country. He estimates that the Pentecostals, Baptists, and Jehovah's Witnesses expanded at a clip of 20–25 percent a year throughout the 1990s and the early years of the twenty-first century. In the streets of Moscow today, new storefront churches seem almost as common as Starbucks.

Russian officials today trumpet their Christian credentials. In February 2012, President Vladimir Putin actually promised leaders of the Orthodox Church that Russia would be on the front lines of defending persecuted Christians in other parts of the world. "You needn't have any doubt that that's the way it will be," Putin said during a meeting with Metropolitan Hilarion, foreign relations chief of the Russian Orthodox Church. Putin also rallied to the defense of Russia's Orthodox identity during the infamous "Pussy Riot" scandal of 2012, when members of a feminist punk band staged an unauthorized performance in Moscow's Cathedral of Christ the Savior—though critics argued that Putin was using the perceived offense to Orthodoxy as a pretext for another crackdown on political opposition.

Yet the end of Communism hardly means that all is well vis-à-vis religious freedom in Russia. Legal regulations for religious organizations have become increasingly stringent under the regime dominated by Putin. In particular, non-Orthodox forms of Christianity in Russia frequently complain of discrimination, suggesting a double standard and alleging a pattern of favoritism and patronage for the Orthodox Church. Leaders of the Orthodox Church sometimes complain that rival Christian factions are engaged in proselytism directed at Orthodox believers.

An October 2012 analysis by International Christian Concern

expresses the situation this way: "Non-Orthodox Christian groups are seen as rooted in the United States in particular and the West in general, competing with the Orthodox Church for membership. Both the government—for which a key priority is to protect 'Holy Russia' from 'foreign devils'—and the Orthodox Church, which is allegedly closely associated with the government, are anti-West. The Russian government also seeks to restrict the functioning of independent organizations that are not allied with it or show any sign of dissent."

Tensions over the return of church properties seized under the Soviets also continue to boil, especially after a controversial law adopted in 2010 that was criticized by Catholics and other minority groups as favoring the Russian Orthodox Church. Catholics, for instance, expressed outrage over the transfer of a former Catholic church in Kaliningrad to the Russian Orthodox. In Lipetsk, Baptists saw a onetime Orthodox church that had been assigned to them taken away and given back to the Orthodox, leaving the Baptists to seek financial compensation.

Threats also continue to face Christians in some contested areas of the Russian Federation, including Chechnya and neighboring Dagestan, where fierce fighting between local Muslims and the Russian army has inflamed sentiments and fed the growth of radical Islamic currents. Formally speaking, Russian legislation is applicable in Chechnya, but the region enjoys limited autonomy, and President Ramzan Kadyrov has signaled his willingness to consider implementing Islamic shariah law. Informally, women who hold public positions are expected to wear head scarves, and men are expected to wear Islamic dress on Fridays, leading many observers to detect a trend toward Islamization. The tiny community of Christians in Chechnya is composed almost entirely of converts from Islam, who face steep social and political discrimination. According to reports, local authorities monitor the activities of these Christians and frequently pressure them to return to Islam. "Honor killings" are also common in families with a member who has converted to another faith.

Most observers believe that for the foreseeable future, believers in Russia will face a twin set of challenges: reconciling genuine religious freedom with the quasi-authoritarian nature of the Putin administration, and dealing with trends toward Islamization and radicalism in some corners of the country.

In February 2009, the governor of Russia's Kaluga region declared that any land owned by the Word of Life Pentecostal Church must be seized "by any means possible," apparently unaware that the meeting at which he made the comment was being streamed live on the regional administration's website. The footage was swiftly posted to YouTube. Most Russian observers said the rare thing was not that a bureaucrat would connive in an assault on a church, but rather that he would be caught doing it. The Word of Life Pentecostal Church has complained of harassment by government officials, who apparently want its land in order to develop a new shopping center.

In October 2009, two Baptist preachers in Kaliningrad were fined after their community was charged with "singing psalms and speaking about Christ" in the streets of the city. Police sources said the Baptists conducted their activity without permission, violating local ordinances. The Baptists, however, insisted that what took place was a service, not a rally, and that requirements for advance authorization did not apply.

In November 2009, Russia's Justice Ministry proposed amendments to the 1997 Religion Law and the Administrative Violations Code to impose more stringent controls on religious activity. Though the measures were bogged down in bureaucratic wrangling, many observers saw them as a worrying indication of new pressures on religious groups.

Also in November 2009, a well-known Russian Orthodox priest named Fr. Daniil Sysoyev was murdered when an unidentified gunman entered his Moscow church and shot him twice. Sysoyev's story will be told at greater length in chapter 11, but the charismatic young cleric had a reputation for evangelizing Russia's Muslim community, and claimed to have personally baptized a large number of Muslim converts to Christianity. Sysoyev frequently reported receiving death threats.

In February 2010, police in Kaluga raided a Sunday-morning service of St. George's Lutheran Church. The local Lutheran archbishop was in attendance in order to ordain a new member of the Lutheran clergy. Reportedly, eleven police officers armed with automatic weapons and assisted by police dogs stormed the church in a search for what they described as "extremist literature." Officers blocked the doors for an hour while the search was conducted, though it ended without any seizures or arrests. Lutheran officials say the church has been harassed since it opened in 2009, apparently disgruntling some locals who see it as a threat to the Orthodox identity of the area.

In May 2010, a seventy-six-year-old Baptist pastor named Yuri Golovin was beaten to death in St. Petersburg outside the home of an elderly member of his congregation he was planning to visit. Golovin died at a nearby hospital as a result of his injuries. Golovin's attackers remain unknown, but local sources suspected they may have been drug addicts looking to rob the pastor. The St. Petersburg neighborhood where the crime took place is reputedly well known for a flourishing drug trade, and sources said that Golovin was aware of the risks but refused to stop his pastoral visits.

In June 2010, authorities backed out of granting permission for members of the Pentecostal Hosanna Church in Dagestan to conduct pastoral visits in local prisons in Dagestan. The Pentecostal pastor asserted that the decision reflected government hostility toward his church.

In July 2010, an evangelical pastor in Dagestan known for founding the region's largest Protestant church was killed by an unidentified gunman, though most observers suspect the involvement of Islamic radicals given that the media in Dagestan had broadcast criticism of the pastor in the weeks leading up to his death. Artur Suleimanov, forty-nine, the pastor of Hosanna Christian Church in Makhachkala, the capital of Dagestan, was shot on the evening of July 15 while leaving his church building. He founded the church in 1994, and it now claims more than a thousand followers, with over 80 percent of its membership believed to be composed of former Muslims.

In June 2012, Sergey Konstantinov, pastor of the Mission Good News Church, and his assistant were attacked in the Leningrad region. According to media reports, the incident occurred early in the morning when morning prayers were being said in the church. Two cars drove up to the church building and more than ten drunken young men tried to enter, while shouting offensive remarks about its ministers and its activities. The hooligans then began to beat the leaders of the congregation, and when they fled and locked themselves in the building, the attackers smashed the windows of both the church and the pastor's car. Konstantinov was left with a broken rib and a broken collarbone in the wake of the assault. A police investigation played down any religious motivation for the assault, but Protestant observers in the area charged that it reflects a growing social climate in which non-Orthodox churches are perceived as fair game.

In September 2012, Russian officials supervised the demolition of Holy Trinity Pentecostal Church in Moscow, leaving more than two hundred members of the congregation to gather near the ruins for worship. Many reportedly do so carrying banners that read THE BUILDING IS DEMOLISHED, THE CHURCH IS ALIVE! Observers say that such demolitions and seizures of church property are becoming more common, with the government often creating a catch-22: it offers new land in a more remote area as compensation, but then makes it virtually impossible to obtain the zoning permits needed to actually construct a new church.

Members of Jehovah's Witnesses, a group situated outside the Christian mainstream, are frequent targets of harassment, especially in light of a new "anti-extremism" law regarded by critics as a tool to exercise control over religious minorities. In February 2012, the Council of Europe voiced specific concern for the situation facing Jehovah's Witnesses in Russia, expressing "deep concern about the misuse of anti-extremism legislation involving the illegal implementation of criminal laws against . . . religious minorities such as Jehovah's Witnesses . . . and the improper banning of their materials on grounds of extremism."

Andrey and Lyutsiya Raitin illustrate the dynamics. They were arrested in February 2011 in Chita, a city in Russia's Zabaykalskiy territory, and charged under the extremism statute. The Raitins were not considered leaders of the denomination, and they held no official positions. Reportedly, their offense was distributing Russian-language versions of a tract called "What Does the Bible Really Teach?," commonly used by the Jehovah's Witnesses in their door-to-door ministry in various parts of the world. Local police searched the Raitins' home, along with the homes of other Jehovah's Witnesses in the city, and confiscated their religious literature. The Raitins were indicted on July 8, 2011, and the Chitinskiy district court began a trial in the criminal case against them on December 22, 2011. During the proceedings the defense called attention to numerous alleged violations committed by law enforcement officers prior to the case being opened and during the investigation, including the disappearance of documents, unauthorized corrections, signs of falsification, and so on. The court refused to consider these allegations, leading spokespeople for the Jehovah's Witnesses to assert "that in trying this case, the court has not put forth the necessary effort to establish the truth."

As of this writing, the criminal proceedings against the Raitins were still ongoing, and no verdict had been reached. Observers say such delays are often part of the pattern of harassing and intimidating religious minorities in the former Soviet Union. The long stretch of time before conclusion is reached tends to sap their energy, and the fear of what might happen sometimes induces them to leave the country. Even if the accused are vindicated, the possibility of rearrest and facing new charges also tends to have a chilling effect.

Other Jehovah's Witnesses face similar harassment, including a church elder named Maksim Kalinin who lives in Yoshkar-Ola in the Mari El Republic, an enclave within the Russian Federation. He was indicted under the extremism law in December 2011, after a police raid in August 2010 on homes and a church service at which he was present. According to a report by Forum 18, the Russian security police had conducted surveillance of Kalinin using a hidden camera. Because Kalinin was too ill to go to the prosecutor's office, officials delivered the indictment at his home. Also facing sanction was Yelena Grigoryeva, from Akhtubinsk in the southern Astrakhan region, who was indicted in December 2011. Grigoryeva was accused of "basing herself on the ideas of inciting religious hatred and enmity, as well as propaganda of the exclusivity and superiority of people on the basis of their religion . . . committed from 2009 to February 2010, a crime of minor gravity against the foundations of the constitutional order and the security of the state." In support of those charges, the indictment noted numerous occasions when Grigoryeva handed a banned tract to someone. The formal indictment came after Grigoryeva's home had been raided by police and her personal religious books confiscated. She was also forced out of her job providing social care in Akhtubinsk, with police compelling her to sign a statement saying she was stepping down "at her own request." Her lawyer was also reportedly pressured to drop Grigoryeva's appeal. Both the Kalinin and Grigoryeva cases went to trial in 2012.

Profile: Fr. Tudor Marin

Though religious animosity is far from the lone force fueling the global war on Christians, it is still part of the mix, as the tragic death of Fr. Tudor Marin illustrates. A beloved Orthodox clergyman in the Romanian city of Focsani, the sixty-nine-year-old Marin was stabbed to death on June 16, 2012, inside his Sfantul Ioan Botezatorul (Nativity of St. John the Baptist) Church on one of the city's main squares. The attack was witnessed by an elderly parishioner who was selling candles inside the church.

Police later arrested thirty-year-old Florentin Puşcoiu, who confessed to killing the Orthodox priest. During a search of Puşcoiu's apartment, investigators found an extensively annotated Bible and rafts of paper with notes concerning various scriptural texts. During a subsequent interrogation of Puşcoiu, he said that he had set out that Saturday morning "to kill a priest." According to his reconstruction of events, Puşcoiu had visited three churches but left the first two because they were too crowded or too well protected. When he arrived at Sfantul Ioan Botezatorul, he approached Marin and asked several questions regarding the interpretation of the Bible. Dissatisfied with his answers, Puşcoiu then produced a knife, stabbed Marin repeatedly, and left him to die.

The case generated controversy, in part because the investigation revealed that Puşcoiu had previously been questioned by police for brandishing a knife at the bread company in Focsani where he worked, but he had been released and no charges had ever been filed. Puşcoiu apparently left Romania briefly after that incident to travel to Italy, spending time visiting churches and developing his own idiosyncratic reading of the Bible. Prosecutors described him as "mentally unbalanced" and "obsessed" with what he believed to be the hidden meaning of various texts from Scripture.

In the aftermath of the attack, the Patriarchate of the Romanian Orthodox Church issued a statement calling on security services to do a better job of protecting churches. The statement deplored that the attack came in a church, "where priests preach peace and love of neighbor, and now a peaceful and venerable prelate was brutally murdered in a horrible crime that shows the alarming state of degradation, violence and insecurity which characterizes society today."

In the wake of his death, Marin was recalled as a humble pastor who remained close to the people he served. He was the father-in-law of a well-known trade union leader named Vasile Marica. Media reports indicate that the community in Foscani was in shock after the attack, given that Marin had been seen as a "kind and gentle" figure with no reputation for generating controversy or taking high-profile positions on political or cultural questions. Observers believe that Marin was killed not for personal reasons but as a symbol of a religious system that his attacker had come to loathe.

Religion famously has the capacity to stir deep passions, for both good and ill. The death of Fr. Tudor Marin is a grisly reminder that even in the twenty-first century, and even in an overwhelmingly Christian society such as Romania, the mere fact of being an ordinary Christian can occasionally be enough to court danger.

PART TWO

Myths About the Global War
on Christians

U.S. senator Hiram Warren Johnson is credited with coining the phrase "The first casualty when war comes is truth," in 1918. Some dispute the attribution, but whoever said it, the experience of the twentieth and early twenty-first centuries illustrates its accuracy. From persistently inflated body counts given during the war in Vietnam to the fabled "weapons of mass destruction" that were nowhere to be found in Iraq, misinformation is as much a weapon of modern combat as tanks and guns.

So too with the global war on Christians, where several chronic misperceptions and erroneous ways of framing the situation get in the way of clear-eyed perception. The chapters in this section tackle five such common myths:

- Christians are vulnerable only where they're a minority, rather than being exposed to danger virtually anywhere, including societies in which they represent the overwhelming majority.
- "No one saw it coming," an assumption that means acts of anti-Christian violence are forever styled as random and unpreventable, rather than the predictable result of a mounting pattern of hatred.

- "It's all about Islam," fueling notions that the war on Christians is exclusively a product of Muslim radicalism, rather than being driven by a bewildering cocktail of social forces.
- "It's only persecution if the motives are religious," rather than seeing Christians as martyrs every time they put their safety at risk on the basis of their faith.
- The war on Christians is a left-wing or right-wing issue, as opposed to the transcendent human rights concern of the early twenty-first century, regardless of ideology or political affiliation.

In various forms, these myths can be found running through much of the public discussion about anti-Christian harassment and violence. In some cases, different constituencies have powerful motives for keeping these myths alive, hoping to exploit the global war on Christians as a wedge issue or to galvanize Christian activism in favor of a pet cause. In other instances, these myths are the result of naive assumptions and partial impressions, which linger because neither the secular media nor the Christian intelligentsia has bothered to examine them critically. In an environment in which press coverage of the war on Christians is often episodic and ill-informed, and in which most Christian conversation is obsessively focused on domestic issues, it's not surprising that these myths have had a long shelf life.

If truth is the first casualty of war, clear perception is the beginning of peace. The reports collected in the previous chapters have already provided the raw material to debunk these myths. The business of this section is to bring it all together so that by the end, to quote St. Paul's Letter to the Corinthians, we can see the global war on Christians "not through a glass darkly, but face-to-face."

7

THE MYTH THAT CHRISTIANS ARE AT RISK ONLY WHERE THEY'RE A MINORITY

On those rare occasions when the war on Christians registers on the public radar screen, there's a tendency to regard it as a problem largely confined to regions where Christians are encircled by some larger force. The Middle East comes to mind, especially because saturation coverage of Islamic radicalism makes the idea easy to accept. Likewise, most people don't have a hard time imagining Christians as victims in China or North Korea, because it's commonly understood that there Christians represent a subculture up against hostile regimes with checkered human rights records. India too seems a plausible setting for anti-Christian hostility, given its overwhelmingly Hindu majority and growing public awareness of the dangers of Hindu radicalism.

To be sure, there's a surface plausibility to this way of thinking about anti-Christian persecution. In the 2012 edition of the annual rundown issued by Open Doors of the top fifty nations in which Christians are at risk, only four are societies in which Christians are a majority (Eritrea, Cuba, Belarus, and Colombia). It's also understandably difficult for people to get their minds around the idea that a war on Christians could take root in overwhelmingly Christian settings, where churches still wield massive social influence, Christian leaders are often culture-shaping celebrities, and Christian institutions command massive financial and human resources. In those environments, it's tempting to presume that Christians ought to be basically safe.

Tempting, that is, but thoroughly false.

First of all, even if it were true that Christians are exposed to persecution only where they constitute a demographic minority, it would not diminish the seriousness of the issue. According to a recent Pew Forum analysis, 10 percent of the world's Christians live in societies in which they're a minority. Given that there are more than two billion Christians on the planet, this translates into more than two hundred million people living in risk-filled circumstances. Any scourge that imperils that many people, whatever the cause, would merit concern. For instance, one leading estimate of the number of people around the world at risk of displacement due to climate change is also two hundred million, and there's certainly no shortage of anxiety about that issue.

Even a moment's reflection, however, is enough to demonstrate that it's not just places where Christians are a minority that form the front lines of this war, and it never has been. The Center for the Study of Global Christianity estimates that seventy million Christians have been martyred since the time of Christ, with forty-five million of those deaths coming in the twentieth century alone. By far the largest concentration of martyrs was in the Soviet Union, with as many as twenty-five million killed inside Russia and an additional eight million in Ukraine. Both Russia and Ukraine are profoundly Christian societies, even during the period in which they were governed by officially atheistic regimes.

Many of the most celebrated martyrs of the late twentieth century came in Latin America, among Christians who resisted the police states of the region. As we saw in chapter 1, the popular estimate that on average one hundred thousand Christians were killed every year over the past decade is heavily influenced by the situation in the Democratic Republic of Congo, where Christians have been slaughtered indiscriminately in what experts at the Center for the Study of Global Christianity describe as a "situation of witness." The Democratic Republic of Congo too is a preponderantly Christian nation.

The basic insight is that anywhere Christians profess their faith openly, anywhere they take controversial stands in favor of social justice and human rights on the basis of their convictions—anywhere, for that matter, where they're simply in the wrong place at the wrong time—they are exposed to danger. Indeed, martyrdom is at least as likely where Christians are in the majority, for the simple reason that it's more probable that the activists and voices of conscience who stir opposition will be Christians.

SNAPSHOTS OF "MAJORITY MARTYRS"

Previous chapters have already brought numerous examples of what we might call "majority martyrs," meaning Christians who suffer violence in places where Christians are a social majority. They include American Sr. Dorothy Stang, the great "martyr of the Amazon" in Brazil, and Maria Elizabeth Macías Castro, a leader in the Scalabrinian lay movement and a popular blogger, beheaded in Mexico in 2011 for exposing the activities of a drug cartel. As we have also seen, sometimes Christians face lethal threats from their fellow Christians, such as Lorenzo López, a twenty-year-old evangelical from San Juan Chamula in Mexico, killed by a band of militant traditionalist Catholics who see evangelicals as a threat to the country's Catholic identity. Brazil and Mexico are the two largest Catholic countries on earth, illustrating that simply being in the majority is no guarantee against harm.

The Vatican-sponsored missionary news agency Fides issues an annual list of Catholic pastoral workers who lost their lives around the world. (The term "pastoral worker" refers to clergy and laity who work for the church, not ordinary faithful.) For the year 2011, Fides recorded twenty-six such deaths. What's striking is that only one died in a country where Christians are a minority: Rabindra Parichha, a lay catechist who was murdered in Orissa in eastern India. All the remaining casualties died in places where Christians form a majority, and most went to their deaths in places where Christianity is the traditionally dominant local religion.

The following are a few representative examples of "majority martyrs," meaning Christians who died in places where Christianity is the dominant religious tradition and where one might think the global war on Christians wouldn't reach.

Sr. Angelina

The story of Sr. Angelina, a Catholic nun and member of the Augustinian order (her last name is not given in any of the reports of her death), neatly illustrates the fallacy of the "only where a minority" myth.

A native and resident of South Sudan, she was killed on January 17, 2011, while traveling in the neighboring Democratic Republic of Congo to bring medical aide to Sudanese refugees. Both South Sudan and the DRC have Christian majorities, and the Catholic Church enjoys strong social prestige. Moreover, Sr. Angelina, a member of the St. Augustine Institute, was attacked and killed by the Uganda-based Lord's Resistance Army, which is both a rebel force and also a sort of new religious movement, blending Christianity with African mysticism and tribal beliefs. In recent years, the LRA has waged a campaign of terror, killing and kidnapping innocent victims in South Sudan. Since 1988, the LRA is believed to have abducted more than thirty thousand children. Boys are forced to become child soldiers, while the girls are abused as sex slaves. Sr. Angelina was thirty-seven at the time of her death at the hands of the LRA militants, who apparently wanted to steal her supplies.

The fact that a self-styled Christian militia exercises this reign of terror in a zone where the local population is largely Christian, and where the churches enjoy enormous respect, forcefully demonstrates that even places where Christians dominate the social landscape are not exempt from the global war.

Fr. Fausto Tentorio

Fr. Fausto Tentorio is another "majority martyr," a Catholic priest and member of the Pontifical Institute for Foreign Missions who was slain in the overwhelmingly Catholic Philippines in October 2011. Tentorio, an Italian missionary priest known by the locals as "Pops," had been serving on the island of Mindanao, the only area of the country with a significant Muslim presence. However, there's no evidence that his death had anything to do with Muslim-Christian tensions. Instead, many locals believe that the gunman arrested in the case had links to a right-wing militia known as the Bagani Forces, who had targeted

Tentorio for his staunch support of anti-mining movements on behalf of the local indigenous population, accusing him of being a supporter of the Communist-affiliated New People's Army.

Tentorio was shot and killed inside the compound of the Mother of Perpetual Help parish church in Arakan, on Mindanao, at around 7:30 a.m. on Monday, October 17, 2011. It was not an ending that came as a complete surprise, given that the missionary priest had faced death threats before over the course of the thirty-two years he spent in the Philippines. In 2003, he had been menaced by the same local militia that many people suspected of orchestrating his death eight years later. Here's his own account of that 2003 experience, drawn from his diary: "On the morning of October 6, 2003, I left the parish of Arakan, Cotabato, at 8:00 together with four of our staff to visit some villages of indigenous people in the area of Kitao-tao, Bukidnon about 30 kilometers away." Tentorio wrote that concerned citizens told him that the Bagani group would cut off his head, roast his ears, and eat them. The people hid him in a hut as the Bagani group began searching for him and another man, Isidro Indao, vice chairman of a group that the Pontifical Institute for Foreign Missions had organized and supported for many years. Tentorio later escaped after the residents diverted the attention of the Bagani group by inviting them to slaughter and roast a pig at another village.

Tentorio was born on January 7, 1952, in Santa Maria di Rovagnate, and raised in Santa Maria Hoè in Lecco, Italy. He was ordained in 1977 and left for the Philippines the following year. He worked with Christian, Muslim, and indigenous B'laan communities in Columbio, Sultan Kudarat, before transferring to the mission in Arakan. He was actually the third priest of the Pontifical Institute for Foreign Missions to be killed in the Philippines, after Fr. Tullio Favali in 1985 and Fr. Salvatore Carzedda in 1992. Like Tentorio, Favali had been accused of being a Communist sympathizer because of his stances in favor of the local poor and against the large-scale corporate interests in the area.

The Philippines is the third-largest Catholic country in the world, and also home to burgeoning evangelical and Pentecostal movements. It's among the most profoundly and tangibly Christian societies on the planet, a place where national leaders are expected to profess Christian beliefs as part of their public discourse, and where clergy often carry more weight in moving opinion than politicians and judges. Obviously, that pervasive Christian ethos was not enough to keep Tentorio and his two confreres safe.

Pastor Julius Mukonzi

Julius Mukonzi of Kenya is an African example of the "majority martyr." He was a popular Protestant police chaplain who belonged to the Utawala Interdenominational Church in Garissa, located in the country's northeast. The church, which is inside a police compound, serves police officers stationed at the compound as well as their families. On November 4, 2012, Mukonzi was delivering a sermon when a grenade was tossed onto the roof of the church; it went off directly above his head, killing him. At least eleven of the estimated forty worshippers inside the church were injured in the attack, most of them fellow police officers. Three were later airlifted to Nairobi for specialized treatment. Other churches ended their services early as news of the attack spread, and church leaders called for an inquiry into an increase in anti-Christian violence. Although no group has claimed responsibility, authorities believe it was carried out by the Muslim extremist group Al-Shabab. According to media reports, Al-Shabab had staged several similar attacks in the past year, including a grenade attack on a Nairobi church in September that killed a nine-year-old boy and an attack in Garissa on July 1 that killed eighteen people.

The vast majority of Kenya's forty-three million people, roughly 83 percent of the population, is Christian. Kenya is among the most Christian societies in Africa, and increasingly it's one of the Christian powerhouses across the developing world. Nairobi is home to several of the best-regarded Christian seminaries on the continent, and Kenya also has the most developed Christian media outlets anywhere in Africa. Yet as the story of Julius Mukonzi illustrates, those things alone are not always sufficient to keep Christians safe.

Archbishop Isaías Duarte Cancino

Archbishop Isaías Duarte Cancino of Colombia was assassinated in 2002. Colombia is the seventh-largest Catholic country in the world, the kind of place where Catholic clergy are often media rock stars and political heavy hitters, and where very little happens without the church being involved. It's also the birthplace of the G12 model for missionary work pioneered by the International Charismatic Mission, based on each church member assembling a group of twelve other believers, which is spreading like wildfire all across Latin America. Yet this pervasive religious climate has hardly been sufficient to insulate Christians from violence—even senior clergy are exposed, as the story of Archbishop Duarte makes clear.

Sixty-three at the time of his death, Duarte was an outspoken critic of the political and drug-related violence in Colombia. On March 16, 2002, two young gunmen shot him to death as he emerged from the church of the Good Shepherd in Aguablanca, one of the poorest districts of his Cali archdiocese. He had just been conducting a wedding ceremony for more than a hundred couples. Cali, in southwestern Colombia, is home to two million people and some of the country's most powerful drug-trafficking organizations. In February, Duarte had publicly accused drug bosses of pouring money into the campaign coffers of local candidates in Colombia's congressional elections, which had taken place on March 10, just six days before his assassination.

Duarte had been in the thick of political controversy for several years. In 1999 he excommunicated leading members of Colombia's second-largest guerrilla group, the National Liberation Army, after they had kidnapped more than 150 people attending Mass in a Cali church. His implacable opposition to the guerrillas earned him praise from some of the right-wing paramilitary death squads that sprang up all over Colombia to challenge the guerrillas. Yet Duarte was equally hard on those groups too, frequently speaking out against the practice of paramilitary killings.

"A rebel who kidnaps and kills, eliminates entire populations and mocks the whole process of peace lacks the virtues proper to a human being and becomes the most miserable of men," Duarte wrote in 2000.

"We ask God that the guerrilla fighters in Colombia may feel deep sorrow in their souls for the evil they commit when they kill an innocent, defenseless brother or sister, and that they may understand that theirs is not a just war, but merely a repeating of savage acts of the saddest times of human history."

The archbishop's death brought tributes from all over the world, including Pope John Paul II. "He paid the highest price for his energetic defense of human life, his firm opposition to all types of violence and his dedication to social development according to the Gospel," the late pope said.

A decade later, a Colombian court tried the founder of FARC and three other senior figures in absentia for involvement in Duarte's death, sentencing each to twenty-five years in prison and ordering them to pay a massive fine to the murdered prelate's family. In reaching its verdict, the court declared, "There is no doubt that the murder of Isaías Duarte Cancino was related to his religious status and position. As archbishop of Cali, he protested the reprehensible acts constantly carried out by guerrillas in this country."

As noted in the chapter on Latin America, Duarte was merely one of at least a hundred priests, bishops, deacons, nuns, and religious brothers to be killed amid the violence in Colombia since 1984. In some ways, Colombia is exhibit A in the case that Christians are at risk not only where they're a minority, but absolutely everywhere.

MARTYRS OF CHARITY

As Notre Dame's Daniel Philpott observed in a November 2012 essay in *America* magazine, "What is most distinctive about today's martyrs is their witness to justice and reconciliation." The emergence of a new class of "martyrs of charity," meaning activists who defy an unjust status quo in whichever settings they find themselves, also helps explain why Christians are vulnerable everywhere. Those who benefit from systems of injustice typically don't appreciate the challenge, and Christian beneficiaries are no exception.

In earlier eras, Christians were put to death for specifically religious reasons, such as refusal to sacrifice to pagan gods. That still happens occasionally, but today's martyrs more often find themselves persecuted for other reasons, often related to social and political positions taken on the basis of their reading of the Gospel. Christians around the world, as Philpott observes, are in the front lines of promoting "religious freedom, unity among the Christian churches, friendship among world religions and the transforming power of forgiveness in politics." To that list could be added other signature Christian causes such as opposition to war, solidarity with the poor, and the robust defense of a "culture of life," implying opposition to abortion, euthanasia, and embryonic stem cell research. In addition, there are core virtues such as honesty, integrity, selflessness, and compassion, the practice of which also has a proven capacity to make some people angry.

Recognizing that these commitments are often the subtext to anti-Christian violence in the modern world, the late Pope John Paul II stretched the concept of martyrdom to include not only those killed in hatred of the faith but also those who died in hatred of the church. Many theologians today are increasingly willing to include also those killed out of hatred for the virtues inspired by the faith.

One classic example is St. Maximilian Kolbe, a Polish Franciscan priest who died under the Nazis in the Auschwitz concentration camp in 1941 after volunteering to take the place of a stranger. This was not a death *in odium fidei*, because Kolbe wasn't put to death on the basis of his religious convictions. Yet when Pope John Paul II canonized Kolbe in 1982, the formal act of declaring someone a saint, he termed the Polish priest a "martyr of charity."

Don Pino Puglisi, from Sicily, is a more contemporary example. Puglisi served in the tough Palermo neighborhood of Brancaccio, and openly challenged the Sicilian Mafia, which controlled its streets. He was shot dead by a Mafia gunman in 1993, on his fifty-sixth birthday. By all accounts, Puglisi was a funny, spitfire pastor who convinced youth in Brancaccio that there are ways forward in life other than the mob, and who helped shape a civil society that challenged its political hold. He is often touted as the "Oscar Romero of Sicily," meaning a man whose life made a difference and whose death changed history.

Francesco Deliziosi is a Catholic layman in Palermo who had

Puglisi as a religion teacher in high school and as a spiritual director for fifteen years, and who served as a volunteer in Puglisi's parish from 1990 until the pastor was gunned down. Deliziosi then began a research project on Puglisi, which became the basis for the historical materials in the diocesan phase of the canonization process. According to Deliziosi, Puglisi's anti-Mafia activism took shape during the 1960s in the tiny town of Godrana, in the hills roughly twenty-five miles outside Palermo. When he arrived as pastor, there had been fifteen recent murders, all related to a feud between two rival clans. Puglisi started going door-to-door, reading the Gospel with people and talking about forgiveness. He encouraged small groups to meet together to pray and read the Bible, at first once a month, then every fifteen days.

Eventually one of the women who had been hosting a group said to Puglisi that she did not feel she could carry on until she had forgiven the mother of her son's assassin. After much time, effort, and prayer, Puglisi arranged a reconciliation between the two women, which endured despite strong disapproval from many in the village. By itself this outcome did not cancel the feud, but it was a start.

"Peace," Puglisi said, "is like bread—it must be shared or it loses its flavor."

In 1992, a year before Puglisi's own death, two famous anti-Mafia judges were assassinated in Sicily, Paolo Borsellino and Giovanni Falcone. Puglisi happened to be with some schoolchildren from his parish when he learned of Borsellino's death. As Deliziosi tells the story, Puglisi was deeply upset, but after a moment he turned to the children and said: "We must be able to forgive the authors of this tragedy and to invite them to conversion."

The kids were incredulous. Puglisis then asked them, "If Judge Borsellino had been in your family, would you forgive his killers?" The youth, raised on the centuries-old Sicilian tradition of the vendetta, said no.

"Then we have a long road yet to follow," he said. "It is the road of Christian forgiveness, seeking justice and not revenge."

A plaque on the wall of Puglisi's old parish in Brancaccio captures his spirit: "To the perpetual memory of the pastor, P. Giuseppe Puglisi.

Priest of the Lord, missionary of the Gospel, former of consciences in truth. Promoter of social solidarity and ecclesial service in charity. Killed for his faithfulness to Christ and to humanity on September 15, 1993." On June 28, 2012, Pope Benedict XVI granted permission for Puglisi to be classified as a martyr, which means that he can be beatified, the final step before sainthood, without a miracle being certified as due to his intercession.

As a footnote, both Kolbe and Puglisi are also examples of "majority martyrs," in the sense that they were killed for choices made on the basis of their faith despite living and working in overwhelmingly Christian cultures. With regard to Puglisi, one might well say that if a Catholic priest isn't safe even in Italy, no further proof of the vacuity of the "minority only" myth should be required.

WHY THIS MYTH IS TOXIC

In addition to being inaccurate, the "minority only" myth is dangerous. It obscures large swaths of the planet from view in thinking about the threats that Christians face, and suggests a false sense of invulnerability for Christians in societies where they represent a majority. It also aids and abets the reluctance of government officials and other leaders in majority-Christian societies to honestly confront the cancers that may be growing in those places. One can imagine Sicilian authorities, for instance, scoffing at the idea of anti-Christian persecution in their own backyard, citing Sicily's overwhelmingly Catholic population. Yet the story of Don Puglisi is the most eloquent refutation possible to such denial.

The myth that Christians are only at risk in certain prescribed places also overlooks the profound suffering faced by Christians in many heavily Christian locations, and often prevents the compelling stories of some of the most heroic martyrs of our time from being adequately told.

For instance, Conchita Francisco was a sixty-two-year-old devout Catholic school principal in the remote province of Tawi Tawi in the southern Philippines who was shot to death in November 2012 as she was leaving Mass. Police were still looking for the gunman at the time of this writing, but many locals suspected the involvement of Abu Sayyaf, an armed Islamic group in the Mindanao region (the group's name means "bearer of the sword"). It would be tragic if either Christians or advocates of religious freedom failed to invest the same energy in Francisco's case, or in preserving her memory, as they would for a Christian targeted in Saudi Arabia or China, simply because the Philippines is a majority-Christian nation.

Debunking this bit of mythology is not only a service to the truth but an important preliminary in turning the tide on the global war. This is a war that can find its victims absolutely anywhere.

8

THE MYTH THAT NO ONE
SAW IT COMING

In the movie *Casablanca*, there's a famous scene in which Captain Louis Renault, played memorably by Claude Rains, declares himself shocked to discover gambling at Rick's nightclub. Immediately after that declaration, of course, an employee of the nightclub hands the captain his winnings from the casino, for which he unashamedly expresses thanks. The scene has become a standard metaphor for the hypocrisy of officials who express surprise and dismay only when a scandal is uncovered, but otherwise condone the behavior, or, as in the case of Captain Renault, actively participate in it.

When it comes to the global war on Christians, there's often what we might call a "Casablanca defense" popular among politicians, police, prosecutors, and other responsible parties, which tends to be invoked on those infrequent occasions when a particular outrage, such as the murder of Shahbaz Bhatti in Pakistan, places these officials in an uncomfortable spotlight. In those circumstances, these officials typically profess dismay, declaring themselves stunned that such a thing could have happened. They heap praise on the victim and vow swift justice for the perpetrators, but also absolve themselves of responsibility by suggesting that no one could have anticipated such a thing.

In addition, they often suggest the perpetrator was an unbalanced or mentally disturbed person, as a way of denying that the act was part of any broader pattern or climate.

More often than not, this "Casablanca defense" is a bald lie. In a strong majority of cases, the act in question did not drop from a clear blue sky. Instead, the warning signs of trouble were usually abundantly clear, even if no one could have predicted the precise time or place when another round of violence might strike. Rather, the act usually speaks to a deeper climate of anti-Christian hostility, for which its leadership often must bear some measure of responsibility—if not for stoking it, at least for standing idly by while it gains force and places innocent people in harm's way. Seeing past the "no one saw it coming" myth is thus an important step toward creating a global culture of accountability.

(By the way, the next time a Christian is victimized in Morocco, the setting for the movie *Casablanca*, no one should let bureaucrats there get away with invoking the "Casablanca defense." Among other signs of hostility, there's a Moroccan convert to Christianity named Jamaa Ait Bakrim who, as of this writing, had served seven years in prison for the crime of proselytizing. Two years ago, the country deported dozens of foreign Christian workers and foster parents.)

THE TURKISH EXAMPLE

Reaction to the brutal June 3, 2010, murder in Turkey of Catholic bishop Luigi Padovese, who had served as the Apostolic Vicar of Anatolia, offers a classic example of the Casablanca defense in action. The bishop's longtime driver stabbed Padovese repeatedly, slitting his throat so deeply that his head was almost detached from his body. In the immediate aftermath of the murder, Governor Mehmet Celalettin Lekesiz of Hatay province insisted that the driver was mentally unhinged, suggesting that the attack was tragic but basically unpredictable and random. According to Celalettin, the incident was "a personal matter" that had no religious or political motive. He promised a "very thorough" investigation, although three years later most Turkish observers believe the inquest was fairly perfunctory.

Turkey's minister for culture and tourism, Ertugrul Günay, issued a message of condolences on behalf of the government. The Foreign Ministry expressed regret to the international media, while also emphasizing the murderer's "psychological problems." The state-run media outlet NTV Turkey announced erroneously that the murderer was not a Muslim but a convert to Catholicism, seen as an effort to deflect any connection between the murder and Islamic radicalism. One police source leaked allegations that the driver had been "forced to suffer abuse" in a homosexual relationship with Padovese, a suggestion that was later retracted following vigorous denials by sources close to both men.

In framing things as unpredictable and not connected to any larger narrative, the Turkish government was not alone. Padovese's murder came just one day before Pope Benedict XVI's June 4–6, 2010, trip to Cyprus. (Padovese had been scheduled to take part in the trip). At the time, it was Benedict's third voyage to the Middle East, and the pontiff was set to present the working document for an upcoming synod dedicated to the Middle East. After a firestorm of protest broke out in 2006 following a speech in Regensburg, Germany, in which Benedict XVI appeared to link Muhammad with violence, the pope had worked hard to put relations with Islam back on track, and he seemed determined not to allow the Padovese murder to cast a shadow over his outing to Cyprus. Aboard the papal plane en route to Nicosia, he told reporters that while he still had "very little information" about the killing, he was convinced that "we must not attribute the fact [of Bishop Padovese's murder] to Turkey . . . What is certain is that it was not a religious or political assassination."

While Benedict undoubtedly had his reasons, his statement left many Turkish Christians perplexed. Looking back with the benefit of three years' hindsight, it seems far less clear today that "religious or political" motives can be ruled out—at least as background to the murder, if not its direct cause.

The archbishop of Smyrna, Ruggero Franceschini—Padovese's successor as head of the country's Catholic Church—rejected the official explanation of his colleague's murder and maintained that the pope had received "bad counsel" prior to his denial of political or religious motives, insisting that he refused to acquiesce in the "usual hastily concocted, pious lie" about the murderer's insanity.

"I believe that with this murder, which has an explicitly religious element, we are faced with something that goes beyond government," Franceschini said at the time. "It points towards nostalgic, perhaps anarchist groups who want to destabilize the government. The very modalities of the murder aim to manipulate public opinion."

In the section on Turkey in chapter 5, we saw that the Padovese murder was the culmination of a growing pattern of anti-Christian violence. The drumbeat included the shooting death of Fr. Andrea Santoro in 2006, attacks on three other prominent Catholic priests also in 2006, the assassination of Protestant human rights activist Hrant Dink in 2007, the gruesome murders of three Protestant missionaries in 2007, and the 2009 revelation of a "Cage Plan" hatched by ultranationalists intended to destabilize Turkey by attacking non-Muslim targets. At the time, a leader of the Turkish Protestant community, Rev. Behnan Konutgan, recorded other cases of violence against church property and the physical harassment of church members, suggesting that the assault on Padovese was eminently predictable, while a noted Turkish sociologist of religion, Ali Carkoglu, argued that no non-Muslim religious gathering in Turkey is risk free.

Moreover, as the previous section also indicated, the specific attacks on Christians listed above unfolded in a broader context of coarsening public attitudes toward Turkey's Christian minority. As momentum toward possible membership in the European Union appeared to gather steam, a growing backlash among Turkish nationalists and Islamist currents became palpable, often expressing itself in public eruptions of anti-Christian hostility. In turn, that animus reflects something deep and ugly in Turkish history and culture.

The oldest Christians retain living memory of the state-sponsored mass deportations and massacres that culminated in the World War I Armenian genocide. More recently, Christian churches have experienced grave setbacks in addition to the abovementioned murders. Those difficulties include a four-year state prosecution of two Turkish evangelical Protestant converts from Islam on charges of "insulting Turkishness." Although these charges were dropped for lack of evidence in October 2010, the converts were forced to pay fines of $3,170 each or go to prison for seven months for "collecting information on citizens." Also in 2010, Turkish authorities under Prime Minister Recep Tayyip Erdogan allowed the right-wing Nationalist Movement Party to conduct Islamic prayers at the ancient Armenian Cathedral of the Holy Virgin at Ani.

Turkey's Christians were especially alarmed by the popular hysteria whipped up by a 2006 blockbuster titled *Valley of the Wolves*, an action-packed adventure film set in post-Saddam Iraq. Reviewing the movie in *Spiegel*, Cem Özdemir—a member of the European Parliament of Turkish descent—decried its pandering to "racist sentiments" and its making "Christians and Jews appear as repugnant, conspiratorial holy warriors hoping to use blood-drenched swords to expand or reclaim the empire of their God." The Christophobia of the popular press and of Turkey's movie industry, often dubbed "Istanbulywood," can also be found in state documents. A national intelligence report, exposed by the newspaper *Cumhuriyet* in June 2005, revealed similar sentiments. Titled "Reactionary Elements and Risks," the report put Islamist terrorist groups on a par with Christian missionaries, who, it claimed, cover Turkey "like a spider's web." According to the report, these Christian evangelizers were seeking to promote divisions in sensitive areas such as the Black Sea region and eastern Anatolia. Also according to the document, the armies of Christian evangelizers in Turkey included Catholics, Orthodox, and Protestants, as well as other groups such as the Jehovah's Witnesses and the Baha'is, with the non-Christians allegedly concentrating on seducing government officials, liberal businessmen, and performing and other artists.

The extent to which an entrenched anti-Christian mentality still influences Turkish society is evident from the findings of a European Union–financed public opinion survey conducted in 2008 by scholars as a part of the International Social Survey Program. They concluded: "Despite laicism, the Turkish state has not been able to overcome the segregation of non-Muslim minorities and to integrate them into the nation as citizens with equal rights. While the Muslim Turks have been the 'we,' the non-Muslim minorities have been categorized as 'the other' . . . they have been rather perceived as 'domestic foreigners.'"

Among the survey's findings were:

- One-third of Turkish Muslims would object to having a Christian as a neighbor.
- More than half believe that Christians should not be allowed to openly express their religious views in printed publications or in public meetings.
- More than half are opposed to Christians serving in the army, security services, police force, and political parties.
- Just under half believe Christians should not be active in the provision of health services.

As John Eibner, CEO of Christian Solidary International, observed in a 2011 essay, "The road from such views to outright discrimination and a heightened threat of violence is very short indeed." In such a context, claims that an assault on a Christian clergyman could somehow be "shocking" simply do not pass the commonsense test for credibility.

THE ZIMBABWE EXAMPLE

On the night of February 17, 2011, unidentified assailants entered the home of an eighty-nine-year-old Zimbabwean woman named Jessica Mandeya in Fusire village in the district of Murewa, located roughly forty-five miles northeast of the capital city, Harare. According to accounts from witnesses who observed the scene afterward, the attackers raped the elderly woman, sliced a large gash across her mouth, beat her with an iron rod, and stabbed her in the leg, then killed her and left her body on the floor. Mandeya was a well-known fixture on the local Christian scene, serving for many years as a subdeacon in her Anglican community.

As word of the gruesome murder began to make the rounds, officials responded with shock and outrage while denying that there was any deeper subtext to the killing. A police spokesperson suggested it was a robbery gone wrong, saying that Mandeya had probably surprised a group of thieves in her home who killed her in order to ensure that she did not report the incident to the authorities.

For those who understand the situation in Zimbabwe, those claims were hard to swallow. Many Christians in the country believe the death of Jessica Mandeya was not an isolated incident, but part of a broader climate of religious tension.

In a nation already reeling from a deep economic crisis and instability under longtime president Robert Mugabe, Christians who stand up against the regime have found themselves facing growing violence and intimidation. The harassment is sometimes delivered by the government itself, and on other occasions by forces purporting to act in its name. A Catholic bishop told Aid to the Church in Need in 2012 that he was seeing the beginnings of a "real persecution" of the church, especially "where Christians refuse to be co-opted by the [ruling] Zanu PF [party]."

Observers say that when Mugabe initially came to power in the 1980s, church/state relations were generally good. Mugabe had been part of the liberation struggle against the white-minority rule government of Ian Smith in what was then Rhodesia. It was a movement supported by a broad cross section of Christian churches, which saw it as an opportunity not merely to correct a racial injustice but also to usher in a state that would do a better job of promoting development, combatting corruption, and protecting the poor. Not so long ago, many Christian leaders in Zimbabwe were actually thought by some to be far too reluctant to offend the Mugabe regime in light of this history.

Over time, however, as Mugabe strengthened his hold on power and fought off efforts at democratic reform, relations with the churches soured. During the first decade of the twenty-first century, senior Christian prelates in Zimbabwe became outspoken in condemning corruption, human rights abuses, and efforts to control any democratic opposition. One turning point came in 2008 when an Anglican bishop named Nolbert Kunonga, a rabid supporter of the Mugabe regime, was formally excommunicated.

From that point on, most observers say, Mugabe and his allies determined that the institutional Christian churches in the country were their enemies, and a new climate of persecution took shape. The regime has backed Kunonga's bid to confiscate Anglican churches, schools, hospitals, and bank accounts, and has committed acts of violence and harassment against those determined to remain part of the wider Anglican Communion. Pro-Mugabe forces often tout Kunonga as the leader of the "real" Anglican Church in Zimbabwe, styling Anglicans who refuse to follow him as enemies of the state.

In October 2011, the archbishop of Canterbury, Rowan Williams, visited Zimbabwe and personally handed Mugabe a detailed dossier reviewing this campaign of violence and intimidation, including several Anglican bishops who had received death threats. The dossier told how congregations were forced to flee after being attacked with tear gas and how parishioners were assaulted and needed hospital treatment. In one diocese, sixty-five churches had been confiscated and a similar number of priests had been evicted from their homes. Church-run schools, clinics, orphanages, and hospitals were also taken over by Kunonga's men. Their senior staff were replaced by people loyal to the excommunicated bishop.

During a homily given in an indoor sports center in Harare, Williams denounced the regime, telling the thousands present: "Their greed and violence have tried to silence your worship and frustrate your witness in churches, schools and hospitals. . . . The message we want to send out from this Eucharistic celebration is that we do not have to live like that—in terror, in bloodshed."

Anglicans have not been the only targets of Mugabe's wrath. In 2011, a Catholic priest named Fr. Marko Mabutho Mkandla was arrested and charged with disturbing public order after holding a church service to recall the victims of an outbreak of violence in the 1980s. Mabutho was indicted for "communicating false statements against the state" and "causing offence to a particular tribe." He was granted bail and released from detention, and a year after the arrest a judge finally dismissed the charges.

In April 2011, armed riot police attacked some six hundred people attending an ecumenical prayer service in Harare. Several people were injured in the assault, while fourteen churchgoers were arrested and charged with offenses against public order. After two days behind bars, they were released. A spokesperson for the United Reformed Church said at the time: "The brutal attack . . . represents a new level of oppression and violence in the long litany of human rights violations by the Zimbabwe Republic Police. . . . Even places of worship can no longer be considered as sacred or safe places—and this raises serious concerns about the fundamental human rights of freedom of thought, conscience and belief in Zimbabwe."

"The greatest irony," said spokesperson Simon Loveitt, "is that people praying for peace were charged with causing public violence, while the only violence was from those charged with the protection of citizens from the very acts they perpetrated."

June 2011 brought another attack on the Anglican Church, as six Anglicans, including an elderly woman, were arrested and detained, while several Anglican clergy were kicked out of their homes in the Harare diocese. When a backer of Kunonga tried to evict yet another Anglican priest, his parishioners fought back and dragged the attacker to a nearby police station. The police, acting on orders, sided with the attacker and arrested the churchgoers. In August 2011, Anglicans who refused to side with Kunonga were denied access to their churches by the police and were forced to worship outside.

In January 2012, police disrupted a retreat for some eighty Anglican clergymen, saying that the gathering had not received the required clearance from state officials. The clergy on hand for the event included two Anglican bishops, and initially they refused to leave. Eventually they dispersed after the police threatened to use force. Anglican bishop Chad Gandiya said afterward: "We deplore this action and call upon the higher authorities to intervene. So much for freedom of religion."

Also in January 2012, an armed band burst into a church-affiliated hospital run by a group of Anglican sisters. According to reports, the intruders told the nuns they would be beaten if they didn't hand over the hospital immediately and leave the area. The sisters had the impression that the group was a militia loyal to the Mugabe regime, which blamed the church for supporting its critics and the Zimbabwean opposition.

This context helps explain why claims of astonishment about the murder of Jessica Mandeya, or suggestions that it was simply a criminal act gone awry, struck many Christians in Zimbabwe as deeply suspect.

Mandeya had been a staunch member of an Anglican community that refused to go along with Kunonga, and most people close to the scene interpreted her killing as a clear signal to other Anglicans that a similar fate might await them too if they continued to defy the regime.

That reading of events seemed especially plausible given that a meeting of Anglican primates in Dublin, Ireland, just two weeks before the murder had issued a statement strongly critical of affairs in Zimbabwe. It said in part: "We believe that the appalling situation experienced by members of the Anglican Church in Zimbabwe seriously infringes their right to justice, freedom of assembly, freedom of religion, and personal security under the law guaranteed by the constitution of Zimbabwe and the United Nations Declaration on Human Rights." The primates called on Mugabe to "use all the power and authority of your office to put an end to these abuses forthwith," adding that this "unmerited, unjust, and unlawful persecution" damaged "the good name and reputation of the Republic of Zimbabwe and results in untold and unnecessary additional suffering for many thousands of people."

In that light, many people in Zimbabwe interpreted the brutal murder of a subdeacon as a response to the Anglican protest—if not a response directly orchestrated by the government, then by one of the numerous militias, gangs, and armed bands given free rein to act in its name. Anglican bishop Chad Gandiya of Harare, speaking at a news conference just two days after the murder of Mandeya, put the situation this way: "My people are going to be killed for the simple reason that they belong to a certain denomination. . . . Our church members should know that we are now an endangered species."

Perhaps no one could have anticipated that violence would come exactly on February 17, 2011, in the middle of the night, or that an eighty-nine-year-old female subdeacon would be the target. Nonetheless, it was clear that a storm was brewing, and sooner or later innocent people would be hurt. Turkey and Zimbabwe are illustrative examples, but a similar case could be assembled virtually anywhere.

WHY THIS MYTH IS TOXIC

There are at least four reasons why debunking the "no one saw it coming" myth is critical to a proper response to the global war on Christians.

First and most basically, it's inaccurate. If we are to arrive at a proper grasp of the situation facing Christians around the world, acts of anti-Christian violence cannot be seen as akin to forces of nature such as earthquakes and hurricanes—in other words, as the result of natural forces that erupt spontaneously. In general, they are the product of deliberately shaped climates of hatred, fueled by propaganda campaigns that often unfold with the connivance of government officials, religious leaders, and other important actors. Spectacular outbreaks of violence are often preceded by less intense incidents, such as believers being harassed on the streets, slurred in the media, shunned in the workplace, and hassled as they gather to worship. The usual cycle is for complaints to be made about these incidents, which are then ignored or dismissed. That failure to act usually serves to embolden the perpetrators, who then may become more likely to move on to even more lethal assaults, in effect testing the limits of official tolerance. Of course, there are also genuinely random acts and outbreaks of madness that afflict Christians, but in the main that's not the story of the global war. To whip up an atmosphere of hysteria and rage and then profess shock when it turns violent is a particularly lethal form of hypocrisy.

Second, grasping that attacks on Christians are generally predictable in light of clear warning signs is an important step toward prevention. If officials in a given country begin to see anti-Christian slurs appear in the media, it should be taken as an indication that trouble may be brewing. That doesn't mean muzzling freedom of speech, because one human rights abuse shouldn't be swapped for another. Moreover, simply prohibiting public expressions of anti-Christian hostility will not make it go away. It can only drive those instincts underground, where they're likely to metastasize and become even more dangerous. However, if officials see a climate of religious antagonism taking shape, they can and should adopt at least three preventive measures:

- Issuing clear warnings that violence directed at religious believers will not be tolerated, including indications of what the sanctions will be for engaging in such criminal acts
- Supporting programs of tolerance education, for example in schools and in state-run media

- Ensuring that Christian leaders have access to the media and to other public opportunities to respond to negative public portrayals, so that an alternative narrative about the Christian presence can be presented

Third, understanding that anti-Christian violence is often the result of deeper movements is also an aid to investigations by police and prosecutors when breakouts occur. Assuming that officials are interested in pursuing justice, knowing that forces hostile to certain denominations or religious leaders may be in the background can be a help in generating leads and shaping an investigation. It suggests skepticism about claims of isolated madmen or simple crimes gone wrong, and opens up a wider panorama of possible accomplices and chains of causation. In addition, understanding that there's often a deeper background to anti-Christian violence offers another tool to human rights groups and pro-democracy activists to keep the pressure on police and prosecutors reluctant to act.

Fourth, getting past the "no one saw it coming" myth is also an important step in promoting accountability whenever innocent people are harmed. If anti-Christian violence were like a tornado, then perhaps one couldn't fault the leaders of the society where it occurs for not preventing it—though even there, one could hold them accountable for failing to act aggressively in its aftermath, as American outrage over the botched federal response to Hurricane Katrina in New Orleans in 2005 illustrates. Given that anti-Christian violence is more often, however, the result of a cancer that metastasizes in a culture well before it turns lethal, then one can hold leadership figures responsible if they don't take swift and decisive steps to excise it.

The bottom line is that the global war on Christians will never be won as long as the myth persists that nobody's really responsible for it.

9

THE MYTH THAT IT'S
ALL ABOUT ISLAM

In a post-9/11 world in which radical Islam is the greatest perceived threat to global stability, there's a natural tendency to presume that almost every conflict, and certainly a war against Christians, must be driven primarily by Islam. That tendency is augmented by several factors, including the fact that the places where the United States has deployed troops since the Twin Towers and Pentagon attacks, Afghanistan and Iraq, are both in the Middle East, so a disproportionate share of American media and foreign policy attention is directed at that region. A car bombing in Iraq is far more likely to register in terms of public attention than a similar incident in Laos or in Mindanao, on the assumption that it has greater potential to affect both military strategy and political fortunes. Moreover, several of the most impassioned writers on anti-Christian persecution in the West are social and foreign policy conservatives, who are disenchanted both with European policies of multiculturalism vis-à-vis the continent's rising Muslim footprint and with the perceived failure of the Western powers to prosecute the "war on terror" more aggressively.

It's not hard to understand the perception that the global war on Christians is primarily about Islam. Christians endure harassment

and various forms of second-class citizenship in many Muslim majority states, often related to pressures for the civil law to reflect shariah.
Especially in the Middle East, a rising tide of Islamic radicalism is
creating dramatic threats to all religious minorities, including Christians. As we saw in chapter 5, a once-flourishing Christian community
in Iraq, which can trace its history back to the era of the Apostles,
has imploded in the arc of two decades. In Egypt, attacks on and harassment of that country's large Coptic Christian minority multiply
on a daily basis, and the country's new legal order threatens to con-
sign Christians to a permanent underclass. In Syria, tens of thousands
of Christians have been killed or dislodged by the fighting. Even where
the Christian population is growing in the Middle East, such as the
Arabian Peninsula, where Christians are being drawn as "guest workers," there's a chronic lack of religious freedom and deep fear about
Christians being exposed to discrimination, exploitation, and physical
violence. Outside the Middle East, the rise of the militantly Islamic
Boko Haram movement in Nigeria and its vicious attacks on churches
have cemented impressions that Muslim radicals are the primary villains in the global war on Christians.

The threats are real. Human rights groups and advocacy bodies
devoted to tracking anti-Christian persecution confirm that the Muslim world is a primary danger zone. In the 2013 edition of the World
Watch List issued by Open Doors, thirty-four of the top fifty nations
have a Muslim majority, and several of the rest are mixed Muslim/
Christian societies. In the 2012 report from the United States Commission on International Religious Freedom, ten of the sixteen nations
designated as "countries of particular concern" have a Muslim majority.
This book itself clearly reflects the peril that Christians face in many
Islamic societies, as the chapter on the Middle East is considerably
longer than the companion chapters on other parts of the world.

Yet the perception that the global war on Christians is all about
Islam is nevertheless misleading, for four reasons.

First, there is a tendency in Western perceptions to identify Islam
with the Middle East and the Arab world, but that way of seeing things
doesn't do justice to the reality of Muslim demographics. Only about

one-quarter of the 1.6 billion Muslims in the world today are Arabs. Just as it's a mistake to identify Christianity with the West, given that more than two-thirds of all Christians today live in the global South, it's equally fallacious to associate Islam exclusively with Arab societies.

Indonesia, for instance, with a population of 238 million people, is the world's largest Muslim nation. To be sure, there's a more militant form of Islam in the country. Open Doors listed Indonesia as the forty-fifth most dangerous spot for Christians in 2013. Yet Indonesia also has a proud tradition of pluralism and a generally tolerant brand of Islam, and it has made a remarkable transition from authoritarianism to democracy. Most experts in Muslim/Christian dialogue say the conversation has an entirely different feel in Indonesia than in Egypt or Saudi Arabia.

On the ground, relations are often strikingly strong. The Muhammadiyah movement is one of Indonesia's largest Islamic organizations, running a network of schools that serves a large population of Christian students. In those settings, a Muslim school actually provides Christian religious education. One can find similar examples from other majority-Muslim nations, such as the former Soviet republic of Kazakhstan. The country's Christian minority arrived in chains as prisoners during the era of Stalin; the Christians were taken in by native Kazakh Muslim families, breeding a strong sense of solidarity. Friendships and marriages between Christians and Muslims are common and generally accepted.

Second, in terms of the body count in the global war on Christians, the highest number of casualties has not come in the Muslim world. That distinction belongs to the Democratic Republic of Congo, a nation of seventy-one million people that's overwhelmingly Christian. As chapter 1 outlined, the Center for the Study of Global Christianity is responsible for the estimate that an average of a hundred thousand Christians have been killed each year over the past decade in what the center calls a "situation of witness," meaning that their death was related to their Christian faith. The bulk of those fatalities have come in the Congo, where a bloody civil war continues at a lower level of intensity, and where thousands of clergy, catechists, and ordinary believers have been slaughtered. Though experts debate precisely how many of these deaths can truly be attributed to anti-Christian hostility, no one doubts that the DRC is a primary killing field in the global war on Christians.

Third, Islamic societies also do not lead the pack in terms of de jure discrimination against Christians, meaning forms of oppression and persecution legally sanctioned by the state. The world's leading manufacturers of state-sponsored oppression are Communist-inspired police states, principally in Asia. There is no Muslim society that operates a chain of prison camps, as in North Korea, where simply possessing a Bible can be grounds to be incarcerated along with three generations of one's family, and where some fifty thousand to seventy thousand Christians presently are believed to languish in detention. Nor does any Muslim society insist that Christians must belong to state-sponsored "autonomous" religious bodies, such as the Patriotic Association in China.

Fourth, Islam also is not the world's only crucible for de facto discrimination against Christians, meaning social harassment and persecution. Consider India, where the country's small Christian minority, estimated at just 2.3 percent of the overall population, is subject to routine forms of verbal harassment, threats, beatings, and ostracism. In 2011, according to the Global Council of Indian Christians, there were 170 assaults on Christians in the country, an average of one every other day. Such incidents occur with regularity in several Islamic societies too, though no Muslim nation in the past decade has witnessed an anti-Christian pogrom on the scale of the mayhem that broke out in the Indian state of Orissa in 2008, which left at least five hundred people dead and fifty thousand homeless.

THE GALAXY OF THREATS

Instead of Islam being the lone protagonist, the global war on Christians is fueled by a complex galaxy of heterogeneous forces, each of which has its own reasons for seeing Christians as a threat. Understanding the nature of this war, and shaping strategies to cope with it, requires a clear-eyed view of the variety of actors in the drama. Beyond Islamic radicalism, those forces include at least the following ten.

Ultranationalists

In societies where national identity is tied up with a particular religion, such as Buddhism in Sri Lanka, Hinduism in India, or Islam in Turkey, nationalist currents tend to be hostile to religious minorities. Christianity is usually a particular source of anxiety, both because of its perceived identification with the West and because Christian ecclesiology emphasizes membership in a "communion of saints" that relativizes national loyalties.

Turkey is a good example, where the primary threats to Christians come not from the most committed Muslims but rather from an ultranationalist underground. (Islam too, with its idea of the *ummah*, the collective body of Islamic peoples, also has a natural tendency to subvert national loyalties.) It's worth remembering that the most spectacular assassination attempt against a Christian leader in the twentieth century came from a Turkish gunman with links to a group of Turkish ultranationalists called the Grey Wolves—Mehmet Ali Ağca, who shot Pope John Paul II in St. Peter's Square on May 13, 1981.

Some elements of the nationalist underground may be influenced by radical Islamic ideas, but there are also important forces in Turkey seeking a stronger public role for Islam, such as movements linked to Said Nursi and his disciple, Fethullah Gülen, which are open to religious freedom. As things play out, Christians in Turkey could well find that their greatest bulwark against the threats of ultranationalists come precisely in alliances with such moderate Islamic currents.

Totalitarian States

The most systematic repression of Christians comes in police states, generally ones with roots in Communism officially committed to atheism as part of national doctrine. North Korea is routinely rated as the most dangerous state in the world in which to be a Christian. Its quasi-religious official state ideology of *juche*, or self-reliance, not only translates into a cult of personality around the "Great Leader" but also makes any religious body with loyalties or ties outside the state suspect. In China, trends toward economic liberalization have not been matched by momentum toward political reform, and religious groups continue to be subject to occasionally severe state control.

Similar dynamics face Christians in other societies that are, to one degree or another, police states, such as Myanmar, Vietnam, and Laos in Asia, as well as Zimbabwe in Africa. In Belarus, Russia, and other post-Soviet states in Eastern Europe, experiments with "managed democracy" often mean the heavy-handed management of religious dissidents. Churches, especially those not identified with the country's dominant religious tradition, are seen with suspicion. In these societies, Christians are often subject to constant surveillance, clergy are either bought off or harassed, religious services are occasionally disrupted, and religious figures who criticize the regime are routinely threatened, deported, incarcerated, or killed.

Hindu Radicalism

Though radical Hindus represent a tiny fraction of India's massive population, they have the capacity to create tremendous grief. A frequent pretext for violence is the claim that Christians engage in duplicitous missionary activity in an effort to "Christianize" India. Groups of radicals sometimes move into Christian villages, preaching a gospel of *hindutva*, or Hindu nationalism, and demand that Christians take part in "reconversion" ceremonies. These groups also routinely stage counterfestivals during Christmas celebrations. Fear of a Christian takeover is pervasive in these circles, often fueled by sensational media accounts of Christian conspiracies. In 2001, when Italian-born Sonia Gandhi ran in national elections, one national newspaper carried the headline "Sonia—Vulnerable to Vatican Blackmail!"

As we have seen, these tensions can turn violent. In April 1995, Hindu nationalists cracked the skulls of two nuns in a convent on the outskirts of New Delhi; another mob broke into a residence of the Franciscan Sisters of Mary Angels and beat the five sisters, along with their maid, using iron rods. In 2006, Archbishop Bernard Moras of Bangalore and two priests were attacked by a mob in Jalahally, ten miles south Bangalore. As described in chapter 3, such assaults have become virtually daily fare in certain parts of India, often with the connivance of local police and politicians.

As the twenty-first century develops, such violence may no longer be confined to India. India is emerging into superpower status, and a wealthy Indian diaspora is spreading around the world, making Hinduism a steadily more global religion. It's possible that at some point observers may came to think of Hindu radicalism the same way they regard Islamic radicalism today, as a primary threat to global stability.

Buddhist Radicalism

Despite stereotypes of Buddhists as tolerant and peace-loving, the reality is that under the right conditions, Buddhist societies are just as susceptible to nationalist and radical currents as anyplace else. Countries such as Sri Lanka, Myanmar, and Laos illustrate the point, having emerged in recent years as primary arenas for the global war on Christians. *Time* magazine captured the trend in July 2013 with a cover story featuring a picture of a militant monk in Myanmar named Wirathu under the headline, "The Face of Buddhist Terror." Wirathu is best known for drawing an aggressive line in the sand with regard to Myanmar's Muslim minority. The government promptly banned the magazine on the grounds that it posed a threat to "religious feelings."

Sri Lanka has adopted a stringent anti-conversion law supported by Buddhist nationalists that tightens freedom of expression for Christians, as well as the country's Sikh, Hindu, and Muslim minorities. Rumors of proselytism by Christians in recent years have also led to a spike in attacks on churches by angry Buddhist mobs. During a 2006 conference of Catholic theologians staged in Padova, Italy, Redemptorist Fr. Vimal Tirimanna, a Sri Lankan, described what he called a worrying rise in "religious extremism" in his society.

In Laos, Christians in general, and the Hmong Christian community in particular, are seen by sections of the Lao society and the authorities as an American or imperialist import, leading to a rising wave of hostility. In 2011, troops from the Lao People's Army stopped a group of Christians belonging to the Hmong community, killing four of the women after repeatedly raping two of them. The husbands and children were beaten, tied up, and forced to witness the gruesome killings. Though the violence was carried out by the military under orders from a Communist-inspired police state, it's often encouraged by religious radicals.

In November 2012, radical Buddhists in Myanmar prevented

humanitarian groups such as Doctors Without Borders from delivering aid to Muslim refugees in the western part of the country, and the same sort of hostility often befalls the country's Christian minority. One aid worker said at the time, "I've never experienced this degree of intolerance."

Economic Interests

Whenever Christians denounce corporate policies that appear to place profit ahead of the well-being of people, or advocate for economic policies in defense of the poor, they may place themselves at risk. The story of Sr. Dorothy Stang, recounted in chapter 4, illustrates the point. She was shot to death in 2005 by gunmen working on behalf of a local rancher who would not tolerate Stang's defense of the human rights and property rights of local farmers.

Sr. Valsa John in India, murdered on November 15, 2011, offers another example. A member of the Sisters of Charity of Jesus and Mary, she worked among the Dalits of Patna and the Adivasis of Santal Parganas, struggling for dignity and justice. In India, the tribals have often been the victims of development. According to national statistics, 40 percent of all people displaced by development projects have been tribals, and the promised rehabilitation has seldom been implemented. Sr. Valsa led a resistance movement to a mining project in her region that would have displaced thousands of poor people, and as a result she was brutally hacked to death by a mob of forty armed men.

Across the developing world, the struggle against corruption has become a signature Christian cause, exposing activists to reprisals from forces with a vested financial interest in the status quo. For instance, Rev. David Ugolor of the New Apostolic Church leads the Africa Network for Environmental and Economic Justice, campaigning for transparency in the oil-rich Nigerian delta. In July 2012, he was arrested and charged with complicity in the murder of a government official and local labor leader, whom Ugolor insisted was a friend. The charges were later dropped, but most observers saw the incident as an attempt by local elites to muzzle Ugolor's criticism.

Organized Crime

In places dominated by criminal syndicates, religious leaders are often the only voices not under their control, and they're often perceived as a serious threat. The 1993 murder of Fr. Giuseppe "Pino" Puglisi in Sicily and the 2011 death of Maria Elizabeth Macías Castro in Mexico, outlined in chapter 4, are both compelling examples. So too was the November 2012 assassination of Maria Santos Gorrostieta, another Mexican woman determined to speak out against the gangs. A devout Catholic, she was a thirty-six-year-old medical school graduate who went into politics, serving as mayor of the town of Tiquicheo. She was outspoken in her criticism of the cartels, which produced death threats and a 2009 assault that killed her first husband and left her badly scarred and in constant pain. On November 12, 2012, as she drove the youngest of her three children to school, she was dragged from her car in an ambush. According to local reports she begged her abductors to spare her child, and when they agreed, she left with them. Her family clung to hopes that she was being held for ransom, but a few days later her badly bruised body was found dumped by a roadside.

After the earlier 2009 attack, Gorrostieta had written: "I have had to bear losses that I would not wish on anyone, and have had to accept them with resignation and with the knowledge that it is our Lord's will, and I have gone on, even with a wounded soul. . . . My long road is not yet finished. I will continue fighting. I will get up however many times God allows me to, to keep on searching, negotiating plans, projects and actions for the benefit of all of society, but in particular for the vulnerable ones. This is who I am."

Even where Christians are not explicitly resisting organized crime, they may nevertheless fall victim to it simply by remaining in place. In lawless zones in which simply moving about is tantamount to taking risks, Christians who choose to continue going about their business may expose themselves to harassment and physical violence. In Mexico, for instance, estimates in January 2013 pegged the number of people killed in drug violence over the past six years to be in excess of sixty thousand, with less than 4 percent of those crimes ever being solved. Guatemalan pastor Neftali Leiva, gunned down by a cartel member as he arrived for a pastoral meeting near the border with Mexico, illustrates the point. A father of five daughters, Leiva was a pastor in Guatemala with the Church of God Ministries, an American Protestant denomination. On the morning of January 30, 2012, Leiva was on his way to a regional meeting of ministers at a retreat center called Prayer Mountain, located in a violent border area near Mexico. As Leiva was arriving at the meeting, according to eyewitnesses, an assailant walked up, pointed a gun at the pastor's head, and fired at point-blank range several times. The shooting was attributed to a member of the Zetas drug cartel. Raul Benitez Manaut, a national security specialist, said that "any person, institution or organization which harms the interests of drug cartels automatically becomes their enemy. . . . These groups are very clear that if any member of the clergy takes positions that challenge them, they become targets."

State Security Policies

Sometimes the authorities of a state may not be driven by an anti-Christian agenda, but their perceived need for security nonetheless harms Christians in a systematic way. Israel offers probably the best example, as the small but symbolically important Arab Christian community inside Israel experiences serious hardships. For instance, Palestinians living in the West Bank and in East Jerusalem hold different residency cards and cannot move back and forth without special permits. Reportedly, there are some two hundred Christian families living apart today, split between members in the West Bank and members in Jerusalem. In January 2013, a group of Catholic bishops from Europe and the United States visited Israel and reported that Christians in the Cremisan Valley between Jerusalem and Bethlehem had complained of "legal struggles to protect local people's lands and religious institutions from the encroachment of the Security Barrier."

Israel, however, is not the only example. In many countries of the former Soviet sphere, security policies intended to curb political dissent end up negatively effecting Christian life, even if Christians aren't specific targets. In Ukraine, for instance, the Greek Catholic University in Lviv has faced persistent harassment.

Although there are roughly 170 universities in Ukraine, most are heavily dependent on state funding and thus tend to stifle dissent. Observers say only a handful foster a climate in which civil society can find its voice, and the Greek Catholic University is perhaps the most visible example. The university has paid a price. In 2010, the rector, Bishop Borys Gudziak, got a chilling visit from security agents suggesting that his students shouldn't protest a visit to Lviv by President Viktor Yanukovych, a pro-Russian figure whom many Ukrainians see as beholden to Moscow and to his country's oligarchs. Rather than kowtowing, Gudziak published a memo describing the meeting and outlining a broader campaign of harassment (including tapping his phones), which elicited support for the university from diplomats, NGOs, and a cross section of Ukrainian intellectuals and activists. In late 2012, the university was facing another round of pressure, with questions from government officials about its accreditation. Leaders at the university have signaled they have no intention of allowing themselves to be muzzled, believing that the road to democracy and an open society doesn't run in that direction.

Christian Radicalism

To the great shame of Christianity, occasionally the protagonists of the global war on Christians are other Christians. As we saw in chapter 4, Mexico offers one example, where traditionalist Catholics have launched assaults on Protestants, mostly evangelicals and Pentecostals, perceived as threats to the country's Catholic roots. These conflicts are also sometimes intertwined with regional, ethnic, and economic factors.

Sometimes Christian radicals become agents of the war on Christians without intending it. Bishop Matthew Hassan Kukah of Sokoto, located in Muslim-dominated northern Nigeria, tells a story that drives home the point. His younger sister, he said, lives in the city of Kaduna in a predominantly Muslim neighborhood. There's a Muslim family across the road who are lifelong friends, and her daughter would often hang out in their home after school. When anti-Christian violence broke out in the city, the Muslim father of the family risked his own neck to come to the shop owned by Kukah's sister and put all of her belongings in his house to keep them safe, while the sister and her family spent a week in an army barracks to escape the mayhem.

Later, Kukah said, armed bands of Christians started attacking Muslims as payback, and this family was among their first targets. They burned down their house, and his sister lost all her possessions in the attack. As Kukah put it, his sister thus fell victim "to a bunch of Christians who had come to save her." The lesson is that whenever Christians become radicalized and take up arms, they don't put only their perceived enemies at risk; they also endanger their fellow believers as well.

Secular Hostility

Although this book does not treat church/state conflicts in the West as part of the global war on Christians, there are times when secular hostility to Christianity can shade off into direct assaults, acts of intimidation, and physical violence. In November 2011, for instance, Cedar Hill AME Zion Church in Ansonville, North Carolina, was desecrated by vandals who spray-painted "God is a lie" on the wall, burned a cross, and reportedly defecated on the altar. In France in 2010, Catholic bishop Michel Dubost of Evry complained of silence and indifference from public authorities after a series of attacks on French churches, with the perpetrators leaving behind slogans such as "Burn your churches!" and the old anarchist dictum "Neither God nor master."

In extreme form, such hostilities can turn lethal. In early February 2012, a forty-eight-year-old man in the United Kingdom named Stephen Farrow murdered a widow named Betty Yates and an Anglican vicar named Rev. John Suddards, apparently after hoping to kill the archbishop of Canterbury but being discouraged by the levels of security around him. Just before the first killing, Farrow reportedly sent a text message to a friend in which he wrote that "the church will be the first to suffer." After killing the vicar, Farrow placed a picture of Jesus and a mirror on the floor along with a Bible on the victim's chest. In the run-up to the attack, Farrow had committed a burglary at a nearby home, leaving a note for the owners, scribbled in red ink and pinned to the kitchen table with two knives, which read: "Be thankful you did not come back or we would have killed you Christian scum. I ****ing hate God." At his trial, Farrow claimed to have been abused by a priest and said he had an "aggressive attitude" toward the church. He was sentenced to two life terms in prison after a jury concluded that while Farrow was obviously disturbed, he was not legally insane.

Religious Delusions

Despite the warning delivered in chapter 8 about the "Casablanca defense," random acts of madness do sometimes occur, especially when religion is in the mix. From time to time, an individual may develop his or her own private set of beliefs, usually augmented by some form of neurosis, and conclude that killing a Christian figure enjoys divine warrant. The story of Fr. Tudor Marin in Romania, presented in chapter 6, illustrates the point. He was stabbed to death in June 2012 inside his church by a man who had developed his own private apocalyptic interpretation of the Bible and was enraged by Marin's unwillingness to endorse it. The thirty-year-old culprit apparently told police that he had set out that morning "to kill a priest."

Mehmet Ali Ağca, who shot and wounded Pope John Paul II in 1981, may well be another example. Though his precise motives remain murky thirty years later, Ali Ağca was apparently influenced in part by bizarre ideas about his own role in cosmic affairs. In a 2010 statement, Ali Ağca said: "In the name of God Almighty, I proclaim the end of the world in this century. All the world will be destroyed, every human being will die. I am not God, I am not son of God, I am Christ eternal."

WHY THIS MYTH IS TOXIC

As with the other misconceptions examined in this section, the first problem with the myth that it's all about Islam is that it's inaccurate. The hard truth about the global war on Christians is that the long-awaited moderate reformation in Islam could arrive tomorrow, yet millions of Christians would still be at risk. That would be true even inside Islamic societies, which could be entirely free of religious extremism and still harbor corporate interests, organized crime, and despotic regimes that could all find good reasons for persecuting Christians. It's even truer outside the Islamic world, because Islamic radicals cannot be blamed for the policies in North Korea or China that put Christians under the screws, or the serial persecution of Christians in India, or the legions of new martyrs in overwhelmingly Christian cultures such as the Democratic Republic of Congo and Colombia. Bringing relief to the victims of this global war requires diagnosing the threats correctly, and that means setting aside the idea that radical Islam is the only villain.

Second, perpetuating the idea that Islam is by far the primary threat facing Christians in the early twenty-first century also stokes the idea of a "clash of civilizations" between the two faiths, adding fuel to the fire of those who long for a new holy war. That doesn't do justice to the complex reality of the situation, as there are examples of both conflict and coexistence, and for every virulent and dangerous current in the Islamic world there are also movements and individuals devoted to peace. Even in Nigeria, where no one can be blind to the threat posed by the militant Boko Haram movement today, Cardinal John Onaiyekan of Abuja insisted in late 2012 that contrary to media images, "Christians in Nigeria do not see themselves as being under any massive persecution by Muslims.

"Most of our problems," Onaiyekan went on, "are caused by the reckless utterances and activities of extremist fringe groups on both sides of the divide."

The right response is not to go quiet about the threats facing Christians in many Muslim societies. Politically correct silence does no one any good, and arguably insults the dignity of those who run risks to life and limb on a daily basis to keep the faith alive. Certainly the failure of Christian leaders in the West, and especially in the United States, to speak out more forcefully in defense of beleaguered Christians in Iraq, Egypt, Turkey, and other places is nothing short of scandalous. However, understanding that reality is a mixed bag suggests a dose of caution and balance, rather than succumbing to the rhetoric of hysteria and the logic of inexorable conflict.

Third and finally, the "all about Islam" myth is dangerous because it obscures from view the many examples of noble Muslims who actually risk their own safety to defend endangered Christians. The story of Italian Consolata missionary Sr. Leonella Sgorbati, who was shot to death in Mogadishu, Somalia, in 2006, and that of the Muslim man who died with her, Mahamud Mohammed Osman, offers a powerful example.

The missionary nun was born Rosa Maria Sgorbati in the Italian town of Gazzola on December 9, 1940, and changed her name to Leonella upon joining the Consolata sisters at the age of twenty. (It's customary in many Catholic orders to take a new name when entering religious life, signifying a change in vocation.) She studied nursing and then served in a series of hospitals in Kenya before heading to Mogadishu in 2001 to open a training center for nurses. She would move back and forth between Kenya and Somalia for the next few years, often getting bogged down because of the difficulties of obtaining visas. Just before her death she had gone to Kenya with three of her nurse candidates to register them for further training, and had returned to Mogadishu on September 13. She would be gunned down, at the age of sixty-five, just four days later.

Many observers believe the attack on the Italian nun came in retribution for Pope Benedict XVI's controversial speech in Regensburg, Germany, six days before, which incited Muslim outrage by appearing to link Muhammad with violence. At the time, Sgorbati was one of only two Westerners left in Mogadishu. Her plan was to deploy her nurse-trainees to deliver medical care to the victims of the country's violence, Muslim and Christian alike.

Mahamud Mohammed Osman, a father of four and a devout Muslim, was Sgorbati's driver, bodyguard, and friend, and was standing next to her when militants staged their ambush. They were shot as they walked from the Mogadishu hospital to the sister's home, where three other nuns were waiting to have lunch. Osman tried to shield Sgorbati's body with his own, and took the first bullet. They died together, their blood mingling on the hospital floor. In that sense, Sgorbati and her bodyguard became not only martyrs but symbols of Christian/Muslim friendship at its best. Many Christian commentators noted that Osman exemplified what Jesus described as the ultimate test of friendship: the willingness to lay down one's life for another.

Sgorbati's last words reportedly were "Perdono, perdono," meaning "I forgive." That spirit, along with with Osman's sacrifice, are perhaps the most powerful refutation imaginable that the global war on Christians is all about Islam.

10

THE MYTH THAT IT'S ONLY PERSECUTION IF THE MOTIVES ARE RELIGIOUS

Although most people find violations of human rights appalling, no matter the target, not everyone is inclined to accept that Christians merit special concern. Those who would deny or minimize the global war on Christians generally have three lines of attack.

THEY'VE GOT IT COMING

The first line is to concede that Christians are being victimized but to argue that they have it coming—either for perceived sins in the past (such as the Crusades, the Inquisition, and the Holocaust) or for political and cultural positions of the present (opposition to abortion and gay marriage, the alleged wealth and privilege of Christian churches, and so on). The problem with this argument is that the wrong Christians are paying the price. Whatever one makes of the Inquisition, its heyday came in Spain in the fifteenth and sixteenth centuries, and it's irrational to suggest that a churchgoer in Nigeria or Nicaragua today carries responsibility for it. Similarly, if the beef is with churches having too much wealth and power, it's tough to see why impoverished Dalit Christians in India and Pakistan, or poor day laborers just trying to get to church in Belarus, ought to be compelled to settle that score.

A related version of the "they've got it coming" argument holds that Christians bring hostility on themselves because they're overly aggressive in their methods of proselytism, offending the religious sensibilities of other cultures. It's certainly true that some Christians, like some followers of other religious traditions, are capable of exceeding the boundaries of decorum. In one famous incident, a group of zealous Filipino evangelicals once made their way through neighborhoods in Riyadh, the capital of Saudi Arabia, tossing Bibles over the walls of estates. A few of those Bibles apparently struck people standing on the other side—meaning that these missionaries were literally hitting people over the head with Scripture.

The problem here is that the punishment is disproportionate to the crime. However obnoxious a given Christian may be, it doesn't merit being consigned to a concentration camp, or being beaten, tortured, and killed. Moreover, as Thomas Farr, a veteran American diplomat who was the first director of the State Department's Commission of International Religious Freedom, observes, "Religious freedom includes the right of individuals and communities to propose their faith." Civilized societies have to find ways to discourage inconsiderate or overly aggressive forms of proselytism without resorting to violence or curbing the legitimate right to freedom of speech.

SKEPTICISM

A second denial strategy is to express skepticism about the scope and scale of the problems Christians face. While skeptics may concede that there are isolated cases in which Christians suffer oppression or violence, they generally deny that there's a wide global pattern of such hostility. They often suggest that such claims have either been inflated or exaggerated—"sexed up," in the political argot of the day—to serve a political agenda, either to make churches look more sympathetic or to bolster their positions in debates over morality and public policy.

The difficulty with those claims is that they dissolve under careful examination. The material presented in this book or in extensively documented reports by respected organizations such as Aid to the Church in Need, Open Doors, the United States Commission on International Religious Freedom, and the Pew Forum demonstrates convincingly that Christians aren't making this stuff up.

IT MAY BE PERSECUTION, BUT IT'S NOT RELIGIOUS

The third way of playing down the war on Christians, and probably the most common, is to embrace the myth examined in this chapter. In essence, it holds that Christians may be subject to harassment, discrimination, and persecution in various parts of the world, but not because they're Christian. The argument is rooted in the perception that in many cases, the architects of persecution that afflicts Christians are motivated by forces other than religious hatred—greed, ethnic rivalry, criminal intent, political ambition, and so on. If a catechist is killed in the Democratic Republic of Congo because she belongs to the wrong ethnic group, that's not hatred of the faith but rather tribal animosity. If a Pentecostal pastor is shot to death in a poor *favela* outside Rio de Janeiro, it's street crime rather than a religious conflict.

In other words, this form of denial holds that a particular act of persecution or brutality counts as "anti-Christian" only if the motives of the perpetrator are specifically religious.

The problem with this way of looking at things is that it suffers from selective focus. If it takes two to tango, it also takes two to persecute—one to do the persecution and the other to suffer it. If that's the case, why should the analysis of motives rest entirely on the perpetrator, to the exclusion of the victim? To grasp whether there was a religious or Christian component to a given incident, we need to understand not only why someone committed the act but also why the target was in a position where it could happen.

The great German Protestant theologian Dietrich Bonhoeffer illustrates the insufficiency of focusing solely on the executioner rather than the executed. Bonhoeffer was a staunch opponent of Germany's Nazi regime, including its euthanasia program and its genocidal persecution of the Jews. He eventually became involved in plans by the Abwehr, the German military intelligence office, to assassinate Adolf

Hitler and was arrested by the Gestapo in April 1943. He was executed by hanging just twenty-three days before the German surrender, after having spent two years in a concentration camp.

Given the facts of the case, one could argue that Bonhoeffer was not a Christian martyr because he was killed as a traitor to the state, not as a religious believer. Looking at it that way, however, leaves Bonhoeffer's own motives out of view. The relevant question is not only why the Nazis killed him but why Bonhoeffer involved himself in an undertaking that he clearly knew could lead to his death.

Bonhoeffer struggled with the choice to try to kill another human being, writing at the time: "When a man takes guilt upon himself in responsibility, he imputes his guilt to himself and no one else. He answers for it. . . . Before other men he is justified by dire necessity; before himself he is acquitted by his conscience, but before God he hopes only for grace." In light of the circumstances of his execution, Bonhoeffer is today commemorated as a martyr by the United Methodist Church, the Evangelical Lutheran Church, and several communities within the Anglican Communion.

The Bonhoeffer example illustrates that unless we bring the motives of the one suffering into consideration, we cannot properly assess whether a given act is a case of religious persecution. Three other case studies drive that insight home.

ERIC DE PUTTER

The murder of a French Protestant missionary and academic named Eric de Putter in Cameroon on July 8, 2012, captures the poverty of leaving the victim's motives out of view. A professor of Old Testament studies and a member of the French Reformed Protestant Church, de Putter was having dinner on a Sunday night with his wife, Marie-Alix, and a mutual friend at their residence in Yaounde, the capital of Cameroon and the location of the Protestant University of Central Africa, where de Putter had taught for two years as a missionary volunteer. Someone knocked at the door, stabbed de Putter when he answered, and then fled. Marie-Alix called for medical help, but de Putter was dead before he reached the hospital. Police would later say that the killer was able to escape because a watchman who normally stood guard over the complex, which also housed the residence of the university rector, was absent. The couple had been scheduled to return to France in just a few days, having completed their two years of service.

Officially the investigation into de Putter's murder remained open at the time this book was written, but two figures already have been arrested and charged with involvement in the crime: a Ph.D. student at the Protestant University of Central Africa and the dean of the Faculty of Protestant Theology. According to police sources, the Ph.D. student ran afoul of de Putter when the French academic charged him with plagiarism. Police believe the murder of de Putter was engineered by the Ph.D. student, with the approval of the dean, in order to clear the way for the student's thesis to be accepted.

If that's correct, at first blush it certainly doesn't look like anti-Christian persecution. It seems more akin to a settling of scores in the workplace, or a particularly violent form of academic infighting. The motive would be professional advancement and the fear of disgrace, not any specifically religious opposition to de Putter's beliefs. Indeed, since both the Ph.D. student and the dean are also Reformed Protestants, presumably they believed themselves to share the same religious convictions.

Yet upon closer examination, there's every reason to regard de Putter as a victim in the global war on Christians.

First of all, even if the lone factor in the slaying was de Putter's refusal to sign off on a plagiarized thesis, that itself is a moral position rooted in his Christian faith. De Putter's writings clearly demonstrate that his view of the world was rooted in his reading of the Gospels. After his death, a friend posted a blog entry containing de Putter's reworking of the beatitudes, in which he has Jesus praising the virtues of "justice, peace, purity, and truth."

Second, there is persistent suspicion that there's more to the story. In the aftermath of the murder, the Protestant Federation of France issued a statement charging that the Protestant University of Central Africa was well known as "a dysfunctional institution where corruption, favoritism, and fraud in examinations had grown." The federation suggested that de Putter had intended to make a report on the situation to church authorities responsible for the university when he returned to France, and that his murder was intended to muzzle his criticism. If so, then de Putter's murder would be an example of how Christians themselves can be protagonists in the war on Christians.

If there is indeed corruption at the university, it would be no surprise. Under strongman President Paul Biya, Cameroon is routinely rated by watchdog groups such as Transparency International as among the most corrupt regimes on earth. Biya earned the dubious distinction of landing on David Wallechinsky's 2006 list of the "twenty worst living dictators." Church leaders in Cameroon who speak out against that corruption often pay a steep price.

The rundown of victims includes:

- Fr. Joseph Mbassi, editor in chief of *L'Effort Camerounais*, the country's Catholic newspaper, killed in October 1988 and his body mutilated
- Fr. Bernabe Zambo, a pastor in the Bertoua archdiocese, poisoned in 1989
- Fr. Anthony Fonteh, principal of Saint Augustine College in Nso, assassinated on campus in May 1990
- Retired archbishop Yves Plumey of Garoua, murdered in 1991
- Srs. Germaine Marie and Marie Leonie of the Congregations of Daughters of Our Lady of Sacred Heart, killed in August 1992
- Jesuit Fr. Englebert Mveng, a noted theologian, killed in 1995
- German missionary Fr. Anton Probst, murdered in 2003

In that climate, allegations of corruption and the suggestion that a leading Christian figure may have been murdered for speaking out against it should surprise no one.

Third and most basically, one has to ask what de Putter and his wife were doing in Cameroon in the first place. They certainly weren't there for the money or professional advancement. De Putter's expertise would have commanded much greater income in France or another

Western location, and in terms of the sort of networking that advances an academic career, Cameroon was not an ideal setting. Instead, the couple came to Cameroon on the basis of their faith convictions, wanting to serve in a missionary setting and to be part of building the church in Africa. Both Eric and Marie-Alix de Putter were bright people with graduate-level educations, so they would have been aware of Cameroon's reputation for corruption and lack of political freedom, and they would have known that Christians sometimes find themselves in harm's way there. In de Putter's case, he followed his moral compass despite knowing that in the context of Cameroon, doing so could be lethally dangerous.

The case for seeing Eric de Putter as a contemporary martyr boils down to this: whatever may have motivated his assailant, the reason de Putter was in Yaounde that fateful night to answer the door is because of his deep Christian faith. That, and not just the rationale of his attacker, must be considered in assessing whether he counts as a victim in the global war on Christians.

SR. LUKRECIJA MAMIĆ AND FRANCESCO BAZZANI

These two Catholic missionaries were killed in Burundi on November 27, 2011, during an attempted robbery at a convent of the Sisters of Charity in Kiremba, in the country's south. Mamić, a Croatian, lived at the convent, while Bazzani, an Italian layman and volunteer, had been called in that night to try to resolve a blackout, a frequent occurrence in the area. When thieves burst in, Mamić was killed right away as she tried to stop them. Bazzani and another nun, Sr. Carla Brianza, were taken as hostages. Nine miles away the attackers stopped and shot Bazzani to death, while Brianza managed to escape. The murderers were eventually arrested and sentenced to life in prison.

Once again, a surface reading of events might conclude that this was hardly a chapter of the global war on Christians. The robbers attacked the convent because they thought it would have items worth stealing, and Mamić and Bazzani got in the way. Yet the question must be asked: What were Mamić and Bazzani doing in this part of Burundi in the first place?

Mamić, sixty-three at the time of her death, was born in 1948 into a Croatian family in Bosnia and Herzegovina, the seventh of eight children (of whom one became a priest and two became nuns). She went on to become a missionary and nurse with the Sisters of Charity, working in Ecuador, where she ministered to the Native American population from 1984 to 2001. She transferred to Burundi in 2002, where she lived and worked among the local indigenous people popularly known as "pygmies." She took special care of poor and sick people in the long-neglected area, especially female victims of sexual violence and children orphaned by AIDS.

This particular corner of Burundi had been one of the epicenters of the genocidal violence in Africa in the 1990s, and it's also one of the corners of the planet hardest hit by the AIDS pandemic. It's a dangerous, largely lawless, and essentially forgotten corner of the world, where the Sisters of Charity and other religious groups are the only institutions that still have a functioning presence in the area.

Mamić accepted such a dangerous mission on the basis of her religious beliefs. Sr. Lucija Baturina, mother superior of the Cyril and Methodius Province of the Sisters of Charity, said at her funeral Mass that Mamić "was always delighted by the universal dimensions of the Church, and the opening of new areas for the proclamation of the Gospel and the spread of the charism of our beloved order." Sr. Klementina Banozić, who served with Mamić in Ecuador, called her "a model of a life of radical Christianity," and said that "her missionary service was her response to Jesus." Mamić was buried in her home city of Split in Croatia on December 5, 2011, where Archbishop Marin Barišić declared her "the pride of the Church among the Croats and the Croatian homeland."

Bazzani, who was fifty-nine at the time of his death, had arrived in Burundi in January 2010 along with his girlfriend, a fifty-two-year-old Italian named Lucilla Volta. He was a lifelong Catholic from Verona, Italy, where he had become part of a group called the Association for Missionary Cooperation, which trained laypeople to take up short-term positions around the world supporting the church's missionary efforts. The association had a thirty-year-long relationship with the Sisters of Charity and their medical complex in Burundi, and Bazzani and four other volunteers from the Verona area had agreed to serve there. Bazzani made his career in Italy as a dental technician, but friends recalled that when he reached his fifties he wanted to do more. He wanted to serve God and to serve humanity, and they said the idea of going to the fifth-poorest country in the world to deliver health care and God's word struck Bazzani as just the ticket. He took courses in French so that he could better converse with the locals.

"Francesco coordinated our personnel, and in concrete he was our ears, our eyes and our mouth at Kiremba," said Giovanni Goppi, president of the Association for Missionary Cooperation, at the time of Bazzani's death. "He was very open, generous, an extraordinary man. He never tired of doing things, of giving someone a hand. He worked basically for free, and he would volunteer for anything. All he ever received was reimbursement for his expenses in order to live in that forgotten land."

Both Mamić and Bazzani were well-educated professionals who certainly knew there were safer and more comfortable places to live and work. In addition to being one of the five most impoverished places on earth, Burundi is ranked by the 2012 DHL Global Connectedness Index as the least globalized of 140 surveyed countries. It has the lowest per capita GDP of any nation and one of the world's lowest life expectancy rates, largely due to warfare, corruption, poor access to education, and the effects of HIV/AIDS. Despite those hardships, Mamić and Bazzani chose to serve there because their faith compelled them to do so.

Given all that, it's inarguable that these two Christians died in what the Center for the Study of Global Christianity calls a "situation of witness." They are a classic illustration of the point that in assessing whether someone has experienced anti-Christian violence, the motives of the victim, not just the perpetrator, are critical to proper assessment.

THE BURUNDI SEMINARIANS

Another group of victims from Burundi offers a final example of the inadequacy of putting the emphasis exclusively on the motives of the killers in trying to judge whether a particular act counts as "anti-Christian."

Thirty-six Catholic seminarians, all between the ages of fifteen and twenty, along with eight members of the seminary's staff, were killed by a Hutu rebel group on April 30, 1997, when a group belonging to the so-called National Council for the Defense of Democracy stormed into the seminary and rousted the young men out of their beds. Armed with rifles, grenades, pistols, and knives, they ordered the seminarians to separate into two groups, Hutus and Tutsis, and it was obvious to everyone that the Tutsis were to be killed. The seminarians refused to split up, and as a result, all forty were murdered, Hutu and Tutsi alike dying together.

The facility in Buta was what Catholics traditionally call a "minor" seminary, meaning it offered basic education and religious formation to younger men, roughly high school age, preparing to enter the major seminary, where they would begin their formal training for the priesthood. Eight of the killed seminarians came from Rwanda, six were from Congo, and one was from Nigeria, while most of the others came from Burundi.

One can certainly admire the courage of these young men, yet it's understandable why some observers might be reluctant to see them as victims of anti-Christian violence. There's no evidence that these Hutu militants attacked the seminary because it was a religious institution, and in fact most of the rebels probably saw themselves as good Christians. Instead, these seminarians were among the fatalities in a bloody cycle of ethnic violence sweeping across their part of Africa at the time. They died because their executioners became frustrated, not because the invaders had any specific intention of killing future Catholic clergymen.

According to a survivor named Jolique Rusimbamigera, the leader of the Hutu rebel group issued the kill order with these words: "Shoot these idiots who won't separate!" (Rusimbamigera, by the way, would later be one of the participants in an ecumenical service to the martyrs of the twentieth century presided over by Pope John Paul II in the Roman Colosseum on May 7, 2000, along with representatives of the Greek Orthodox Church and a number of other Christian churches.)

Concluding that this was not a chapter in the global war on

Christians, however, doesn't do justice to the reasons that Christians shaped by the environment of this particular place refused an order to separate themselves along ethnic lines.

According to the *Dictionary of African Christian Biography*, the Buta seminary, located in southern Burundi, had long been a refuge from the violence that had pitted Hutus and Tutsis against one another, which had waxed and waned since 1972. The seminary had made a special point of resisting the tug of ethnic animosity, explicitly organizing its life around the doctrine of Christian fraternity—the idea that the common brotherhood born of baptism was more important than ethnic origin or any other source of identity. Just prior to their massacre, the seminarians had gone through an Easter retreat dedicated to precisely this theme.

Fr. Nicolas Niyungeko, rector of the Sanctuary of Buta in the Diocese of Bururi, wrote of the seminarians:

> At the end of the retreat, this class was enlivened by a new kind of spirit, which seemed to be a preparation for the holy death of these innocents. Full of rejoicing and joy, the word in their mouths was "God is good and we have met Him." They spoke of heaven as if they had just come from it, and of the priesthood as if they had just been ordained. . . . One realized that something very strong had happened in their heart, without knowing exactly what it was. From that day on, they prayed, they sang, they danced to church, happy to discover, as it were, the treasure of heaven.
>
> The following day, when the murderers surprised them in bed, the seminarians were ordered to separate into two groups, the Hutus on one hand, the Tutsi on the other. They wanted to kill some of them, but the seminarians refused, preferring to die together. Their evil scheme having failed, the killers rushed on the children and slaughtered them with rifles and grenades. At that point some of the seminarians were heard singing psalms of praise and others were saying "Forgive them Lord, for they know not what they do." Others, instead of fighting or trying to run away,

preferred helping their distressed brothers, knowing exactly what was going to happen to them.

Their death was like a soft and light path from their dormitory to another resting place, without pain, without noise, nor fear. They died like Martyrs of the Fraternity, thus honoring the Church of Burundi, where many sons and daughters were led astray by hatred and ethnic vengeance.

Forty days after the massacre, the small seminary dedicated its church to Mary, Queen of Peace, and it has since, according to Fr. Niyungeko, "become a place of pilgrimage where Burundians come to pray for the reconciliation of their people, for peace, conversion, and hope for all. May their testimony of faith, unity, and fraternity send a message for humankind and their blood become a seed for peace in our country and in the world." When asked for a comment on the armed men who slaughtered his seminary brothers, the survivor, Rusimbamigera, replied: "I pray that the sacrifice of the murdered students and our suffering will lead the soldiers who caused this suffering to their own conversion."

Given that background, one has to conclude that if the death of these forty young men does not count as a Christian act, and that their deaths were the direct result of their Christian beliefs, then it's hard to know what would.

WHY THIS MYTH IS TOXIC

As with the other myths we've examined, the most basic problem with the "only if the motives are religious" way of seeing the global war on Christians is that it's inaccurate. It's a model borrowed from a secular justice system, premised on the idea that to establish the degree of criminal liability for an act, the focus has to be on the motive of the perpetrator. For instance, to ascertain if a particular act falls under a hate-crimes statute, one has to examine the motives of the person committing the crime. Did the perpetrator target a particular individual on the basis of race, politics, or religion? Or was this simply a question of robbery or rage unrelated to the victim's identity or beliefs?

If our aim, however, is not to establish criminal culpability but rather to establish the true scope of the global war on Christians, the focus must be different. The first step toward an accurate assessment must be establishing what counts as "Christian" activity, and there it's the motives of the person undertaking the activity that are most relevant. For instance, if a Christian from the United States or Europe goes to a zone of Colombia dominated by narcoterrorists and FARC guerrillas in order to exploit the area's mineral wealth and ends up killed, that would not count as a "situation of witness," because the person's motives for being present in that place were not related to any Christian convictions, even if he or she was quite devout in terms of personal spirituality.

If, however, a Christian moves to Colombia in order to serve in a mission hospital, and understood that service as a form of religious commitment, then his or her death in an ambush might well be seen as a casualty in the global war on Christians. The motives of the perpetrator would be identical, but the self-understanding of the victim is different, and that's what is relevant for purposes of this analysis.

On the moral plane, placing the emphasis on the motives of the perpetrator also does a serious injustice to the victims of the global war on Christians. Eric de Putter, Sr. Lukrecija Mamić, Francesco Bazzani, and the forty-four victims of the massacre at the Buta seminary in Burundi all gave their lives for the faith, just as surely as the great saints persecuted under Nero for refusing to participate in the imperial cult. They deliberately chose to give up their own comfort and security, placing themselves in dangerous situations because they believed their faith compelled them to do so.

To suggest that their sacrifice is somehow less religiously meaningful, that it doesn't fully count as a Christian act, because their persecutors were not driven by specifically religious motives would be both morally unfair and spiritually hollow.

11

THE MYTH THAT ANTI-CHRISTIAN PERSECUTION IS A POLITICAL ISSUE

Of all the myths about the global war on Christians, the idea that the suffering of Christians around the world is either a left-wing or right-wing concern is arguably the most pernicious. If members of the various political tribes can agree on anything, surely it ought to be that violent persecution of people on the basis of their beliefs—whatever those beliefs may be—is indefensible, and not as a matter of any ideological position but on the basis of universal human rights.

Over the years, the global war on Christians has undeniably been exploited by various forces in Western politics. During the 1970s and 1980s, the martyrs of the liberation theology movement in Latin America were touted by left-wing voices in order to criticize the Reagan Doctrine in the United States, which was premised on supporting anti-Communist regimes and movements regardless of their human rights record. In Latin America, that policy sometimes put the United States in the position of propping up police states that suffocated dissent and brutalized their own people, with El Salvador being an emblematic example. The assassination of Archbishop Oscar Romero became exhibit A for opponents of the Reagan Doctrine, and for a time it seemed that in political terms, the new Christian martyrs skewed to the left.

After the upheavals of the 1970s and 1980s, anti-Christian perse-cution receded in public consciousness, only to make a strong comeback in the 1990s. This time, the issue was propelled by the right rather than by the left. It was put on the American political map by a constellation of conservative activists and intellectuals, such as Michael Horowitz, Nina Shea, and Paul Marshall—in part as an element in a broader cri-tique of secular hostility to religion, and in part as a pre-9/11 version of the "clash of civilizations" with Islam. Writing in the *New York Times Magazine* in 1997, Jeffrey Goldberg called the newfound concern with persecuted Christians "an issue manufactured in the mile-square sec-tion of Washington that produces the most priceless of political com-modities: the wedge issue."

Goldberg went on to describe how the crusade to defend per-secuted Christians pitted several important domestic constituencies against one another:

- Mainline church groups versus evangelicals and conservative Catholics. (The general secretary of the National Council of Churches, Joan Brown Campbell, groused in 1997 that the movement smacked of an "overly muscular Christianity.")
- Social conservatives versus pro-business groups and the for-eign policy establishment. (China tended to be the focal point: Do we impose sanctions because of China's record on reli-gious freedom, or not?)
- Traditional human rights groups such as Human Rights Watch and the American Civil Liberties Union versus faith-based movements.

To some extent, those divisions still exist. One could add that in the post-9/11 era, anti-Christian violence by Muslims is a terrific rally-ing cry for hawks on the American right, which may help explain why some liberals remain skittish. All this, however, says much more about American politics than about the nature of anti-Christian persecution. Alas, the United States has developed a political culture that could turn Mom and apple pie into wedge issues.

The truth is that, ideologically speaking, persecution against Christians is an equal-opportunity enterprise. Looking around, it's clear that the traditional villains for both the political left and the political right, the bête noire for both ideological camps, are equally among the protagonists in the global war on Christians.

Take the 2012 murder of a Protestant Christian named Asif Masih in Mirpur Khas, a village located in south Pakistan. Masih, an evangelical who was twenty-six at the time of his death, was a member of the Dalit underclass and the only breadwinner for his family, which comprised his parents, his younger brothers, and a sister. Masih was reportedly shot to death by gunmen acting at the behest of an influential area landowner named Faisal Kachelo, just one month before his planned wedding date. According to a medical report, Masih was hit by five bullets, including one to the head. He was a manual laborer with ties to a local nongovernmental organization that advocated for the rights of Dalits and tribals, and he was apparently killed over a petty dispute involving some bags of sand used by locals as construction material. Observers charged that the Pakistani authorities did not investigate the murder with vigor, part of what they charged is a pattern of not taking crimes against non-Muslims seriously, especially where they are perceived to belong to low-caste groups that don't enjoy any social standing or protection.

Standing back from the details, one sees that Masih died not from religious and ethnic discrimination but as a result of a social and economic system premised on defending the privileges of wealthy landowners over the rights of exploited laborers. In effect, one could say that Masih was a martyr to a particularly savage form of capitalism, and thus he is a classic icon of the political left—precisely the sort of figure that one could imagine on Che Guevara–style T-shirts and banners, inspiring progressive uprisings for social change.

Now consider Bishop John Han Dingxiang, an underground Catholic prelate in the Chinese region of Yongnian, a division of Hebei province. A staunch Roman loyalist, he was ordained to the priesthood in 1986 and became a bishop in 1989. Even before his ordination, Dingxiang had refused to take part in the state-controlled Patriotic

Association, erected by the Chinese authorities as an "autonomous" form of Catholicism independent of the Vatican but which in reality is subservient to the government. As a result, Dingxiang spent his entire life as a member of China's Catholic underground, often referred to as the "church of the catacombs," worshipping mostly in secret in house church services for fear of harassment and arrest.

Those fears were hardly idle. Dingxiang was imprisoned at a labor camp for almost twenty years, from 1960 to 1979, and during his tenure as a bishop he was imprisoned eleven separate times, which meant that he spent thirty-five years of his life in some form of official custody. Repeatedly during those incarcerations, he was beaten, subjected to various forms of "reeducation," and otherwise mistreated. He had been placed under arrest again in 1999 and remained in custody until his death in 2007, having been kept in several locations, including a housing complex for Chinese police and their families. As a final indignity, when the bishop died in 2007, Chinese officials refused to allow anyone to be by his bedside. They said that he died of lung cancer, but his body was hastily cremated just six hours after his death, preventing any autopsy from being conducted. His remains were then placed in a large public cemetery without any headstone marking the spot.

Aid to the Church in Need, the Catholic humanitarian group that monitors anti-Christian persecution around the world, has preserved a bit of grainy footage of Dingxiang shot by a fellow Chinese Catholic just prior to his death from one of the locations where the bishop was held under arrest. It shows an obviously weakened Dingxiang on a balcony surrounded by iron bars, clinging to the bars for support, but defiantly waving a cross in the air. The Aid to the Church in Need report also featured comments from some of the mourners who gathered in secret to mark the bishop's passing, one of whom was quoted as saying: "We are so tired of these difficulties." Then, with a smile, he quickly added: "But the sufferings of this time are as nothing compared to the glory of God."

China, of course, is an officially atheistic and socialist society. In that light, one could say that Bishop John Han Dingxiang was a martyr to Communism. Dingxiang could be styled as a classic icon of the political right, someone who went to his death upholding the right to personal freedom against the Leviathan of the state. Taking both Masih and Dingxiang into view, the bottom line should be obvious: there are victims in the global war on Christians whose stories reflect the instincts and worldview of both the political left and the right, and no one has any monopoly on suffering.

As mentioned in the introduction, politics distorts perceptions of the global war on Christians in another sense. Ideological bias tempts observers in the West to see only part of the picture. Those on the political left may celebrate martyrs to corporate greed or to right-wing police states, but fear to speak out about the suffering of Christians behind the lines of the Islamic world. Conservatives may be reluctant to condemn the situation facing Christians in the state of Israel or in regimes that are presently in fashion on the right as allies in the "war on terror." Either way, the result is a reductive reading of the true score of anti-Christian persecution, and a double standard when it comes to engaging its protagonists. If we want to see the global war on Christians clearly, we have to stop looking at it through the funhouse mirror of secular politics.

The following vignettes are designed to bolster the point that there are martyrs aplenty in our time who appeal both to the political left and to the right, making the point that no ideological camp can make any exclusive claim confirming this war.

BISHOP JUAN JOSÉ GERARDI CONEDERA OF GUATEMALA

Born in 1922, Juan José Gerardi Conedera was the grandson of Italian immigrants to Guatemala. Seventy-five at the time of his death in late April 1998, he devoted the latter stages of his life to promoting justice and reconciliation in the wake of Guatemala's long-running civil war, which in one form or another had lasted from 1960 to 1996. Gerardi knew the story from the front lines: while he was serving as bishop of the rural El Quiché diocese in the late 1970s, he repeatedly received death threats because of his advocacy on behalf of the indigenous Mayan people, and several of his clergy were actually killed by paramilitary groups in league with the Guatemalan military. At one stage, the violence directed at the church became so intense that Gerardi took the unprecedented step of closing the diocese rather than watch as the army picked off more of his priests. Gerardi was forced to take refuge in neighboring Costa Rica for two years until the overthrow of a military junta allowed him to return.

Carrying the scars of those experiences, Gerardi was later named to a national reconciliation commission. He said that he had had two goals for his work: keeping the memory of the suffering endured by his people alive, and promoting a national climate of forgiveness that would allow society to recover. Within the offices of the Archdiocese of Guatemala City, Gerardi spearheaded a project called Recovery of Historical Memory, designed to catalogue in detailed fashion the human rights violations and other atrocities that had occurred during the civil war. The project presented its final report on April 24, 1988, laying the lion's share of blame for what had happened at the feet of the Guatemalan government and the army.

Two days later, Gerardi was bludgeoned to death in the garage of his home in Guatemala City. His attackers beat Gerardi with a crude concrete slab, disfiguring him to the extent that his face was completely unrecognizable and identification of the body was possible only by means of his episcopal ring.

Fr. Ricardo Falla, a Jesuit anthropologist who first got to know Gerardi in the 1970s, said the manner in which Gerardi was killed is significant. He contrasted it to the 1980 assassination of Archbishop Oscar Romero in El Salvador.

"Romero was killed with a bullet to the heart, as if to kill off the love and the passion that drove people to struggle," Falla told reporter Paul Jeffrey in 1998. "Gerardi was killed by someone who smashed his brain, as if they were trying to wipe out his memory."

If that was in fact the aim, it backfired. In the wake of Gerardi's death, archdiocesan officials increased the press run on the four volumes of the church's report from three thousand copies to twenty thousand copies, and to this day it remains the most widely circulated report chronicling human rights violations in Guatemala, despite the fact it's definitely not easy reading. Besides a statistical breakdown about who did what during the war, there are dozens of selections from victim testimonies. Here's an example: "Many of the women were pregnant, and they cut open the stomach of one of them who was eight months pregnant. They took out the creature and played with it as if it were a football," said one survivor of a 1981 army incursion.

In a section titled "Mechanisms of Horror," the report describes the practices of death squads and other clandestine organizations spawned by the military. Besides the organization of hit squads and descriptions of domestic spying, the report also includes anecdotes of how novice assassins would practice their skills on street people, in preparation for political jobs. Testimonies of former soldiers relate how troops were trained in a step-by-step process for conducting massacres, such as how military agents would conduct "disappearances"—characterized in the report as a particularly vicious form of social control. The report also relates how civil defense patrols were designed to extend the army's reach in the countryside and induce civilians to kill one another.

Presenting the report on April 24, Gerardi said: "As a church, we collectively and responsibly assumed the task of breaking the silence that thousands of victims have kept for years. We made it possible for them to talk, to have their say, to tell their stories of suffering and pain so they might feel liberated from the burden that has been weighing down on them for so long."

Authorities in Guatemala initially tried to deflect blame for Gerardi's murder, at one point making the ludicrous suggestion that the killer was the parish dog, named Baloo, which they hinted had attacked Gerardi at the direction of a priest who lived in the same residence. The "arrest" of Baloo was briefly a mini soap opera. In response, the Catholic Church in Guatemala took the controversial decision to form an investigative team of young men who called themselves "Los Intocables," or "the Untouchables," to find the killers.

Eventually in 2001, three army officers, including a colonel and two junior officers, were convicted of Gerardi's assassination and sentenced to thirty-year terms in prison. A priest identified as an accomplice received a twenty-year sentence. The verdicts were historic, in that they marked the first time members of the Guatemalan military were tried before civilian courts. Upon appeal, two of the officers had their sentences reduced to twenty years, while one was killed in prison before the appeals process reached completion. One of the convicted officers was paroled in July 2012, while the priest, Fr. Mario Orantes, was released in January 2013 for good behavior after serving twelve years.

The court had also requested that thirteen other people be investigated, including a handful of senior government officials, but to date no additional charges in the case have been filed. Many observers in Guatemala believe that the real masterminds of the affair remain at large and are unlikely ever to be identified or tried.

Fr. Cirilo Santamaría, a Carmelite priest and veteran of the Recovery of Historical Memory project, said at a public forum in 2003 that Gerardi's legacy continues to challenge the church to reach past its institutional boundaries.

"Gerardi was a bishop who went beyond the frontiers of the church," Santamaría said. "He was a bishop who incarnated himself, who knew how to walk with the poor, listen to the indigenous, who knew the way down into the gullies where the urban poor live, who attended to the victims without asking them their religion. The victims were simple people, and Gerardi embraced them where they were."

Santamaría encouraged Gerardi's followers to pick up where the bishop left off.

"Gerardi wanted this country to break out from the years of fear and death that have reduced the majority of Guatemalans to silence," he said. "That's why we're today starting to continue the task he began, to recover our memory so that history won't repeat itself. All of us are learning to shout together, 'Never Again!' Never again violence, never again massacres, never again assassinations."

In 2010, a dramatic film was made of the bishop's life and death, titled *Gerardi*. He is celebrated as a "martyr for truth," someone who gave his life so that the suffering of the Guatemalan people, especially the Mayans with whom he lived and worked for most of his life, would not be lost or forgotten. By encouraging the remembering of the past, his aim was to shape a better future.

In political terms, Gerardi profiles as a classic martyr for the left, someone who challenged poverty and oppression associated with a right-wing regime. The witness of Gerardi, and countless other Christians like him in various parts of the world, offers proof that defending Christians at risk is hardly an exclusively "conservative" enterprise.

FR. DANIIL SYSOYEV

The November 19, 2009, slaying of a celebrated Russian Orthodox priest in Moscow is the equal and opposite version of Gerardi's story. Fr. Daniil Sysoyev's story presents a classic instance of a new martyr whose death stirred immediate sympathy and outrage on the political right, not just in Russia but across the world.

A gunman wearing a hospital mask shot Sysoyev four times at point-blank range inside an Orthodox church in southern Moscow, where he served as rector, and he died on the operating table in a nearby hospital. The assailant was identified as a Muslim radical and Kyrgyz citizen who was later killed during an attempted arrest. A militant Islamic group based in the North Caucasus took credit for the assassination of the Orthodox cleric, saying in a statement that "one of our brothers . . . expressed his desire to execute the damned Sysoyev."

In the Orthodox world and beyond, Sysoyev has become an icon of the dangers of radical Islam and the failure of authorities to confront the threat with sufficient vigor. He's a clerical analogue, in some ways, of Theo van Gogh, the Dutch filmmaker whose 2004 assassination by a Muslim fanatic made him an posthumous darling of hawks and neo-cons.

Thirty-five at the time he died, Sysoyev was married with a wife and three children. After his ordination to the priesthood in 1995, he became a leading figure in the post-Soviet renaissance of the Russian Orthodox Church, having graduated from the Moscow Spiritual Academy and later founding an academy for street preachers in Moscow. He was an active member of the center for the rehabilitation of the victims of totalitarian sects and pseudo-religious movements. Sysoyev authored dozens of books, including a work titled *Son of Man*, styled as an introduction to the life of Christ for people in the former Soviet sphere. He founded the Orthodox Open University, launched one of the first Sunday schools in Russia, and helped to found a charity group at the Russian Children's Hospital in Moscow. Sysoyev clearly belonged to the conservative wing of the mainstream Russian Orthodox Church. He was critical of Darwinian evolutionary theory and famously instructed Orthodox believers that they were not to participate in yoga, karate, Latin American dances such as the tango or salsa, or belly dancing, because, in his view, all those activities had non-Christian origins and thus posed the risk of syncretism and religious relativism. Sysoyev also struck out against what he saw as the growing influence of "paganism" and the occult in Russian society, becoming a specialist in trying to bring people attracted to New Age spirituality back into the church.

For most Russians, however, Sysoyev's real claim to fame was his strong opposition to Muslim immigration and his insistence on the need to confront Islamic radicalism, making him something of a celebrity on the political right and among some nationalist currents in Russian society. (Ultranationalists had a cool view of Sysoyev because he wasn't a monarchist.) He conducted two celebrated public debates with a former Orthodox priest named Vyacheslav Polosin, who had converted to Islam and taken up a mission to spread his new faith. Sysoyev published a book titled *Marriage with a Muslim*, in which he asserted that God and the Orthodox Church condemned marriages between Christians and non-Christians—in context, meaning mostly Muslims. The cochair of Russia's Council of Muftis and a Muslim journalist both sued Sysoyev over the book, accusing the priest of inspiring hatred against Russia's Muslim minority of roughly twenty million, basing their complaints on Russian federal statutes banning "hate speech."

Sysoyev made a special point of missionary outreach to Muslims and at one point claimed to have personally baptized eighty Muslim converts, "among them Tatars, Uzbeks, Chechens and Dagestanis." The fiery priest pointedly charged that many of his fellow Orthodox clergy were unwilling to follow his lead because "they are afraid of revenge from the Muslim world." One prominent leader in Russia's Muslim community, Mufti Nafigulla Ashirov, branded Sysoyev "the Russian Salman Rushdie." In a 2008 television interview, Sysoyev testily insisted, "As I see it, it is a sin not to preach to Muslims, for I am half-Russian and half-Tatar myself," meaning that his family hailed from a Tatar region with a heavy Muslim presence. Sysoyev organized weekly missionary courses in his parish, explicitly designed to prepare Orthodox Christians to attempt to spread the faith to Muslims.

As a result, Sysoyev routinely received death threats. In one instance, the priest said that he had received an anonymous email threatening to "cut his head off and let his guts out." In 2008, a man identifying himself as a Muslim called the parish in which Sysoyev was serving and said that the priest would be killed if he continued to publicly express his negative attitude toward Islam. On the basis of those threats, Sysoyev twice asked Russia's Federal Security Bureau to assign agents to protect his personal security. In October 2009, he posted this note in an online service called LiveJournal: "I have news again. Today, you'll laugh, but Muslims once again have promised to kill me. Now by phone. Already tried. The 14th time. I've got accustomed. . . . And so, I ask you all to pray."

According to a friend and colleague of Sysoyev's, Fr. Oleg Stenyaev, an Islamic warlord had sentenced the Orthodox priest to death in absentia on the basis of two charges: that Sysoyev conducted open debates with Muslims, challenging core principles of their faith, and that he baptized Muslim converts to Christianity. (Stenyaev would later claim that several more Muslim converts were baptized in the wake of Sysoyev's death.)

After his death, Patriarch Kyrill I of Moscow, the leader of the Russian Orthodox Church, proclaimed Sysoyev a "confessor of the faith" and a "martyr" for the cause of evangelical preaching. The murdered priest is popularly celebrated as a martyr even outside Russian Orthodox circles; in Greece, he is venerated as a saint and martyr by many Greek Orthodox believers, who place him in the same category as their fellow believers who were martyred during the Turkish occupation.

Looking back on the murder three years later, Stenyaev wrote of his friend: "Saints are difficult people. They always have an inspirational impulse, and they are ahead of others in ideas, words, and actions. It looked as if he [Sysoyev] was in a hurry. But actually, it was us who were behind. Father Daniil was not in a rush, he was a measured person. But he set the pace and the tension and it wouldn't let one rest idly."

Given the circumstances of his assassination, Sysoyev became a hero to critics of policies of "multiculturalism," which many social and political conservatives believe to be overly accommodating of radical currents in the Islamic world, failing to insist that Muslim immigrants assimilate to the values of their host societies. More broadly, Sysoyev is hailed by many conservatives as a martyr in the "clash of civilizations," whose death illustrates the need for a more muscular response to Islamic-inspired terrorism.

To be clear, neither Gerardi nor Sysoyev understood himself as a politician or an ideologue, and neither man lived or died in order to advance the interests of a particular party or faction. Though Gerardi's own political and theological instincts were probably to the left of Sysoyev's, both men probably would have said what they shared as Christian believers, despite the denominational divide between Catholics and Orthodox, was more important than any political differences. The relevant point here is that the stories of Gerardi and Sysoyev show that both the right and the left have their martyrs, that no political position is excluded from the global war on Christians, and therefore that raising an alarm over the kind of violence that claimed the lives of these two clergymen, and that continues to afflict Christians all over the world, is not a political exercise.

WHY THIS MYTH IS TOXIC

As ever, the basic problem with the "political issue" myth is that it's inaccurate. The forces driving the global war on Christians don't skew predominantly in one political direction, and the fact of this global war does not support the ideological diagnosis of any given faction. There are martyrs on all sides of contemporary political divides; liberals and conservatives both can be found both among the victims and among the protagonists. For every Dorothy Stang or Oscar Romero, there's a Bishop John Han Dingxiang or a Fr. Daniil Sysoyev. Beyond such well-known figures, there are also anonymous casualties like Asif

Masih in Pakistan, people victimized by every imaginable kind of political ideology and interest. To suggest that attempting to mobilize a response to this global war is in some sense a political exercise thus misrepresents the situation on the ground.

In addition, the "political interest" is also an impediment to galvanizing a coherent and nonpartisan response to the global war on Christians, perhaps especially in the contemporary West—where everything is perceived to have a political subtext. As long as some sectors of opinion in the West suspect that political axes are being ground whenever someone speaks out against anti-Christian persecution, the response will be hamstrung. The threat must be framed in terms of universal human rights, not partisan interests. Crystal clarity needs to be achieved on this point: calling for more aggressive action on behalf of suffering Christians, in terms of both direct humanitarian efforts and a policy response at the government level, does not carry any direct political payoff, because Christians of all political persuasions, and of none, are equally at risk.

Finally, the "political issue" myth is also spiritually offensive because it taints the sacrifice of the new martyrs, suggesting that they went to their deaths for a political agenda rather than on the basis of their religious beliefs. In terms of both secular politics and Christian doctrine, today's martyrs represent a wide range of instincts. Simply because people understand themselves to be religious believers does not mean that they cease to be citizens, or stop having their own opinions on political questions. What the people described throughout this book have in common is a profound conviction that faith matters. Their life choices were fundamentally rooted not in secular ideology but in their own reading of the Gospels, however different that reading may be from one person to another. First and foremost, these martyrs lived and died as Christians, not as participants in the culture wars, and to attempt to exploit their legacies in order to score political points is both crass and dishonest.

PART THREE

Fallout, Consequences,
and Response

As we have seen, the global war on Christians is in many ways the greatest story never told about the early twenty-first century. Anti-Christian violence is often masked by silence and indifference, or touted only when publicizing a particular atrocity happens to serve someone's interests. Like all generalizations, however, this assessment paints with too broad a brush, because it's not as if no one is paying attention. Beyond the victims themselves, consciousness is beginning to grow both at the grass roots across the Christian world and at the leadership level.

On September 12, 2012, the Catholic bishops of the United States organized a symposium devoted to the issue, "International Religious Freedom: An Imperative for Peace and the Common Good." Cardinal Timothy Dolan of New York, president of the United States Conference of Catholic Bishops, called for greater consciousness-raising and advocacy, saying: "Many Christians experience daily affronts and often live in fear because of their pursuit of truth, their faith in Jesus Christ and their heartfelt plea for respect for religious freedom. This situation is unacceptable, since it represents an insult to God and to human dignity; furthermore, it is a threat to security and peace, and an obstacle to the achievement of authentic and integral human development."

Looking forward, it seems likely that the defense of persecuted Christians will increasingly become a front-burner priority for the various churches and denominations around the world, in part because of an inexorable demographic reality: a robust two-thirds of the 2.2 billion Christians in the world today live outside the West, a share destined to reach three-quarters by midcentury. These people live on the front lines of the global war on Christians, and as their numbers afford them greater influence in shaping the agenda in church affairs, inevitably the realities of anti-Christian violence and persecution will rise up the to-do list. In part too, growing attention to the fate of the persecuted will be the result of a sort of spiritual "amplifier effect." Average believers in the West may not yet have heard the stories of the new martyrs, but once they do, it's hard not to be stirred.

As that happens, it is likely to have consequences across the board—for how Christianity chooses to spend its political and social capital, for the theological and spiritual interests of the different churches, and for the ways in which Christians attempt to make a difference. This section tries to sketch those implications.

In chapter 12, we examine the observable, this-worldly fallout of the global war, suggesting that Christianity is likely to experience three broad consequences:

- First, growing attention to the global war on Christians is likely to accelerate the emergence of leadership from the developing world, both in terms of internal doctrinal wrangles within Christian churches and in terms of Christianity's external agenda.

- Second, consciousness about the often violent persecution of Christians around the world will cement religious freedom as the paradigmatic social and political concern of Christian churches in the twenty-first century. That's a development already in progress, often driven by perceived new restrictions in the West, but it will be turbocharged by a growing wave of alarm about the global war on Christians.

- Third, the mounting preoccupation with anti-Christian persecution, and new leadership from believers and churches suffering harassment, will make Christianity a stronger pro-democracy force around the world. Scholars say that religious actors are most likely to be strong promoters of democracy when they're not controlled by the state, and they have an occasionally rocky relationship with the ruling powers. Research shows those same dynamics also tend to make religious actors more ardent activists in peacemaking and social justice, which is also likely to have an echo in Christianity as a result of leadership from cultures where Christian suffering is most intense.

Chapter 13 then ponders the spiritual fruits of a growing focus on the global war on Christians. It outlines what many experts describe as a new "ecumenism of the martyrs," meaning a renewed commitment to Christian unity as a result of the common experience of persecution. It also hints at the implications for a new "theology from below," meaning a new Christian self-understanding rooted not in a context of power and privilege but in one of suffering and deprivation. The chapter also proposes that the witness of the martyrs could prove to be a central ingredient in the success or failure of Christian efforts at evangelism in the twenty-first century, with a considerable body of empirical evidence suggesting that martyrdom may well be the most powerful tool in the missionary toolbox.

Finally, chapter 14 considers practical steps that both individuals and communities can take to try to express solidarity for the victims of the global war on Christians, ranging from personal prayer to widespread education campaigns, from humanitarian relief to advocacy of a more muscular defense of religious freedom at the policy level. The core idea is that while Christianity celebrates its martyrs, Christians also have an obligation not to stand by and watch new martyrs go to their deaths when there are practical steps to be taken that might curb their suffering.

In terms of the bottom line, this section is designed to make a very simple argument: rallying to the defense of Christians who find themselves on the firing line in this global war would obviously be good for them, but that's not the whole story. This effort ought to have extraordinarily healthy consequences, both in human terms and in matters of the spirit, for the rest of us too.

12

SOCIAL AND POLITICAL FALLOUT

One paradox about Christianity is that while it's not a political party, it has always had massive political implications for any society in which it takes root. In his famous eighteenth-century treatise *Decline and Fall of the Roman Empire*, English historian Edward Gibbon blamed Christianity for the fall of Rome, charging that the turn-the-other-cheek ethic of Christianity sapped Rome's warrior spirit. Gibbon also believed that financial support of monasteries and convents siphoned off Rome's public resources, and that theological disputes exacerbated factionalism and weakened the state from within. Ever since, historians have debated whether the introduction of Christianity was good or bad for ancient Rome, but everyone acknowledges that it mattered.

That point is by no means an artifact of history. Throughout the twentieth century, totalitarian states of all stripes waged war on churches, understanding that if you want to control the population, you have to control its religion. In the early stages, totalitarians tried to wipe out religious institutions. When that proved impossible, they tried to buy the churches off. Nazi Germany, for instance, promoted a policy of *Gleichschaltung*, meaning "bringing into line," which included rewarding compliant churches and pastors and punishing defiant ones.

After the Nazis fell, Christians were also prominent in the recovery from fascism. Many of the architects of the European Union after the Second World War were laity inspired by Christian social teaching. One of them, French statesman Robert Schuman, is now a candidate for sainthood in the Catholic Church.

Perhaps the best contemporary example of the church's political muscle is the role the late John Paul II played in the collapse of Communism. It is, however, far from an isolated case. From the People Power movement in the Philippines that deposed Ferdinand Marcos in 1989 to the independence of East Timor in 2002 and the birth of the world's newest nation, South Sudan, in 2011, Christians have played lead roles in a staggering share of political turning points across the developing world.

Whenever a new issue or concern seems to be rippling across the Christian world, savvy political thinkers take notice. In 1980, for instance, the Council for Inter-American Security produced a report that came to be known as the "Santa Fe Document," and which was influential in shaping the foreign policy agenda of the incoming Reagan administration. Among other points, the Santa Fe Document warned against the growing influence of liberation theology among Catholics in Central America. During the 1980s and 1990s, the emergence of the "culture wars" in the West over issues such as abortion, gay marriage, euthanasia, and embryonic stem cell research have confirmed Christianity's political relevance.

For those reasons, it's not only legitimate, but very smart, to consider what the political implications might be of the emergence of the global war on Christians as a signature concern in the twenty-first century. Though prediction is a hazardous business, three such consequences seem plausible as this transition plays itself out.

THE AGENDA OF THE DEVELOPING WORLD

As the stories of the new martyrs begin to exercise a tighter grip on the Christian imagination, this new awareness about what it means to be a believer today in Mali, Honduras, and Indonesia should have ripple effects in several zones.

First, Christians in the West will become more accustomed to thinking of themselves as members of a global family of faith, because they will be privy to greater insight about the previously hidden lives of their fellow believers from other corners of the planet. Some share of those Western Christians will become more inclined to factor the experiences and perspectives of their coreligionists into their thinking about social and political matters, as well as taking them into greater consideration on ecclesiastical questions.

Second, clerical stars from the developing world will play a steadily more influential role in terms of leadership inside their own denominations and church organizations. That process is already under way; for instance, Samuel Koiba, a Methodist from Kenya, served as president of the World Council of Churches from 2004 to 2009. In November 2012, Pope Benedict XVI took the unprecedented step of holding a consistory, the event in which a pope creates new cardinals, in which there wasn't a single European and only one Westerner (an American). The new cardinals came from Lebanon, India, Nigeria, Colombia, and the Philippines. Not long afterward, in March 2013, the cardinals of the Catholic Church elected the first pope from the developing world in Jorge Mario Bergoglio of Argentina, who took the name Francis. The election of a Latin American to the most visible and consequential leadership position in all of Christianity is a perfect illustration of this trend.

Third, a variety of different grassroots Christian actors, from committed individuals to movements, associations. and spiritual groups, will find a more receptive audience for their messages in the West, and will become bolder about proposing them. There is a mounting conviction among Christians in the global South that their historical moment to lead has arrived, which means they are progressively shedding what has sometimes been a reluctance to project themselves as equals in the global Christian conversation. No longer content to act as branch officers of a multinational enterprise, they're ready to join the board of directors. Today's tools of social communication mean it's easier for people to reach large audiences, and growing sensitivity to the martyrs means that Christians in the developing world are more likely to find fellow believers in the West open to what they have to say.

The cumulative effect of these three developments should be enormous, and it won't end with implications for internal ecclesiastical life, such as who's chosen to lead denominations or which liturgical styles are permitted. The rise of the developing world also means that the social and political outlook of Christians in the global South will have greater influence in their churches.

What might we expect to see and hear from Christians in the global South when it comes to the intersection of faith and politics?

Naturally, generalizations are dangerous. To suggest that a massive bloc of 1.5 billion people hold identical views would be ridiculous. For every assertion one can make about Christians in the global South, there are millions, if not tens or hundreds of millions, of exceptions. Further, Western categories of "liberal" and "conservative" are often misleading when applied to the developing world, because they presume a taxonomy that is an artifact of Western culture ("left wing" and "right wing" are terms that date from the French Revolution) and that doesn't always occur naturally to the people we're trying to describe.

Nevertheless, with allowances both for the overgeneralization and for imposing artificial categories, one could say that Christianity in the developing world tends to be "morally conservative and politically liberal."

By Northern standards, Southern Christians typically hold conservative attitudes on moral questions such as abortion, homosexuality, and the family. This dynamic is clear within the Anglican Communion, where a minority of liberal Anglicans in the North, especially the United States and Canada, is pressing ahead with the ordination of gay clergy and the blessing of same-sex unions, against a determined majority in the developing world which strongly opposes such measures. That opposition is concentrated above all in Africa. Today, there are an estimated forty million Anglicans in Africa, more than half the global total of seventy-six million, and African prelates have been extending ecclesiastical recognition to traditionalist Anglican communities in many parts of the West. The Convocation of Anglicans in North America, for instance, under the authority of the Anglican hierarchy in Nigeria, claimed sixty-nine congregations as of 2012.

Across much of Asia and Latin America, similar attitudes on sexual ethics often prevail. According to a 2006 Pew Forum survey, 72 percent of Indians, 78 percent of South Koreans, and 56 percent of Filipinos believe that homosexuality is "never justified." Even in sexually liberal Brazil, a strong 49 percent of the population agrees that homosexuality is "never justified." In Guatemala, 63 percent of the population takes that view. On the abortion issue, 79 percent of Brazilians, 85 percent of Guatemalans, 68 percent of Indians, and 97 percent of Filipinos are opposed to abortion, and solid majorities in almost every country want abortion to be against the civil law. In general, the rise of Christianity in the developing world seems destined, at least in the short run, to bolster the conservative position on the Western culture wars. It will make Christian churches more committed to defending traditional positions and less inclined to make accommodations for dissent.

Yet when one leaves the ambit of personal morality and enters the terrain of economic, political, and military matters, the typical attitudes of Southern Christians often strike Northern observers as remarkably "liberal." To be specific, Christian clergy and laity in the developing world often are:

- Skeptical of capitalism and globalization.
- Wary about the global influence of the United States.
- Abolitionist on the death penalty.
- Favorable to the defense of immigrant rights and concerned about the fate of their countrymen in Western societies.
- Pro-Palestinian and, by implication, often critical of Israel and the Western powers that back Israel.
- Pro–United Nations and in favor of a strong multilateralism in foreign policy, as opposed to domination of global affairs by a handful of wealthy and powerful states.
- Antiwar, including overwhelming opposition to the U.S.-led war in Iraq.
- In favor of a robust role for the state in the economy and suspicious of neoliberal, laissez-faire economic models.

These views can be found embedded in both official statements of church bodies in the global South as well as in their working structures. For instance, in a 127-page report issued in 2004, the Catholic bishops of Asia declared that "neoliberal economic globalization" destroys Asian families because it is the primary cause of poverty on the continent. In June 2005, a group of Catholic bishops from Eritrea, Ethiopia, Kenya, Malawi, Tanzania, Sudan, Uganda, Zambia, Somalia, and Djibouti declared, "We are particularly horrified by the ravages of unbridled capitalism, which has taken away and stifled local ownership of economic initiatives and is leading to a dangerous gap between the rich few and the poor majority."

The Association of Evangelicals in Africa is one of the continent's leading Protestant bodies, representing an estimated one hundred million evangelicals who belong to thirty-six national evangelical fellowships made up of numerous local churches. The group has become an outspoken force on behalf of peace, poverty relief, and broad economic justice, despite the irony that many of its clergy would be seen as staunch conservatives on other matters, such as whether their churches and denominations ought to be more receptive to homosexuality or women clergy.

For a broad swath of Christian opinion across Latin America, Africa, and Asia, these views do not seem "liberal" or "progressive." Rather, they reflect a meat-and-potatoes social consensus that holds across most of the usual ideological, linguistic, geographical, and ethnic divides. Of course there are prominent dissenters and critics of this consensus, but they fall mostly into the category of exceptions that prove the rule.

In other words, the political agenda of Christianity in the developing world tends to defy the political dichotomies of the West. It's highly conservative on some matters, strikingly liberal on others. It tends to cut through the frequent division in Western Christianity between pro-life forces and the peace-and-justice camp, toward something like what some Catholics refer to as a "consistent ethic of life," suggesting that Christianity's pro-life and peace-and-justice commitments belong together. In any event, this mixture of highly traditional positions on the "culture wars" and highly progressive stances on the economy, war and peace, the death penalty, immigration, and so on seems poised to exercise greater influence in shaping the agenda of global Christianity. That's in part the result of simple demographics, but also too because the stories of the martyrs will foster a climate of growing sympathy and solidarity with the developing world.

RELIGIOUS FREEDOM AS THE SIGNATURE CAUSE

Even if there were no such thing as the global war on Christians, the defense of religious freedom would still be a source of mounting concern for Christianity. For one thing, mounting restrictions on religious freedom affect the followers of other faiths too, people with whom Christians are in long-standing dialogues and whose fate matters to them.

A September 2012 report by the Pew Forum concluded that "a rising tide of restrictions on religion [has] spread around the world." Among other points, the study found that 37 percent of nations in the world have high or very high restrictions on religion, up from 31 percent a year ago, a six-point spike in just twelve months, and that three-quarters of the world's population of 7 billion, meaning 5.25 billion people, live in countries with high or very high restrictions on religion. That's up from 70 percent in the previous year. Facing those trends, any person of conscience, including the leadership of the various branches of Christianity, would obviously be concerned.

For another thing, many Christian leaders in the West are deeply worried about what they perceive as a rising tide of restrictions on religious liberty, with the dispute between the Obama administration and a cross section of religious organizations in America over insurance mandates being merely the tip of the iceberg.

When Archbishop William Lori of Baltimore, chair of the Catholic bishops' new Ad Hoc Committee for Religious Liberty, testified before the House Judiciary Committee in October 2012, he said that "the bishops of the United States have watched with increasing alarm as this great national legacy of religious liberty . . . has been subject to ever more frequent assault and ever more rapid erosion." (At the time, Lori was still the diocesan bishop of Bridgeport, Connecticut.) Beyond the insurance mandates, Lori cited several other causes for alarm:

- Directives from the Department of Health and Human Services requiring faith-based relief agencies to offer a "full range" of reproductive services in anti-trafficking and migrant care programs that receive federal funding.

- A similar requirement from the United States Agency for International Development that contraception be included as part of international relief and development programs promoted by all nongovernmental groups that received federal funding, including faith-based agencies.

- A brief filed by the Department of Justice in opposition to the Defense of Marriage Act, or DOMA, which labeled opposition to same-sex marriage as a form of "bias" and "prejudice." (That language raised fears among some religious groups that their resistance to gay marriage, even in terms of their internal practice, might eventually be prosecuted as a form of prejudice.)

- Another brief filed by the Department of Justice, this one arguing for reversal of the "ministerial exception" to federal employment laws in the case of *Hosanna Tabor v. Equal Employment Opportunity Commission*, which could have eroded the ability of faith-based groups to hire and fire in keeping with the tenets of their faith. (The Supreme Court eventually upheld the ministerial exception in its ruling.)

- The absence of strong conscience protections as part of gay marriage laws at the state level, which among other things could threaten the ability of faith-based social service providers, such as adoption agencies, to decline to serve same-sex couples. Already a handful of conscientious objectors in New York who work in county clerks' offices and who declined to register gay marriages have been fired, and in locations such as Boston, Illinois, San Francisco, and the District of

Columbia, Catholic Charities effectively has been driven out of the adoption and foster care business.

Most observers would say that these sorts of church/state tensions are even more frequent in Europe. In the United Kingdom, the 2006 Equality Act made it illegal for adoption agencies to refuse to place children with same-sex couples. The English government announced that private adoption agencies refusing to serve gay couples would no longer receive reimbursements for their services, resulting in the loss of over $9 million in annual payments to Catholic charities in the United Kingdom. At least eleven Catholic adoption agencies have closed their doors in the United Kingdom while others cut their ties to the church and reincorporated as a civil entity. Critics of this aspect of the law saw it as especially tragic, given that Catholic adoption agencies had a reputation for serving the poorest sectors of English society and finding homes for children considered the hardest to place, such as children with Down syndrome and other disabilities.

Such pressures are multiplying, especially around the issue of homosexuality. In 2004, a Pentecostal pastor was convicted in Sweden under laws against hate speech for declaring that homosexuality is "a deep, cancerous tumor on all of society." The country's Supreme Court later set aside the conviction, under provisions in the European Convention on Human Rights concerning freedom of religion. Swedish prosecutors, however, have vowed to revisit the issue. In British Columbia, Canada, in 2005, a local branch of the Knights of Columbus was taken before a regional Human Rights Tribunal for refusing to rent a hall to a lesbian couple for a wedding reception. Their right to refuse the rental was eventually upheld, but the Knights were ordered to pay each woman $1,000 for offense to their "dignity, feelings and self-respect." In France in 2004, a new federal law added "anti-gay comments" to a class of prohibited speech that already includes racist and anti-Semitic insults. Though no religious figure has yet been prosecuted, French Catholic leaders have expressed concern that the law might prevent bishops from opposing gay marriage.

In light of these trends, some Christians today view the idea of going to prison for defending traditional positions on issues such as gay marriage somewhat the way their predecessors in Eastern Europe once looked at the possible consequences of defying the Soviets, or the way that Chinese priests and pastors do today for spurning the official government-sponsored Catholic association—nothing to be desired, but have your affairs in order just in case.

The global war on Christians is destined to turbocharge this preoccupation with religious freedom. What's at work is a triple whammy: growing pressure on Christian institutions in the West, the suffering of other faiths, and the staggering global scale of anti-Christian violence and persecution. These three forces are combining today to make religious freedom a Christian idée fixe.

The three prongs of this whammy will reinforce one another. Someone already persuaded that there's a "war on religion" in the West, for instance, is more likely to be concerned about the victims of such a war in other parts of the world, where the cost is measured not in lawsuits and ballot measures but in human lives. Likewise, someone concerned about assaults on the religious freedom of believers in other cultures may be more inclined to ponder whether Western societies really can be counted upon, in the long run, to uphold the liberty of believers—or whether today's debates over insurance mandates and hiring exemptions may be the beginnings of a slippery slope that has its logical conclusion in martyrdom. Religious freedom advocates in the West will likely find that their strongest argument is to tell the stories of the victims of the global war on Christians, pointing to their suffering as a harbinger of where things may be headed.

As religious freedom becomes set in cement as a defining Christian preoccupation, it will likely be styled not as a confessional exercise on behalf of beleaguered Christians but as a principled defense of the rights of all—even if there's a "preferential option" for Christians because Christians are the world's most persecuted religious group.

Such an across-the-board approach will strike most Christians as just, given that what's at stake is the defense of human rights believed to be universal. Influential Christian leaders also understand that the defense of religious freedom will be more effective if it's supported by a broad coalition, including a variety of different religious perspectives. That's already the approach taking shape in Western debates, and Christian leaders and organizations will want to apply that experience globally, looking to build the most extensive ecumenical and interreligious coalitions possible. The next chapter explores the ecumenical implications of the global war on Christians, but it's worth noting here that this effort to build alliances among churches and other faiths in defense of religious freedom could itself be a boon to good relations across denominational lines.

CHRISTIANITY AS A PRO-DEMOCRACY FORCE

In their 2011 book *God's Century: Resurgent Religion and Global Politics*, scholars Monica Duffy, Daniel Philpott, and Timothy Samuel Shah documented religion's comeback over the last forty years as a protagonist in geopolitics. They demonstrate that the "secularization thesis," which once forecast an inevitable decline for religion, has been refuted by events on the ground, including examples given earlier—the collapse of Communism, the People Power movement, and the rise of Islamic radicalism. The authors call this boom both "dramatic and worldwide." They quote the famed sociologist of religion Peter Berger, who once believed in the inexorable triumph of secularism, but who changed his mind in 1988: "The assumption that we live in a secularized world is false. The world today . . . is as furiously religious as it ever was, and in some places more so than ever. This means that a whole body of literature by historians and social scientists loosely labeled 'secularization theory' is essentially mistaken."

Beyond making the point that religion matters, the authors of the book are also interested in *how* religion matters, meaning the nature of the influence that religion exercises on political affairs. They want to understand which circumstances direct its energies down one path or another. In typical scholarly fashion, they craft a lot of complicated charts and invent some tongue-tying neologisms, but essentially their findings boil down to this: religious actors are most prone to defend democracy, and to support a healthy distinction between church and state, when they have a relationship with the ruling authorities of "conflictual independence." The term refers to a situation in which religious groups are autonomous from the state, and experience various degrees of conflict with it.

Here's how the authors explain the dynamic: "Having eked out and defended a protected area of independence from an authoritarian regime that wants to suppress them, they seek a regime whose laws guarantee the practice of their faith." As examples, they cite Islamist parties in Turkey and the Tamil Hindu minority in Sri Lanka. Both are groups that have emerged as effective political actors, out of the crucible of frequent conflicts with an often hostile state.

Two case studies from different parts of the world, one in the recent past and another unfolding today, show the same principle in action.

Malawi

In the early 1990s, Malawi was still under the eccentric rule of its dictator-for-life, a British- and U.S.-educated strongman named Hastings Kamuzu Banda, who had governed the country since independence from the United Kingdom in 1964. Though he's largely forgotten today, Banda was the quintessential African dictator of his era. He sashayed around in elegant three-piece English suits, with matching handkerchiefs and a homburg, along with a fly whisk that symbolized his absolute authority over life and death. His unofficial motto was "My word is the law." Church groups suffered along with the rest of civil society, as prominent religious leaders typically faced a choice between being bought off or being treated as a dissident.

In March 1992, the seven Catholic bishops of Malawi, led by Archbishop James Chiona of Blantyre, issued a dramatic pastoral letter titled "Living Our Faith," instructing that it be read aloud in all 130 parishes in the country. The bishops denounced the vast disparity between rich and poor, as well as human rights abuses by both Banda's political party, the only one allowed under national law, and the government. They called for an end to injustice, corruption, and nepotism, and demanded recognition of free expression and political opposition. They also criticized substandard education and health systems. While none of this was new, it was the first time prominent Malawians had said it out loud and signed their names.

"Every human being, as a child of God, must be free and respected," the letter began. "We cannot turn a blind eye to our people's experiences of unfairness or injustice. These are our brothers and sisters who are in prison without knowing what they are charged with, or when their case will be heard." In a direct challenge to Banda's assertion that his word was law, the bishops said: "No one person can claim to have a monopoly on truth or wisdom."

The bishops managed to get sixteen thousand copies printed and distributed without Banda's intelligence services catching on. On the Sunday the letter was read out, attendance at Mass across the country swelled. Reportedly people wept, shouted gratitude, and danced in the aisles. Emboldened by the pastoral letter, grassroots opposition found its voice. In the country's largest city, Blantyre, poor squatters in illegal shantytowns—where cholera was rampant and sewage flowed openly in the streets—stood up when security forces tried to run them out. Student protests broke out on university campuses. Opposition figures began returning. As news of the uprising circulated internationally, pressure grew for Western powers to take a stand. In 1994, donors froze all foreign aid to Malawi, forcing Banda to call free elections. In effect, his regime was over. Today Malawi remains chronically underdeveloped, but it's a multiparty democracy led by the country's first female president.

The Middle East

Where people stand often determines what they see, meaning that perspective is critical in framing any question. The Christian reaction to secularism is a classic case in point. It may be the bogeyman of many believers across Europe and the United States, where it often conjures up Gay Pride parades, legalized abortion, and scorn for traditional religious belief. But for Christians in the Middle East, secularism is more like a survival strategy. In a neighborhood where Christians are a small minority often perceived as a beachhead for the West, state support for religion generally means heartache, and a secular understanding of church/state separation offers a shelter from the storm.

As a result, nowhere on earth are Christian leaders more zealous apostles for a legal order that protects both pluralism and freedom of conscience, and that keeps the state out of religious affairs. Historically, Christians were among the founders and strongest supporters of secular parties across the Middle East, such as the Ba'ath Party in Syria and Kemalist parties in Turkey, because they saw them as the best way to ensure the protection of minority rights. Similarly, Coptic Christians in Egypt today are in the vanguard of pressing for a secular democratic state, as opposed to what they fear will be a process of creeping Islamization.

In part, this advocacy reflects a basic law of religious life: secularism always looks better to minorities who would be the big losers in a theocracy.

If it doesn't disappear first, Christianity in the Middle East actually may be ideally positioned to inject balance into global Christian reflection about the relationship between faith and secular society. One proof of the point came in a 2001 survey by the Pew Forum of evangelical leaders around the world, which revealed a dramatic contrast between evangelicals in the developed world and in the Middle East. A stunning 90 percent of evangelical leaders from North America defined secularism as a "major threat" to the faith, but only 37 percent of evangelicals from the Middle East had the same view. On the contrary, almost two-thirds of evangelicals in the Middle East were highly favorable toward secularism.

Likewise, a working document for a 2010 Vatican meeting on the Middle East read like a manifesto for secular politics. It calls upon Christians to work for "an all-inclusive, shared civic order" that protects "human rights, human dignity and religious freedom." Twice the document dwells on the concept of "positive laicity"—meaning, in effect, a positive form of secularism. It cites a September 2008 speech in France by Pope Benedict XVI, who in turn borrowed the term "positive laicity" from French president Nicolas Sarkozy.

"Catholics, together with other Christian citizens and Muslim thinkers and reformers, ought to be able to support initiatives at examining thoroughly the concept of the 'positive laicity' of the state," the document said. "This could help eliminate the theocratic character of government and allow for greater equality among citizens of different religions," it asserted, "thereby fostering the promotion of a sound democracy, positively secular in nature, which fully acknowledges the role of religion . . . while completely respecting the distinction between the religious and civic orders."

PEACEMAKING AND JUSTICE

Research by Duffy, Philpott, and Shah also supports the conclusion that religious actors in a milieu of "conflictual independence" tend not only to be more pro-democracy but also more active in peacemaking and advocacy on behalf of social justice. They are often pioneers in national reconciliation in societies torn by war, and activists on behalf of solidarity with the poor in countries struggling with chronic underdevelopment.

In the Christian realm, the authors cite the role played by churches in several Latin American countries, such as Guatemala, Brazil, Chile, and Argentina, in steering the transition from military juntas to democracy, and in accounting for human rights abuses under the former regimes. The story of Guatemalan bishop Juan José Gerardi Conedera, recounted in chapter 11, offers one such example. They also point to the South African Truth and Reconciliation Commission, noting not only the leadership of Anglican archbishop Desmond Tutu but also the fact that religious bodies in the country supplied "staff, publicity, spiritual and psychological counseling for victims, encouragement of their own members to take part, and appearances at hearings for faith communities."

The authors also offer the example of Albanian Orthodox archbishop Anastasios Yannoulatos, a figure who knows the war on Christians firsthand. Under dictator Enver Hoxha, Albania unleashed a ferocious crackdown on religion. Hoxha declared in 1967 that Albania was "the world's first atheistic state, whose only religion is Albanianism." Churches were shuttered, clergy sent to prison or executed, and atheism widely propagated in schools and in the media. Out of that experience Yannoulatos emerged as a leading voice for reconciliation and dialogue across ethnic and religious boundaries. He came to fame when he sheltered thousands of Muslim refugees from Kosovo in Orthodox facilities during the violence of the 1990s. Yannoulatos serves as the honorary president of the World Conference of Religions for Peace and has been a candidate for the Nobel Peace Prize.

In terms of other religious traditions that illustrate the same dynamics, the authors point to the influence of "engaged Buddhism" in Cambodia, where Pol Pot's Khmer Rouge was responsible for two million deaths, and where the regime had tried to exterminate Buddhism as a "force of reaction." Amid the carnage, a Buddhist monk named Samdech Preah Maha Ghosananda began leading "peace walks" around the country. Ghosananda had lost his entire family and most of his friends during the genocide, and he was determined to teach peace, drawing on a tenet of Teravada Buddhism holding that social peace and inner peace are both inseparable and interdependent. The first peace walk began in a refugee camp on the Thai border and worked its way toward Phnom Penh. Stories are told of soldiers laying down their arms along the way and marchers meeting relatives they hadn't seen in decades because of the fighting. Now repeated annually, the marches have become an important force in the reconstruction of Cambodian society and have also helped to support causes such as refugee repatriation and landmine removal. Ghosananda is known as the "Gandhi of Cambodia" and has been nominated several times for the Nobel Peace Prize.

The conclusion is that suffering can sometimes be a crucible for imagination and for activism. As Christians shaped by such experiences become more influential, their instincts for peacemaking and social justice advocacy therefore may also gain momentum.

13

SPIRITUAL FRUITS OF THE GLOBAL WAR

Tertullian, one of the great fathers of early Christianity, famously said that "the blood of the martyrs is the seed of the church." It's a rare case of a theological formula for which there's empirical proof. Historically, waves of persecution have fueled major advances for Christianity. Crackdowns during the Roman Empire earned Christianity admiration across the ancient world, and were perhaps the single most important ingredient in its success. The sacrifice of missionaries during the Era of Exploration helped bring the Gospel to the New World. Today, it's no accident that zones where persecution of Christians is the most intense, such as China and parts of India, are also the places where Christianity is growing the most dramatically.

In addition to providing missionary momentum, martyrdom has also stimulated theological breakthroughs. During the Roman era, Christian communities had to wrestle with what to do about members who lapsed under pressure and then sought readmission to the church. That question forced thinkers to wrestle with the issues of grace and forgiveness, and contributed to the development of the sacrament of penance. Similarly, churches had to face the question of sacraments administered by clergy who had knuckled under, such as priests dur-

ing the Diocletian period in the early fourth century who handed the
Scriptures over to the imperial governor in a gesture of submission.
Some rigorous Christian groups, such as the Donatists, insisted that
sacraments celebrated by these traitors were invalid, while mainstream
Christianity worked out a theology of *ex opere operato*, meaning that a
properly celebrated sacrament is effective apart from the worthiness of
the minister.

Many thoughtful Christian leaders believe that today's global war
on Christians has a similar capacity to energize the church with new
missionary momentum and important theological insights. In September
2009, a cross section of evangelical leaders from around the world
gathered in Bad Urach, Germany, at the invitation of the Religious
Liberty Commission of the World Evangelical Alliance and other
bodies. By the end, they issued the "Bad Urach Call," a four-page declaration insisting that persecution of Christians around the world calls
the church to deeper theological and spiritual meditation.

"Persecuted Christians have learned truths about God that Christians under less pressure need to hear in order to experience the fullness
of God," the statement reads. "The spiritual insights of the persecuted
are vital to the transformation of the lives of the rest of the Body of
Christ. One of these essential insights is that we will all be—if witnessing for Christ—in some sense persecuted. There is a grander, greater
narrative of God's action underneath the stories of individual pain, suffering, deliverance, and endurance."

The Bad Urach Call ends with a plea to Christians everywhere: "We
call on the Body of Christ to take up the cross of Jesus actively, will-
ingly, and corporately, in order to implement the mission of Jesus. This
will include remembrance of those persecuted (with prayer and assistance), understanding (joined with informed efforts to reduce persecution), and transformation (so that the entire Body of Christ is renewed
through the insights of those who are persecuted and martyred)."

For those inclined to answer the Bad Urach Call, the question is,
what are some of the insights to be gleaned from the new martyrs?

There are three zones of Christian life today where the impact of
the global war seems most discernible, and it's at least worth pondering

whether they are among its spiritual fruits—places, so to speak, where it's possible to glimpse the logic of salvation history in action.

"ECUMENISM OF THE MARTYRS"

For many people, the division of Christianity into various branches, denominations, and independent churches probably seems both familiar and natural. We live in an era of consumer choice, so the idea that there are different flavors of Christianity to appeal to different tastes has a clear market logic. Yet for Christians, division (as opposed to diversity) is a problem, because it flies in the face of Christ's final prayer on earth that his disciples "may all be one." The push to put the ecclesiastical Humpty-Dumpty back together again, meaning to restore unity among the various branches of the Christian family, is known as the "ecumenical movement."

The middle of the twentieth century, in the aftermath of the Second World War, saw a major surge in ecumenical activity. The first meeting of the World Council of Churches came in 1948, while the Second Vatican Council (1962–65), a gathering of bishops from all over the world, renewed the ecumenical energies of the Catholic Church. In 1965, a major breakthrough came when Pope Paul VI and Patriarch Athenagoras I of Constantinople formally revoked the mutual excommunications their predecessors had issued at the time of the rupture between East and West in 1054. This ferment created hopes that an era of new Christian unity was about to dawn. Today some of those fires have cooled, as the differences between the various Christian denominations have proven more durable. Some pessimists have suggested that Christianity now finds itself in a new "ecumenical winter."

Ecumenists more inclined to optimism, however, believe there is a new impulse breathing life into the movement today, locating one center of gravity precisely in the global war on Christians. The common experience of martyrdom, these figures argue, has the potential to generate a new Christian consciousness, emphasizing what Christians have in common rather than what divides them, and prioritizing spiritual essentials rather than secondary matters of history and practice. These experts believe the "ecumenism of the martyrs" is key to the future of the press for Christian unity in the twenty-first century.

Historically, there's logic to that proposition. Many of the pioneers of the ecumenical movement in the mid-twentieth century had been in the Nazi concentration camps and the Soviet gulags, where they shared their suffering with other Christians. Their clandestine worship services and prayer meetings were necessarily ecumenical, and they developed deep friendships across confessional lines. Writers at the time called it the "ecumenism of the gulags." Protestant, Orthodox, and Catholic believers witnessed the strength of faith, the spiritual nobility, of their fellow Christians in the most harrowing circumstances imaginable, and came away much more inclined to relativize older confessional rivalries.

There are three compelling reasons to believe that such an "ecumenism of the martyrs" could have a similar sort of impact today.

As Christians from outside the West begin to play a greater leadership role in church affairs, they'll bring their cultural experience with them, and often it contains a strong ecumenical dimension. Where Christians are a minority, their instincts are generally to minimize intra-Christian differences, and often the majority tradition in the culture reinforces that instinct by lumping all Christians together. To the typical Indian Hindu, for instance, a Christian is a Christian. In China, the government scrutinizes Protestant Christianity just as it does Catholicism. Across much of the Middle East, the same dynamic is visible. In many Middle Eastern societies, Orthodox Christians and followers of Eastern Catholic churches happily worship in one another's churches, and ordinary believers are often hard-pressed to explain the difference between the two. About the only time of year they're conscious of the difference is usually Easter, because Orthodoxy follows the Julian calendar and thus celebrates Easter on a different date than Catholicism does. Africa is also a case in point. In Europe and the United States, mainline Protestants and Catholics may perceive themselves as quite different from one another. In many parts of Africa, however, they're not divided by the issues of sexual morality that loom large in the West, and their focus tends to be on their commonalities vis-à-vis their Muslim and animist neighbors.

Second, the defense of persecuted Christians is itself an ecumenical undertaking. Protestants, Anglicans, Catholics, and Orthodox find themselves increasingly making common cause, both to bring humanitarian relief to those Christians most in need and to press governments around the world to take stronger action to protect people at risk. As an example, the Anglican archbishop of Canterbury and the Catholic archbishop of Westminster jointly hosted an international conference on Christianity in the Holy Land at Lambeth Palace, the headquarters of the Anglican Communion, in July 2011.

One natural by-product of such efforts is that they afford Christians a chance to come together not to talk about their theological or ecclesiastical differences but to pool resources in pursuit of a shared social and political aim. In other words, it creates a space in which Christians from the various traditions can build bonds of friendship, and once people become friends, it often takes the edge off perceived differences.

Third, the stories of the martyrs have a deep spiritual resonance, and when people are exposed to them, they often come away changed. As these stories become better known—as pastors and priests recount them from the pulpit, as they loom larger in Christian media, as an entire literature is generated lifting up the new martyrs, and so on—the result could help shape a new climate within global Christianity, one that's both more appreciative of other Christian traditions because of the witness of their martyrs, and more inclined to focus on essentials rather than the arcana of doctrinal debates. Hearing the story of John Ian Maina, for instance, a nine-year-old Anglican in Kenya who was killed in October 2012 when Muslim radicals tossed a bomb through the window of his Nairobi Sunday school, most Catholics would likely be inclined to sympathy and solidarity, not to reflection upon Pope Leo XIII's 1896 edict declaring Anglican ordinations "absolutely null and utterly void."

One veteran of the press for Christian unity who has laid out a compelling vision of this "ecumenism of the martyrs" is Catholic cardinal Kurt Koch from Basel, Switzerland, who today heads the Vatican's department for ecumenical work (formally known as the "Pontifical Council for Promoting Christian Unity"). During a speech at an ecumenical and interreligious meeting in September 2011, Koch began his reflection with some thoughts about the special love for the poor in Christianity, and then turned to the import of today's Christian martyrs. It's worth quoting him at length:

> Because today all the churches and ecclesial communities have their martyrs, we must talk about a real and true "ecumenism of the martyrs," which contains within itself a beautiful promise: The drama of divisions among the churches notwithstanding, these noble witnesses of the faith have demonstrated that God himself maintains a communion of faith among all the baptized at the deepest possible level, which is witnessed with the supreme sacrifice of one's own life. As Christians and as churches, we live on this earth in a communion that's not yet perfect, but the martyrs in their heavenly glory are already in full and perfect communion.
>
> Today, as Christians, we must live in the hope that the blood of the martyrs of our time will become one day the seed of the complete unity of the Body of Christ. But we must testify to this hope in a credible manner by offering effective help to the persecuted Christians of the world, publicly denouncing the situations of martyrdom and committing ourselves in favor of respect for religious liberty and human dignity. The ecumenism of the martyrs, therefore, not only constitutes the nucleus of ecumenical spirituality, which is highly necessary today, but it is also the best example of why the promotion of Christian unity and the privileged love for the poor are absolutely inseparable.

As a final note, much of what's been said here about the ecumenical significance of the defense of persecuted Christians can also be applied to interfaith relations. In many parts of the world, Christians stand shoulder to shoulder with the followers of other religions in their exposure to persecution. As Christians mobilize to defend religious freedom, they will naturally find themselves working in coalition with members of other religious traditions, creating a space in which friendships will develop organically. Finally, as the stories of the martyrs from other religions become better known in Christian circles, they will inevitably create a deeper atmosphere of sympathy and respect.

In other words, in addition to an "ecumenism of the martyrs," there's an "inter-faith dialogue of the martyrs" to be developed as well.

THEOLOGY FROM BELOW

A classic distinction in Christian thought runs between an approach crafted "from above" versus one shaped "from below," sometimes referred to as the difference between a "high" or a "low" angle of vision. A "high" Christology focuses on Jesus as the Eternal Son of God, the second person of the Trinity, and the King who will return in messianic glory. A "low" Christology emphasizes the Jesus who was born the humble son of a carpenter, who lived as a poor itinerant preacher, and who suffered an unjust death at the hands of an occupying power. In terms of orthodoxy, both are fully legitimate, but they lead to different accents and a different spiritual response. In the course of history, a "high" Christology has been associated with a muscular and triumphal version of Christianity, while the "low" approach has tended to produce a Christianity that's more humble, oriented to service, and keen on solidarity with the poor and oppressed.

For obvious reasons, contact with martyrdom and suffering tend to nudge the church in the direction of a theology "from below." The great German Protestant thinker and martyr Dietrich Bonhoeffer presents a classic example. In 1930, Bonhoeffer traveled to the United States for postgraduate study and a teaching fellowship at New York's famed Union Theological Seminary. Ever the German academic, he found Union not quite up to snuff; his famous quip was, "There is no theology there!" Yet Bonhoeffer's life was profoundly changed by the experience, largely through his friendship with Frank Fisher, a black seminarian at Union who introduced Bonhoeffer to the Abyssinian Baptist Church in Harlem.

Bonhoeffer ended up teaching Sunday school in Harlem, and developed a deep love for African American spirituals. He saw firsthand the racial and economic oppression suffered by black Americans, he witnessed how the Christian faith of the people in Harlem sustained them in the teeth of the hardships of their lives, and he also saw how the institutional church, in his eyes, was failing to make a sufficiently strong stand against prejudice and in favor of racial justice.

Bonhoeffer would later write about his experience in Harlem: "Here one can truly speak and hear about sin and grace and the love of God . . . the Black Christ is preached with rapturous passion and vision." He would later add of those Harlem years, "I turned from phraseology to reality." Most experts who have studied Bonhoeffer's life believe it's not too much to say that the path that led him to a martyr's death at the Flossenbürg concentration camp on April 9, 1945, in some ways began in the black churches of Harlem.

Looking around, many observers of the Christian scene believe contemporary martyrs and victims of anti-Christian violence may once again be steering the church away from phraseology and toward reality. During a conference at the University of Notre Dame in September 2012, Fr. Angelo Romano of the Community of Sant'Egidio described how his community has turned the Basilica of St. Bartholomew on Rome's Tiber Island into a shrine to the new martyrs at the urging of the late Pope John Paul II, who said, "Their witness should not be lost to the church." Romano described the various chapels, icons, and relics present in the basilica, and then turned to what he called the "inestimable gift" of their spiritual legacy.

"In the martyrs we see a more human vision of the world, one that's unarmed and fragile," Romano said. "Their memory is important because those memories can build a better future."

In his 2008 work *To Share in the Body: A Theology of Martyrdom for Today's Church*, Protestant scholar Craig Hovey echoes the view that victims of anti-Christian persecution are an important source of theological wisdom. For instance, he suggests they offer a new lens for reading the Gospel of Mark, which was originally written for a martyr-church in the first century. Most basically, Hovey suggests that the martyrs can help comfortable Christians in the West recover a "proper and appropriate antagonism to the world," meaning a sense of the countercultural thrust in Christianity and its willingness to challenge prevailing social assumptions and values.

Anglican priest Samuel Wells provides the foreword for Hovey's book and recalls delivering a sermon in 2004 shortly after the Abu Ghraib scandals broke out that illustrates the point.

"I felt the best way to preach was not simply to denounce the horrific practices and the culture that made them imaginable," Wells wrote. "Such was timely and appropriate but did not seem to be the stuff of a sermon. Instead I wondered aloud whether if our country were invaded by a foreign power, we—the congregation and I—would be considered enough of a threat to be worth torturing. Not a political threat, necessarily, and probably not a military threat, but a living presence of hope and truth whose continued witness would become intolerable to an invader bent on submission and destruction."

Posing such provocative questions to the Christian conscience, Wells suggests, is what the martyrs do. He writes that the martyrs, if taken seriously by the wider body of Christians, "make God's people a disciplined and responsive community whose witness constitutes a rival claim," one that Hovey describes as "instrumentalism" and "the world."

Imagine, for instance, a theology written from the perspective of Yang Caizhen, a Chinese Protestant who spent almost two years in prison after being arrested for organizing a prayer rally in September 2009. She was released on parole in May 2011 after nearly dying in detention as a result of a high fever and liver inflammation. Because Caizhen lived to tell her tale, she's a precious resource for understanding the situation facing today's suffering Christians. One suspects a theology informed by her experience might have very different contours and points of emphasis than a theology emerging, for example, out of the "culture wars" in the United States.

Or, consider what theology might develop from the experience of the predominantly Dalit and tribal Christian community in India. These Christians carry the stigma of a triple form of discrimination: ethnic, on the basis of being born into the lowest rungs of the traditional caste system (in the case of Dalits) or outside the system altogether (the tribals); economic exploitation, because they've been largely left outside India's economic miracle and its exploding middle and upper classes; and religious discrimination on the basis of their Christian faith. It's an arresting thought exercise to ponder what might result if Ph.D. students in Christian theology were required to spend a year living and working among India's Dalit and tribal Christians before completing their degrees—what new insights might result, and how their theological approach might take on new aspects.

As the stories of the new martyrs become better known, a new wave of theological interest in martyrdom may well be formed. More doctoral theses will be written about contemporary martyrdom, more college courses will be taught on the subject, more books will be written, symposia organized, and so on. Over time, this ferment will undoubtedly have a leavening effect on Christian thought, moving it in the direction of a spirituality and a theological style "from below," forged by the perspective of the gulags and concentration camps, by the bombed churches and terrorized Christian neighborhoods of the world.

One example of how profoundly this theological impulse can reshape conventional ways of doing business is the Greek Catholic University in Lviv, Ukraine. The rebirth of the university in 1994 is part of the revival of the Greek Catholic Church after the fall of the Soviet empire, when it was the largest illegal religious body in the world. The biggest of the twenty-two Eastern churches in communion with Rome, it has more than 3 million followers in Ukraine and around 5.5 million worldwide. With an enrollment today around 1,600, this is the only Catholic university in the former Soviet sphere; as they like to say, it's the only Catholic university "between Poland and Japan."

The bold aim in Lviv is nothing less than to "rethink" what a Christian university can be in the twenty-first century. During a reflection process on what the university should become in the early 1990s, planners identified two core challenges:

- Building on the legacy of the Ukrainian martyrs during the period of Soviet oppression, when the Greek Catholic Church was the most important source of social opposition. On a percentage basis, no country produced more martyrs in the twentieth century. The university's ambition, according to

Bishop Borys Gudziak, the rector, is to pioneer "a new social, intellectual, and theological synthesis" of that experience—a theology, so to speak, of the catacombs.

- Repairing a deficit of social trust, Gudziak said, because "the Ukrainian soul and psyche have been profoundly marked" by the Soviet period, in which "the system killed systematically." In that milieu, he said, Ukrainians were taught from early childhood "to think one thing, say another and do a third," and so they learned to wear masks, to hide themselves, and never to trust anyone else.

The response has been as acute as the diagnosis. With regard to the martyrs, Gudziak believes a theological synthesis of their suffering will have less to do with doctrinal theory than an "ecclesiastical style," which he describes in terms of "humility" and "being close to the people."

"When times are difficult, you're stripped down and forced to look at the essentials," he said. "You fall back on the basic Christian experiences of being together, supporting one another, praying together and being community . . . overcoming the negation of the gospel without any pretense or imposition."

Gudziak believes that style is a "tangible presence" in Greek Catholicism. It allows the university, he said, to be a place where a church that prizes humility, closeness to the people, and taking the lay role seriously becomes self-reflective.

As for the trust deficit, the response has been even more innovative. To help people learn to take off their masks, the university turned to the insights of Henri Nouwen, Jean Vanier, and L'Arche, a Catholic movement founded by Vanier that emphasizes building friendships with disabled people. (Gudziak studied under Nouwen at Harvard.) Guided by their inspiration, the university has invited mentally handicapped people to become part of their community. At the Ukrainian Catholic University, the mentally handicapped actually serve as "professors of human relations."

"This is not some kind of handout," Gudziak insists. "We need the gifts they have. They don't care if you're a rector, a doctor, or how rich you are. What they force us to confront is the most important pedagogical question of all: Can you love me?" New residences include apartments for these professors of human relations to live among the university's students, becoming part of the daily fabric of their lives.

Has all that made the Greek Catholic University a more loving place?

"It's as if you put a shot of rum into some chocolate chip cookies," Gudziak said. "There's a different flavor, and if you know what rum is, you'll recognize it." Similarly, he said, if you know what love is, you'll feel it in the relationships forged at the university, shaped by the legacy of the martyrs and the imprint of the disabled.

EVANGELIZATION AND MISSION

Scholar Todd Johnson of the Center for the Study of Global Christianity likes to tell a story about his renowned predecessor and mentor, David Barrett, who died in 2011, and who pioneered the quantitative study of Christian martyrdom. As Johnson tells it, Barrett was once speaking to a group of Christian industrialists and CEOs. Being a practical group of hard-nosed business people, they got quickly to the bottom line. What, they wanted to know, is the single most effective form of evangelization? Barrett didn't duck the question, informing them that a considerable body of empirical research suggests it's martyrdom.

The response left the crowd quiet for a minute, until one of the industrialists finally had the nerve to ask: "Dr. Barrett, could you tell us what the second most effective form of evangelization is?"

The question reflects a core human instinct: no matter how much we may admire the martyrs, most of us aren't in a hurry to join them. The proper Christian understanding of martyrdom is that of St. Thomas More, who did everything in his power to avoid death except renouncing his faith. Yet all the evidence suggests that when martyrdom does occur, it's an enormously powerful resource for introducing people to the faith, or renewing it in those for whom the faith has grown cold. Even for people hostile to religion or to Christianity in particular, the martyrs represent Christianity at its most attractive.

Like pretty much everything in Christian life, the subject of mission has become controversial today. At the liberal end of some de-nominations, there's a current wary of the whole idea of trying to convert others. In part, that's because of the historical association between evangelization and colonization, and the embarrassing memory of the faith being imposed down the barrel of a gun. In part too, that's because when people look around, they often find the most aggressive Christian missionaries to be a bit repulsive—too pushy, too self-righteous, too insensitive to the wisdom of other peoples and cultures. Critics also may feel there's something offensive about insisting that followers of other religions need to convert in order to be right with God.

While appreciating those cautions, most Christians feel that the church can't just throw in the towel on missionary work, because doing so is impossible to square with the risen Christ's final command: "Go forth and make disciples of the nations, baptizing them in the name of the Father, the Son and the Holy Spirit." Christianity is by nature a missionary religion, and most Christians rejoice when they see someone join the family of faith. The mainstream Christian consensus probably boils down to something like this: The faith must always be proposed, never imposed. Do it with great respect, do it gently, and don't measure success in terms of head counts and market share—but at the same time, do it.

Surveying the landscape of the early twenty-first century, we may be entering a time of renewed Christian missionary ferment. In the Protestant world, there's a powerful movement among evangelicals and Pentecostals who call themselves "Great Commission Christians," referring to the commission given by Christ after his resurrection. The most determined current in Great Commission Christianity today focuses upon what its architects call the "10/40 window," meaning a swath of the globe between 10 degrees latitude north of the equator and 40 degrees south of the equator. It includes North Africa, the Middle East, India, and China, representing the part of the world with the lowest percentage of Christians. Of the fifty-six countries in the 10/40 window, forty-four are majority-Muslim states, and these Great Commission Christians are determined to bring the Gospel to those regions of the world.

This isn't just an ambition among Western Christians. The most audacious Christians in China today dream of carrying the Gospel beyond the borders of their own country, along the old Silk Road into the Muslim world, in a campaign known as "Back to Jerusalem." As journalist David Aikman explained in his 2006 book *Jesus in Beijing*, some Chinese evangelicals and Pentecostals believe that the movement of the Gospel for the last two thousand years has been westward: from Jerusalem to Antioch, from Antioch to Europe, from Europe to America, and from America to China. Now, they believe, it's their turn to complete the loop by carrying the Gospel to Muslim lands, eventually arriving in Jerusalem.

In the Catholic world, Popes John Paul II and Benedict XVI made what they call the "New Evangelization" the church's highest internal priority. In broad strokes, the idea is to exit a period in which the Catholic Church's energies were largely consumed by internal debates and to turn once more to the external challenge of spreading the faith. As it's been conceived by church leaders, the New Evangelization is directed in the first instance at people who have already been baptized as Christians but who for one reason or another are no longer practicing the faith. In the United States, for instance, the "Catholics Come Home" campaign founded by Arizona layman Tom Peterson is one example of the New Evangelization in action. Featuring slick TV, radio, and Internet presentations (such as a commercial during the 2013 college football national championship game with former Notre Dame coach and TV commentator Lou Holtz), the campaign claims an average increase of 10 percent in Mass attendance rates in the dioceses in which it's been rolled out.

As this evangelical momentum gathers steam, in tandem with rising consciousness about the global war on Christians, it's reasonable to suspect that the stories of the martyrs will become an increasingly important resource in Christian missionary efforts. That's not only because the martyrs will simply be on people's minds but also because, from a missionary perspective, the martyrs work.

From the point of view of bringing people to the faith, or bringing them back if they've walked away, it's one thing to sit down and give them a theological lesson about Christian notions of sacrifice, human dignity, and love for one's neighbor. It's another thing to tell them the story of Fr. Fadi Jamil Haddad, an Orthodox priest who was kidnapped and killed near Damascus, Syria, in late October 2012.

Haddad was born to a Christian family in the Syrian city of Qatana on February 2, 1969. In 1994 he graduated from the University of Balamand, and in 1996 he began serving in Qatana, a city with a mixed Muslim-Christian population, which had a population of fifteen thousand before the war. He was ordained a priest of the Greek Orthodox Church on July 14, 1995. He quickly became a beloved local activist on behalf of victimized people, regardless of their religious affiliation. He reached out to Sunnis, Shi'ites, and Alawites equally, as well as Catholics, Orthodox, Anglicans, Protestants, and those with no religious ties. Because he was considered a man of tact and discretion, he was often asked to negotiate for the release of kidnapped Syrians on behalf of their families. Despite the risks to his own life and safety, he always agreed, and frequently was able to engineer their safe release. Haddad purposely did not take sides in the political conflict in Syria, and gained the reputation of a "man of God, trusted by all."

Days before his own death, Haddad acted as a mediator for the family of a Muslim doctor who had been abducted. He communicated with the kidnappers, who demanded a ransom of more than 50 million Syrian pounds (roughly $700,000). He managed to reduce the ransom to 25 million pounds ($350,000) and traveled with the doctor's father-in-law to hand over the money. The transaction turned out to be a ruse, and both Haddad and the father-in-law were themselves taken prisoner. The kidnappers then demanded 750 million pounds ($10.5 million) to free all three men.

When the money wasn't forthcoming, the kidnappers decided to kill Haddad to prove they were serious—perhaps on the assumption that the church was the least likely party to pay for his release anyway. The forty-three-year-old priest was found shot in the head on a highway near the town of Drousha. Sources say an examination of the body revealed that Haddad had been tortured, including gouging out his eyes, before death finally came.

Haddad swiftly was declared a martyr by Orthodox believers in Syria. They see him as a believer willing to risk his own life to try to liberate people who had been taken captive, in the spirit of Jesus as portrayed in Luke 4:18: "The Lord has sent me to proclaim liberty to the captives and recovering of sight to the blind, to set at liberty those who are oppressed." Syrian state television stated of Haddad, "He was one of the most prominent workers for national reconciliation and the healing of wounds."

As a question of missionary strategy, the Haddad story has a capacity to capture imaginations and stir hearts that a catechetical lesson or a sermon simply cannot reproduce. One spiritual fruit of the global war on Christians is providing the contemporary church with more such stories, both those told about the dead by others and those that survivors can tell for themselves. They represent a powerful missionary resource at a time when the churches are struggling to renew their evangelical commitment.

For believers, that coincidence might well smack of divine providence.

14

WHAT'S TO BE DONE

Authors are an idiosyncratic bunch, with different strategies about the best way to write a book. Some play their cards close to the vest, refusing to reveal anything about what they're up to until the book is actually published, so that it falls upon an unsuspecting world like a thunderclap. The idea is to maximize impact and, naturally, sales. I generally take a different tack, developing my books like open-source software. I trot out the material along the way, in columns I write for the *National Catholic Reporter* and other media outlets, and in speeches I give on the lecture circuit. That's partly a product of sloth, in that I don't have the energy or the time to come up with anything else to write about or think about, but in my experience this kind of public exposure to my ideas prior to publication also results in a better finished product. I'm able to figure out which verbal formula capture ideas most effectively, which questions people are likely to ask, and where my initial assessments are half-baked or need development.

By the time I publish a book, I've usually written articles and given speeches about it hundreds of times, and also given scores of interviews to other reporters on the subject, giving me a pretty good sense of what the typical responses are likely to be. In many cases, especially when the topic stretches over a lot of ground, there's no single dominant reaction. When it comes to the global war on Christians, however, the clear winner in terms of a response from the grass roots is: "What can we do?"

That reaction speaks to a couple of basic truths. First, the scope and scale of the global war on Christians is almost invariably news to audiences in the West. They may have heard a few of the individual stories—many Catholics could probably identify Archbishop Oscar Romero of El Salvador, for instance, and lots of folks at least have heard of Asia Bibi in Pakistan. However, most people are staggered to hear that a leading estimate says that eleven Christians are killed somewhere in the world every hour, or that 80 percent of all acts of religious persecution in the world today are directed at Christians. They've never asked themselves what ought to be done about the global war on Christians, because quite honestly they didn't know it's being waged.

Second, the "What can we do?" question reflects basic Western instincts toward both decency and activism. It's about decency, in the sense that most people are well-intentioned and compassionate souls inclined to generosity. Having learned that Christians around the world are in trouble, they'd like to help. It's also about activism, in that Westerners generally are not inclined to passivity or contemplation in the face of suffering and evil. Our instinct instead is to roll up our sleeves and get to work. All this reflects a sort of good news, bad news situation. The bad news is that consciousness about the global war on Christians is slow in reaching the grass roots. The good news is that once people pass from ignorance to awareness, there's precious little debate over the merits of the cause. Instead, the vast majority are ready to act.

This final chapter presents a set of suggestions for responding to the global war on Christians, in an effort to answer the question "What's to be done?" It is not intended to be comprehensive, as there are many additional possibilities beyond those mentioned here. In that sense, this is more like a primer, or a stimulus, than an encyclopedia. The idea is not to imply that these are the only things that can be done, because additional steps and strategies always emerge when momentum around a cause begins to build. Rather, these are among the immediate things that can be done, right here and right now, which stand a plausible chance of making a difference.

As a broad observation, the ideal is always that any response to the global war on Christians ought to be worked out in conversation with the victims themselves, to avoid ending up in Hell down the road of good intentions. Arab Christians in Palestine, for instance, often complain that they are not consulted by evangelical groups that come into the region and make pronouncements. Many Indian Christians were outraged in 2012 when prominent American politicians declared their support for providing a travel visa for a visit to the United States by Narendra Modi, chief minister of Gujarat state, because of his reputation as a fierce opponent of Islamic radicalism. These Indian Christians pointed out that Modi is also responsible for a notorious 2003 anti-conversion law in Gujarat that frequently serves as a pretext for violence and harassment against Christians. In colloquial language, their point was that the enemy of my enemy is not always my friend. The rule of thumb should be to look before leaping, paying special heed to the people who'll have to live with the consequences of whatever we do.

PRAYER

For believers, the first and most natural response to a situation of suffering is prayer. Mainstream Christian theology holds that pain is always regrettable, but when it's unavoidable, it can have spiritual value. Mediated through prayer, pain allows a believer to enter into the spirit of Christ on the Cross and to open oneself more deeply to the suffering of the world. In prayer, people experiencing pain turn to God to ask for consolation and strength, to struggle with their doubts and despair, and to summon the will to endure.

Aside from such spiritual fruits, one also should not underestimate the importance of prayer in shaping a culture in the church. Catholicism has the saying *lex orandi, lex credendi*, meaning "the law of prayer is the law of belief." The idea is that what Christians pray for shapes what they believe and how they see the world. In that light, the more that Christians learn to pray on behalf of the persecuted, both individually and in public liturgical settings, the more conscious they will be of the nature of the global war on Christians, and the more inclined they will become to want to do something about it.

As an example of the point, consider the Catholic Church's custom prior to the Second Vatican Council of including a prayer for the "conversion of Russia" at the conclusion of each Mass. It was part of a cluster of prayers to be said at the end of each low Mass, known as the "Leonine Prayers" because they date from 1884 during the papacy of Leo XII. The prayer for Russia was added in 1930 at the direction of Pope Pius XI, following the Bolshevik Revolution. It was not actually for the conversion of Russia, but rather that "tranquility and freedom to profess the faith be restored to the afflicted people of Russia." It was popularly known as a prayer for conversion, however, because of its association with a reputed appearance of the Virgin Mary at Fatima in Portugal, where the visionaries reported that Mary had directed Catholics to pray for the conversion of Russia.

Naturally, this was before the ecumenical momentum unleashed by Vatican II, and today the idea of praying for the "conversion" of Russia would be seen as ecumenically insensitive. Russia is a profoundly Christian nation, and remained so despite seven decades of Soviet oppression. Recent popes have worked hard to restore good relations with the Russian Orthodox Church, and today most Catholics would see the aim of those relationships not to be the conquest of Russia for the papacy, but a form of mutually acceptable unity in diversity.

However politically incorrect, the prayer served the purpose of reminding Catholics that there were people suffering for the faith in Russia, and that the church cared. It created a popular consciousness about the "Church of Silence," the catacombs church behind the Iron Curtain, which was important in keeping Christian attention riveted on the fate of believers in the Soviet sphere. Such concern alone did not cause the collapse of Communism, but Christians in Poland and other Eastern bloc nations, sustained by networks of support in the West, were instrumental in setting the dominoes in motion, and it's reasonable to ask if that Western support would have been as strong without the culture of concern shaped by the practice of prayer on behalf of the persecuted.

In today's context, similar prayers on behalf of the victims in the global war on Christians could help raise consciousness and steel resolve. In order to maximize effectiveness and to cement ecumenical solidarity, it would be desirable for such a prayer to be worked out among the various Christian churches and then authorized for common use, both in terms of personal devotion and for public liturgical functions. Such a gesture would not only say something important about how committed the churches are but also promote and enhance the spiritual fruits of martyrdom described in the previous chapter.

RAISE CONSCIOUSNESS

On September 16, 2012, I found myself in the middle of a vast crowd gathered in Beirut, made up of people who had come from all across the Middle East to attend Pope Benedict XVI's open-air Mass. It was the culmination of the pope's three-day trip to Lebanon, which had begun just two days after U.S. ambassador Christopher Stevens was killed in Benghazi, Libya, triggering a spasm of anti-American and anti-Western violence. Benedict's presence seemed to lift up a different face of the Middle East, one characterized by mutual respect and welcome. Even Hezbollah, seen in the West as a terrorist organization but which acts as a social and political movement in Lebanon, festooned Beirut with banners welcoming the Holy Father. Lebanon's *Daily Star* hailed the three-day trip as a "symbol of tolerance."

During the Mass, I made my way toward a group of people in the crowd waving a Syrian flag. It turned out they were a group of Christians from Syria who had fled the bloody civil war, packing their bags and boarding a beaten-up minivan, not sure if they would ever be able to return, and hoping that someone in Lebanon would take them in. A member of the group told me they had found temporary refugee with a Christian family living in a village near the Syrian border, but they weren't sure what their long-term solution would be. They described losing family and friends, hearing anti-Christian slogans shouted by the Free Syrian Army, watching Christian churches and shops being bombed, and being afraid to take their children to services on Sunday.

At the end of our conversation, I asked the typical Western question: What can we do? I was expecting them to suggest sending money, helping them to get visas, or tell the American government to do more to stop the violence. All those points came up, but by far the most common response was much simpler: "Don't forget about us." Over and over, these refugees said that the core reason they chose to leave Syria was because of a sense that they had been forgotten by the rest of the world and left to fend for themselves—that no one cares about their fate or is even paying attention.

One concrete response to the global war on Christians, therefore, is for individuals in the West to do whatever they can to raise consciousness, ensuring that the victims of the war are not forgotten. That might mean volunteering to lead an adult faith formation group in one's local parish or congregation. It might mean volunteering to deliver a sermon on the subject during a Sunday service. It might mean asking a Bible study group or a Marian sodality to introduce a special prayer for persecuted Christians into their devotions. It might mean writing a letter to the editor of a church newspaper, or to the leadership of one's denomination, calling for greater attention to the issue. It might simply mean making a point of talking about persecuted Christians within one's own spheres of influence, such as one's school, neighborhood, and workplace. Whatever form it takes, such small efforts can help break the silence.

Another form that speaking out can take, especially in the new world of social media, is reaching out to persecuted Christians directly. There are numerous websites, for example, set up by congregations and religious communities that still have a presence in Syria, which provide an opportunity for people from around the world to post messages of solidarity and support. Egypt's Coptic Christians have a significant presence in social media such as Twitter and Facebook, which creates channels of communication with the outside world. Various organizations that assist embattled Christians also have means of communicating directly with the people on the front lines of this global war, and are generally delighted to pass along expressions of sympathy and concern. As hollow as it may sound, sometimes simply reassuring the victims of violence that their pain has not occurred in a vacuum, that someone is paying attention, can be enormously reassuring.

THINKING GLOBALLY ABOUT THE CHURCH

Though individual Christians can't control how the leadership of their denominations responds to the global war on Christians, let alone what politicians and bureaucrats do, they at least have power over their own thinking—which issues to pay attention to, what they care about, and what they see as the real priorities. In the context of twenty-first-century Christianity, that means one thing above all: learning to think globally about the church.

As we've seen, adopting a global perspective in the first instance is no more than a simple reflection of the realities of Christianity on the ground today. The United States, with roughly 225 million Christians, is conventionally described as the largest Christian nation in the world. Yet the United States represents only 10 percent of the 2.2 billion Christians in the world, which means that 90 percent of the Christians on the planet aren't necessarily like Americans. They have different experiences, different perspectives, and different needs. In this era, Christians really only have two choices when it comes to how they think about the issues facing their churches. They can learn to think globally, or they will think dysfunctionally.

Given the drama of the global war on Christians, the urgency of shifting to a global perspective becomes even clearer. It's one thing, perhaps, to focus entirely on domestic concerns and debates when people are basically safe and sound in other parts of the world. When leading estimates indicate that some one hundred million Christians around the world face the threat of interrogation, arrest, torture, and death on the basis of their faith, such insularity becomes much harder to defend.

In part, taking a global perspective means appreciating that the issues dominating Christian conversation in the West do not always loom so large elsewhere. Debates over gay marriage and female clergy, for instance, raise important questions about Christian tradition, ecclesiastical justice, sexual morality, and other matters, and there's certainly a need for reflection on them. However, to allow one's attention to be entirely consumed by such matters, either advocating for them or opposing them, would strike most victims of the global war on Christians as either ridiculous or tragic, and perhaps both at once.

As an American Catholic, I have often been struck by the juxtaposition over the last decade and a half of the unraveling of the Christian community in Iraq and the "liturgy wars" that have gripped English-speaking Catholicism, which pivoted on the best way to render the original Latin of texts for worship into English. Those debates dominated Catholic attention in the United States at the same time that U.S.-led military interventions in Iraq were creating a context in which Christians have become an endangered species. With no disrespect to liturgists, and without taking a position on the new translation of the Mass, I will just say this: if we American Catholics had invested in gestures of solidarity with our fellow Christians in Iraq one-tenth of the time and treasure we have spent over the last fifteen years debating whether we should say "And also with you" or "And with your Spirit," we could have changed the world.

MICRO-CHARITY

It's the perennial question that haunts anyone moved by reports of tragedy half a world away, when something awful happens to people they've never met and in places they've never been: It's terrible, yes, but what can I possibly do about it? Fortunately for forty poor and illiterate widows whose husbands were killed during a ferocious anti-Christian pogrom in the Indian state of Orissa in 2008, Rita Larrivee wasn't daunted by the challenge of finding an answer. Her response illustrates the power of what some experts call "micro-charity," meaning relief efforts that aren't organized by governments or large NGOs but by individuals acting under their own steam and aimed to address specific, manageable problems.

A Catholic physician now living in Greensville, South Carolina, Larrivee immigrated to the United States from India as a young doctor. She's a devout believer, and heard about the anti-Christian violence in India by watching a report on the Eternal Word Television Network (EWTN). Even though she felt an immediate connection to the story, at first she was stumped about what she could possibly do. She grew up in southern India, while Orissa is in the northeast, where she didn't know anyone and still doesn't speak the local language. Eventually

Larrivee set out to make contacts, with the idea of trying to meet what she calls a "bite-sized portion" of need. The result is a modest and eminently practical program that provides goats, chickens, and vegetable seed to forty widows who lost their husbands in the pogroms, to ensure a source of food for them and their families. It also provides microloans to help them bring small local crafts to market and scholarships to send twenty-five of their children to Catholic schools.

In Orissa, a local congregation of religious women, the Sisters of St. Joseph of Annecy, runs the effort, coordinated with the help of a Divine Word missionary, Fr. Richard Vaz. They call the project "Widows of Persecution," aimed at helping Christian women in Orissa whose husbands died amid the rampage of violence in 2008, and who now face the challenge of caring for themselves and their children alone. Against that backdrop, Larrivee decided she had to do something, initially contributing her own money and whatever she could raise from family and friends.

Through the sisters who run the Widows of Persecution project, Larrivee said she's received a crash course in how to run a humanitarian program—including the insight that good intentions, by themselves, aren't enough. For instance, she said, she learned it's not enough to help poor women in rural areas develop crafts or produce for sale. It's also critical to help get those products to market, because otherwise middlemen will suck up most of the modest profits. In addition, she said, it's also been important to extend some parts of the program, such as the crafts training, to Hindu women too. Otherwise, the effort might have boomeranged and produced additional hostility toward Christians.

Now that she's reaching retirement, Larrivee said she plans to make solidarity with India's persecuted Christians her "lifelong project." In the first place, she wants to extend the existing program to sixty additional widows. Eventually, she said, she'd like to help rebuild some of the churches and community centers that were destroyed.

Larrivee's experience teaches two important lessons about bringing relief to the global war on Christians. First, one doesn't need a large pool of resources or a massive infrastructure. Gumption will do. Second, it's not true that simple individuals are powerless, incapable of doing something to effect change. Although few may be willing to invest the time and effort that Larrivee has, her example illustrates that one doesn't always have to wait for the train to leave the station. Sometimes the better strategy is to build your own train.

INSTITUTIONAL HUMANITARIAN RELIEF

People motivated to do something on behalf of persecuted Christians around the world can also support one of the many organizations devoted to humanitarian relief on behalf of suffering believers. To offer simply one example among many, there's a Catholic organization called the Catholic Near East Welfare Association that has a sparkling record of identifying the most pressing needs of Christian groups in the Middle East, organizing effective programs, and ensuring that resources are actually directed to the people on the ground, as opposed to being consumed by administration and overhead.

A compelling example of their efforts that was unfolding at the time this book was written was the group's emergency appeal on behalf of Christians in Syria. As we have seen, the situation facing Christians in the country is harrowing, especially in Aleppo and Homs, where the carnage has been the most intense. Among other nightmares, one challenge facing many Christian congregations in Syria is to come up with enough money to ransom the mounting number of Christians kidnapped by militant groups, who see extortion as a way to finance their mayhem. The spike in kidnappings is also, naturally, another force driving Christians out of the country.

The Catholic Near East Welfare Association is among the largest providers of aid to Christians in Syria, if not the largest. Realizing the urgency of immediate relief, their first priority is to help Christian refugees get through the winter. The idea is to deliver "winter survival kits" to two thousand families, at a cost of $210 each. Issam Bishara, a representative of the Catholic Near East Welfare Association in Lebanon, said in October 2012 that because Syria's Christians generally have not headed for massive refugee camps in Turkey or Jordan, they're not getting help from international relief agencies. Fearing exposure to further hostility, they've headed to other parts of Syria and to Lebanon, taking refuge with family and friends, but in many cases those folks are running out of food, water, heating oil, and other supplies. Without the help provided by CNEWA and other groups, these Christian refugees faced the prospect of a long, cold, and deadly winter.

In the Catholic world, Aid to the Church in Need is another such leading supplier of humanitarian assistance to suffering Christians. Among Protestants, groups such as Barnabas Aid, Christian Freedom International, Open Doors, and Voice of the Martyrs play a similar role. Most mainstream Christian denominations have some organization or relief agency that provides aid to persecuted and impoverished Christians in locations around the world, and all are chronically in need of resources. Many of these groups also blend direct humanitarian efforts with other aims, such as political advocacy, consciousness-raising, support for evangelization, and church-building in various regions of the world. Christians of various stripes will likely find some of these organizations more appealing than others, depending on how aggressive a missionary posture they strike, for instance, or whether their emphasis is more on immediate aid or long-term policy strategies. As always, careful discernment is in order before making a decision about which outfit one may choose to support.

The point is that there are options at hand for people wanting to be part of the solution to the global war on Christians. These groups generally do heroic work with little fanfare and with perennially limited resources. Donating $210 online to aid one Christian family in Syria may seem a drop in the bucket, but change often begins with such small steps.

POLITICAL ADVOCACY

Beyond trying to put out the immediate fires of persecution, Christians obviously should be involved in crafting better fire containment strategies to prevent them from forming in the first place. That means using the usual tools of political life to bring pressure to bear on leaders to make the defense of religious freedom a priority, and to give special attention to members of the world's most persecuted religious body. Sixteen years ago Paul Marshall argued that since Catholics and Protestants together make up a strong majority of the American population, it is "neither unreasonable nor unachievable" that they could mobilize political opinion in the country to make protecting Christians at risk a priority. That diagnosis remains as true today as it was then.

These efforts at advocacy vis-à-vis the global war on Christians can take at least five forms.

First, Christians can stand in the front lines of insisting that political debates in the West generally take more cognizance of the international situation, especially the fate of suffering peoples whether they're Christians or not. The famous adage has it that all politics is local, which is perhaps especially true of political discourse in the United States. The Center for Responsive Politics estimates that the 2012 election in the United States was the most expensive in history, with a final bill of around $6 billion. Beginning in late October, spending on behalf of the two American presidential candidates reached an astronomic level of $70 million per week. Yet despite those enormous sums, the foreign policy discussion during the race was remarkably impoverished. Aside from some skirmishing over places where American troops are engaged, such as Iraq and Afghanistan, a casual observer of the 2012 race could be forgiven for concluding that, in political terms, the rest of the world didn't even exist. Simply as a matter of global justice, not to mention spiritual solidarity, Christians ought to be the first to insist on a broader vision of what's at stake in political life.

Second, Christians can insist that the defense of religious freedom internationally becomes a more central element of the foreign policy of Western governments. In part, that means ensuring that governments do more than pay lip service to the cause, and not backtrack on their commitments. In 2011, for instance, the American Congress reauthorized the United States Commission on International Religious Freedom just hours before it was scheduled to go out of business, a delay that had left both staff and those invested in the commission's work uncertain for months about its fate. Symbolically, such dithering sends a signal that the United States isn't truly serious about the issue. Christians can also hold policymakers' feet to the fire when hard choices have to be made—demanding, for example, that China not get a free pass for its oppression of religious minorities simply because it's in the perceived economic and geopolitical interests of the West. At the same time, Christians should also insist that the rhetoric of religious freedom not be exploited to advance ideological interests—that criticism of Iran for its treatment of Christians, for instance, not be swept up into broader debates about nuclear policy or anything else, and that any sanctions be commensurate with measures imposed on other states with a similar track record.

Third, Christians in the West can also insist that their leaders take the perspectives of Christians on the ground into consideration when crafting foreign policy. For instance, they could find ways to bring the voices of Syria's Christian minority more thoroughly into debates about Western policy with regard to the Assad regime and Syria's ongoing civil war. Many of those Syrian Christians are less enthused about the prospect of regime change than some in the Western foreign policy establishment. While listening to them doesn't necessarily mean endorsing their position, it at least ought to be part of the conversation—if for no other reason than because they're the ones who will have to live with the consequences. In late July 2013, I interviewed Bashar Khoury, a twenty-nine-year-old Latin rite Catholic from Syria, during the Catholic Church's World Youth Day gathering in Brazil. He told me that if the Assad regime falls he'll leave Syria for good, on the conviction that Christians will have no place in a country led by the opposition. Whatever one makes of his diagnosis, voices such as Khoury's should be heard.

Fourth, Christians in the West can also mobilize when disaster strikes to ensure that their governments bring their resources to bear in situations of special need. In Nigeria at the moment, for instance, many Christian leaders are asking Western governments to offer military and law enforcement resources to assist the Nigerian authorities in combatting the militant Boko Haram movement—identifying its leadership, tracking its financial support, ascertaining who precisely is responsible for its various attacks, bringing the perpetrators to justice, and offering security to vulnerable Christian communities, especially in the country's north. Christian advocates in the West can demand that their governments make those resources available, in dialogue with Nigeria's

Christian leadership, and even engage in some gentle arm-twisting to convince potentially reluctant Nigerian officials that they actually need the help.

Fifth, Christians can demand that policies on refugee admission and resettlement in their societies recognize persecuted Christians as a protected category. In recent years, scores of Christians fleeing situations of violence and oppression have encountered difficulties when applying for status as refugees, because in many nations "Christians" are not specifically identified as a persecuted group. In other cases, basic bureaucratic forces compound the difficulties. Many Iraqi Christian refugees, for instance, were either turned away or faced lengthy delays in their applications to enter the United States after enhanced background checks due to terrorism concerns plugged the pipeline. As author Lela Gilbert has noted, "Christians have no Israel," meaning no place they can go when facing repression that will automatically accept them. Christians in the West can at least help ensure that their nations remain receptive to Christians seeking a safe harbor from the global war.

As is always the case in political life, there is no guarantee that these efforts will be successful, and advocacy is no substitute for the other measures described here. At the same time, most of the other strategies outlined in this chapter fall into the category of responding to crises after they've occurred. A more robust climate of protection for religious freedom at the level of both law and political administration, on the other hand, can help prevent the crises before they occur.

RESETTLING REFUGEES

Given the realities of the global war, it's hardly surprising that millions of vulnerable Christians today find themselves living as refugees or displaced people. Christian churches and organizations have done admirable work assisting these refugees, often providing visa assistance, aid with housing and finding work, providing breaks so that the children of refugees families can attend church-run schools, offering legal aid and help with navigating the immigration systems of host countries, providing pastoral care in their native languages, and so on.

All that assistance is urgently needed, and may well have to be ramped up. Churches and denominational structures should be mobilizing now to identify the most likely areas of need and to organize an effective response. (Syria and Egypt, for instance, may soon be generating new waves of Christian exiles.) Further, it's important to remember that a truly effective resettlement program is not a one-and-done affair. Refugees need monitoring and ongoing support well after the initial challenge of finding a home and a source of income is resolved, and church organizations need to be with them along the journey.

One caution, however, is in order. In trying to understand the Christian exodus out of the Middle East, some experts wonder if the good intentions of Western churches aren't actually fueling the phenomenon. One reason that Christians are disproportionately more likely than other groups to choose to leave is precisely because they have access to networks of care and support, many run by Western churches, that are not always as readily available to others. Jabbar Yassin Hussein, the most prominent living Iraqi poet, who's been in exile in France since 1976, has said that "if America and Australia opened their borders, not a single Christian would be left in Iraq."

Some pastors and church officials in the West have openly asked whether the extensive refugee programs they operate will end up accelerating the demise of Christianity in places where it's most at risk. Of course, no one becomes a refugee on a lark; the choice to leave behind one's home, and often members of one's family, is always traumatic, and people who feel compelled to make that wrenching decision certainly merit support.

A thoughtful refugee program that's sensitive not only to the welfare of the church in the host society but also to the one in the country of origin will come with a guarantee: "We're with you now, when you've chosen to leave because you believe circumstances required it and we trust that judgment. However, we will also be with you if the situation changes and you believe it's possible for you to return. We welcome you here, but we're also in solidarity with your church back home, and we will match every dollar and every hour we've invested in helping you get out with a commensurate amount of resources to help you go back, if you ever reach the conclusion that's what you want."

NORTH/SOUTH PARTNERSHIPS

Relationships between churches and congregations in the developed and developing worlds have deep roots, such as the "twinning" of parishes in, say, Iowa and El Salvador, or Italy and Burundi. Sometimes these relationships arise organically, for instance when a pastor from a mission country happens to spend time at a congregation in Europe or the United States, and a natural bond is formed. Other times these relationships are the result of an organized effort at the denominational level, or they come from a direct request made by a congregation in the developing world for support. Typically, these relationships involve mutual prayer, financial support, missionary exchanges, and other forms of solidarity.

Such partnerships have the capacity to deepen a sense of membership in a global church, as well as to spread resources around the world in a more equitable fashion—often drawing upon the human capital of the churches in the South, and the financial and logistical capital of churches in the North. In light of the global war on Christians, such North/South partnerships are likely to be challenged to expand in three ways.

First, churches and congregations in the North will feel pressure to become more deliberate about which relationships they undertake, and in particular to try to identify fellow believers most at risk of becoming the victims of anti-Christian persecution. At the moment, congregations looking for potential partners would likely feel inclined to turn to Syria, Egypt, India, or Nigeria, understanding that many churches in those societies are exposed to special risks. The nature of these relationships will likely also evolve, coming to focus more intensely on advocacy on behalf of Christians in the society where the partner is located, as well as on more extensive humanitarian aid when members of the partner community find themselves in need.

Second, many people in Western churches and congregations will likely feel pressure not merely to support their partners at a distance but to go and see for themselves what the situation is like. These personal exchanges already take place in the form of missionary and humanitarian expeditions, and that will doubtless continue. Increasingly, however, partners in the West may also want to organize delegations of "observers," whose role is not necessarily to evangelize or to build homes but rather to document the persecution facing Christians in that society and then to report back both to church officials and to policy makers. Such outings must be organized with care, because responsible church leaders will not want to put their people in harm's way. At the very least, however, in places where basic calm has returned after an eruption, these observers would be able to witness the aftermath and to collect testimonies before memories fade. Doing so would not only change the participants' perspectives but also help to build a broader consciousness around the world as they talk with others back home about what they saw and heard.

Third, North/South partnerships will also be pressured to grow beyond the realm of parishes, churches, and congregations and include to a greater degree faith-based institutions such as schools, hospitals, and social service agencies. Such relationships already exist, for instance in the form of partnerships between religiously affiliated universities. There will be accelerating pressure to expand such ties, both to address immediate situations of crisis and to build long-term networks of solidarity. For instance, Christian hospitals in the United States and Europe will likely feel new pressure to mobilize medical assistance for Christians who suffer violent persecution in areas where local health care systems are overwhelmed. In situations where Christian schools are damaged or destroyed, Christian educators in the West will be asked to dispatch assistance, both to address the physical damage and to provide stopgap support while repairs are under way. Even Christian businesses that aren't part of any denominational structures may be pressed into service; Christian CEOs, for instance, may be asked to target regions where Christians are at risk to open new franchises, to offer employment, and to engage in commercial transactions to support the local economy.

Across the board, any Christian with institutional responsibility in the twenty-first century is likely to feel new pressure to exercise a kind of "preferential option" in deploying the institution's resources to support the victims of the global war on Christians.

POSTSCRIPT

When a Christian reflects on religious violence, it's tempting to forget all about embarassments such as Anders Behring Breivik, the Norwegian lunatic who bombed a government building in Oslo on July 22, 2011, killing eight people, and then opened fire on a Labor Party youth camp, leaving sixty-nine people dead, mostly teenagers. Breivik imagines himself as a "modern-day crusader," a protagonist in a vast cultural struggle to save Norway from Islam, Zionism, Marxism, feminism, and a host of other "isms." For someone with such a grandiose and delusional sense of his own importance, perhaps the most fitting punishment would be to ignore him altogether.

Alas, that's not an option open to thoughtful Christians. It's part of the record that Breivik described himself as "100 percent Christian" in his rambling manifesto, declared that he prayed to God for help during his attacks, and asserted that only the "Cross of Christ" could bring Europe back to its senses. Though he is apparently not terribly spiritual, he claims to be a devoted cultural Christian. He wants to overthrow the existing authorities in both Protestant and Catholic churches, whom he regards as weak, corrupt, and fatally given to make nice with Muslims, to be replaced by a "Great Christian Congress" to establish a newly militant European church.

In other words, Breivik imagines himself as a miniature Christian version of Al-Qaeda.

In the aftermath of Breivik's atrocities, many well-meaning Christians insisted that he could not actually be a Christian, because the loving teachings of Christ could not possibly justify such horrors. The Norwegian head of the World Council of Churches, Rev. Olav Fykse Tveit, accused Breivik of "blasphemy" for citing Christianity as a justification for his actions. Of course, that's the same reasoning many Muslims use to insist that jihadist terrorists are not real Muslims, because Islam is a religion of peace. Both may have a point in terms of orthodoxy, but the fact remains that Breivik saw himself as a Christian, and he acted, at least in part, to defend the faith. His story illustrates a point that Christians dare not forget: Christians are as much in the grip of sin as anyone else, and Christianity is as capable of being perverted to support cruelty and inhumanity as any other system of belief.

This book is devoted to documenting the vast scale of anti-Christian violence and persecution around the world, and to debunking the chronic mythology that too often impedes a clear understanding of this global war on Christians. At the close, however, it's apposite to add a brief word regarding possible abuses of the story I've tried to tell.

First, the focus on Christians as victims should not suggest that Christians are incapable of being perpetrators. Beyond rare madman such as Breivik, we've already seen that some of today's new martyrs go to their deaths at the hands of their fellow Christians. The irony can sometimes seem especially cruel, as in April 1994, when the Catholic bishops of Africa gathered for a synod meeting in Rome and exhorted their followers "to join together in the service of life . . . in justice and peace." At the same moment that message was issued, the genocidal frenzy in Rwanda was erupting. An estimated 1.2 million people were slaughtered over a period of one hundred days between April and July, which adds up to ten thousand killed every day, four hundred every hour, seven every minute. While the vast majority of the victims were Catholics, so too were their murderers. The bishops were forced to acknowledge that something had gone wrong in the evangelization of Africa, because if baptized Christians had refused to participate, the genocide could not have happened. It's an old story, one that applies with equal force to other dark chapters of history such as the Shoah in Nazi Germany. In every case, to celebrate the victims is not to diminish the responsibility of the victimizers, whatever their religious affiliation may be.

As a related point, it's sometimes suggested by apologists for Christianity that there is no Christian form of violent fundamentalism akin to "Islamic radicalism" or "Hindu radicalism." While perhaps not on the same scale, Christian radicalism does exist. It too can give lethal expression to religious passions that are often intertwined with national, political, economic, and cultural antagonisms.

In March 2007, I met a Nigerian Pentecostal preacher named James Wuye, who's become internationally renowned for his efforts at Muslim/Christian harmony along with his partner, Imam Muhammad Ashafa. It wasn't always that way. Born a Baptist, Wuye entered the Catholic Church while attending Catholic school, then gravitated to the Assemblies of God. When the first waves of religious violence hit northern Nigeria in the late 1970s, Wuye said he watched as Christians were targeted by Muslim extremists, with no support from the local police or army forces. Wuye and other young Christians decided to organize themselves into secretive paramilitary bands. These groups were designed to protect churches and Christian populations, and members took oaths never to strike first. Yet, Wuye concedes, as the logic of violence took over, the militias eventually took on a more provocative role. In one case, he said, they blew up a bridge in a Christian area and blamed it on Muslims, in order to radicalize Christian opinion.

Having grown up the child of an army officer—"in the barracks," as he put it—Wuye was a natural drill sergeant. He told chilling tales of how young Christians were indoctrinated to justify violence against Muslims, including selective use of Biblical texts. (For example, Luke 22:36: "If you do not have a sword, sell your cloak and buy one"). He paid the price in his own flesh. In 1992, he lost his right hand during a pitched battle to defend a church against Muslim militants in Kaduna; today, he wears a prosthetic limb due to the injury.

"In my heart," Wuye said, "my hatred for Muslims knew no bounds."

His conversion moment came in 1999, when he attended a local revival where he heard a well-known local Pentecostal pastor thunder from the pulpit, "You can't preach Christ with hate . . . you have to take on the mind of Christ!"

Today Wuye is an interfaith hero, and I suspect most Christians would agree with the Pentecostal pastor that his activity became authentically Christlike only after 1999. Descriptively and psychologically, however, Wuye also understood himself to be fully, even heroically, Christian while he was slaughtering Muslims.

Eric Rudolph is an American example of the impulse. Convicted of a series of bombings between 1996 and 1998 that left two people dead and injured 150 others, Rudolph has described himself as a Christian warrior in the struggle to end the "holocaust" of abortion. Aside from the Olympic bombing in 1996 in Atlanta, Rudolph targeted two abortion clinics and a lesbian bar. He was linked to a movement known as Christian Identity, which includes militia groups in its network. While it's exaggerated to style Rudolph as a harbinger of a looming Christian jihad, it's equally disingenuous to suggest that he doesn't count as a "Christian" extremist because his beliefs are heterodox. If Christians don't have to take responsibility for Rudolph, then Muslims ought to get a free pass for Osama bin Laden. This is not, of course, to suggest that the two figures are mirror images, or that their crimes are of equivalent moral gravity.

Put simply, the notion that Christianity is insusceptible of fomenting radicalism and terrorism is bunk, and nothing in this book should be taken to suggest otherwise. Christians must always be on guard against the stirring of prejudice in their own hearts, and should not use the suffering of their coreligionists to evade that examination of conscience.

Nor is this book intended as a form of Christian apologetics, an exercise designed to bring people to the faith or to persuade them that Christianity is spiritually or morally superior to other religions. Christians may be suffering persecution today in greater numbers than other faith traditions, but that doesn't automatically mean that Christianity is nobler than, say, Zoroastrianism or Buddhism, or for that matter atheism. Spiritually, many Christians may well see today's persecution as part of a cosmic struggle between good and evil, between God and Satan, which validates the claims of the faith. Logically, however, there's no correlation between violence directed at a belief and the ultimate truth of that belief. The effort here is not to convert anyone to a religious position but rather to bring individuals to a humanitarian conviction that the suffering of innocent people is being ignored and merits attention.

Finally, the reality of a war on Christians should not suggest that everyone who makes a principled argument against Christianity or who clashes with representatives of the faith is a bigot. It's quite possible to believe that religion is a delusion, that Christian churches in the West enjoy too much wealth and power, or that orthodox Christian teachings on sexual morality are wrong without succumbing to religious hatred. In the same way that opponents of gay marriage aren't all religious fanatics, its supporters are not all bent on destroying the Christian foundations of the West. The global war on Christians is the most chilling human rights story of our time, but not every critic of contemporary Christianity is among its authors.

Yes, some Christians have blood on their hands; yes, Christians and their churches often take controversial positions on political and social issues that are fair game for debate; yes, Christians can sometimes be overly attached to systems of privilege and too quick to see any questioning of those privileges as an assault on their rights. Nothing in this book suggests anything to the contrary, and Christians themselves should be in the front lines of asking hard questions about their own conduct, in the spirit of Matthew 7:3: "Why do you notice the splinter in your brother's eye, but do not perceive the wooden beam in your own?"

At the same time, the various ways in which some Christians fall short, or court controversy, are no excuse for a stubborn unwillingness to acknowledge the very real threats far too many Christians face. Just as two wrongs don't make a right, two versions of moral blindness don't constitute vision.

Index

Read on for an excerpt from John L. Allen Jr.'s

The Future Church:
How Ten Trends Are Revolutionizing
the Catholic Church

IMAGE

Available everywhere books are sold

INTRODUCTION

In Thomas Friedman's enormously popular book about globalization, he summarized the essential message in four words: the world is flat. Globalization is knocking down one barrier to opportunity after another, creating a world in which smart, hungry go-getters in India, China, or Brazil can compete not just for the low-wage jobs Americans don't want, but for the high-tech, high-pay jobs they definitely do want. For that reason, Friedman's book came with a warning: Americans need to hustle in this century or they'll find themselves run over by this phenomenon.

This too is a book about globalization. Its subject is the oldest globalized institution on earth, the Roman Catholic Church. Its bottom line can also be expressed in a few words: the church is upside down. By that, I don't mean that the Church is topsy-turvy or out of whack. I mean that the issues, party lines, and ways of doing business that have dominated Catholicism in the forty-plus years since the close of the Second Vatican Council in 1965, that watershed moment in modern Catholic life, are being turned on their head by a series of new forces reshaping the global Church. This book comes with a warning too: Catholics in the twenty-first century won't just need hustle (though they certainly will need that), but above all they'll need imagination. They'll need the capacity to reconsider how they think about the Church, and what they do with their faith, because otherwise Catholicism won't rise to the occasion of these new challenges—it'll be steamrolled by them.

Consider the following ways in which the Catholic Church is upside down in the twenty-first century:

- A Church dominated in the twentieth century by the global North, meaning Europe and North America, today finds two thirds of its members living in Africa, Asia, and Latin America. Catholic leadership will come from all over the world in this century to a degree never before experienced.

- A Church whose watchword after the Second Vatican Council (1962–65) was *aggiornamento,* meaning an "updating designed to open up to the modern world," is today officially reaffirming all the things that make it different from modernity: its traditional markers of Catholic thought, speech, and practice. This politics of identity is in part a reaction against runaway secularization.

- A Church whose primary interreligious relationship for the last forty years has been with Judaism now finds itself struggling to come to terms with a newly assertive Islam, not just in the Middle East, Africa, and Asia, but in its own European backyard.

- A Church that has historically invested a large share of its pastoral energy in the young now has to cope, beginning in the North, with the most rapidly aging population in human history.

- A Church that has long relied on its clergy to deliver pastoral care and to provide leadership now has lay people doing both in record numbers and in a staggering variety of ways.

- A Church used to debating bioethical issues that have been around for millennia—abortion, birth control, and homosexuality—finds itself in a brave new world of cloning, genetic enhancements, and trans-species chimeras. Its moral teaching is struggling desperately to keep pace with scientific advances.

- A Church whose social teaching took shape in the early stages of the Industrial Revolution now faces a twenty-first-century globalized world, populated by strange entities such as multinational corporations (MNCs) and intergovernmental organizations (IGOs) that didn't exist when it crafted its vision of the just society.

- A Church whose social concern focuses almost exclusively on human beings finds itself in a world in which the welfare of the cosmos itself requires new theological and moral reflection.

- A Church whose diplomacy has always relied on the Great Catholic Power of the day is now moving in a multipolar world, in which most of the poles that matter aren't Catholic, and some aren't even Christian.
- A Church accustomed to thinking of the Christian "other" as the Orthodox, Anglicans, and Protestants today is watching Pentecostals march across the planet, shooting up from 5 to 20 percent of global Christianity in barely a quarter century—in part by siphoning off significant numbers of Catholics. The Catholic Church is itself being "Pentecostalized" through the Charismatic movement.

An old car commercial carried the tagline, "This isn't your grandfather's Buick." I would submit that what we're looking at today isn't your mom and dad's Catholic Church—and it may not even be your older sister's.

The aim of this book is to survey the most important currents shaping the Catholic Church today, and to look down the line at how they might play out during the rest of the twenty-first century. The word I'm using to describe these currents is "trend." To explain what I have in mind, let me quote the historian Arnold J. Toynbee from his book *Civilization on Trial*:

> The things that make good headlines are on the surface of the stream of life, and they distract us from the slower, impalpable, imponderable movements that work below the surface and penetrate to the depths. But it is really these deeper, slower movements that make history, and it is they that stand out huge in retrospect, when the sensational passing events have dwindled, in perspective, to their true proportions.

Those "slower, impalpable movements" are what I mean by "trends." (I lay out the six criteria I employed for what counts as a trend in the chapter on "Trends That Aren't.") In several cases, there are plenty of headlines associated with one or another aspect of the trends, but usually they're treated in isolation, as random events, rather than being seen as part of deeper historical patterns. I hope to put the pieces of the contemporary Catholic puzzle together, so we can see what the picture looks like.

Each of the examples of an upside-down Church given above corresponds to one of the ten trends surveyed in this book:

1. A World Church
2. Evangelical Catholicism
3. Islam
4. The New Demography
5. Expanding Lay Roles
6. The Biotech Revolution
7. Globalization
8. Ecology
9. Multipolarism
10. Pentecostalism

The ten chapters of the book correspond to the ten trends listed above. They are not listed in order of rank or priority, as if number one were more important than number ten. To be completely honest, the sequence simply reflects the order in which I wrote the chapters. No additional significance should be attached to why one trend is number two, for example, and another number eight.

The format in each chapter is to give the lay of the land first, examining what's driving the trend and what impact it's having on the Catholic Church, in a section called "What's Happening." I then move into more speculative territory, trying to anticipate what the trend could mean for the Church as the century unfolds. That part is called "What It Means." These are not really predictions, but possible lines of development that could still be redirected, blocked, or turned in the opposite direction by forces not yet on the radar screen. In each chapter, I offer four categories of outcomes: near-certain, probable, possible, and long shots. Not only does the degree of probability go down with each category, but the projections venture farther out in time. Near-certain consequences are usually short-term extensions of developments that we can already see happening. Long shots, if they happen at all, are usually far on the horizon. The arc of time under consideration here is the rest of the century, meaning roughly ninety years. Farther out than that, all bets are off.

The book's conclusion is intended as a stand-alone summary of what impact the trends will have in the century to come. I condense the likely profile of upside-down Catholicism into four points. They're styled as sociological notes of the Church in the twenty-first century, inspired by the theological notes in the Nicene Creed: "One, Holy, Catholic, and Apostolic." My notes are intended not as theological claims about the Church's inner essence, but rather as descriptive terms for what Catholicism will actually look and feel like in this century. The four notes are: "Global, Uncompromising, Pentecostal, and Extroverted." Readers who just can't wait to arrive at the bottom line may want to read the conclusion first, then work backward.

Descriptive, Not Prescriptive

It's important to be clear at the outset about what this book is and what it's not. I'm a journalist, not a priest, theologian, or academic. My role is to document what's happening in Catholicism and to provide context for it, not tell readers what to think. This book is therefore an exercise in description, not prescription. I'm not trying to argue that these trends are the way Catholicism *ought* to go, or the issues it *ought* to face. I'm saying instead that they accurately express the way Catholicism *really is* going, and the issues it *really is* facing. I invite readers to bracket off the immediate instinct to debate whether any given trend is positive or negative, and to try to understand it first on its own terms. After that, I entrust the prescriptive debate to better minds than my own.

I stress this point because in writing about these trends, I find that many Catholics immediately want to challenge one or another of them on prescriptive grounds: "I don't think evangelical Catholicism is what Vatican Two had in mind," or "Ecology is just another word for pagan pantheism." I understand those reactions. Religion is about someone's ultimate concern, their deepest passion, and naturally Catholic blood boils when someone says the Church is moving in direction "x," if a given Catholic happens to regard "x" as obtuse, or heretical, or reactionary. In principle, that kind of argument is terrific. Part of the dynamism of Catholicism is that so many people help keep the Church alive by being passionate enough to push the Church to realize the best version of itself. To move immediately to forming opinions, however, is to miss the point of what I'm trying to do here. There will be time later to argue whether a given trend is a good idea or a bad one. For that sort of prescriptive debate to be useful, it first has to be based on solid analysis, and that's the work of this book.

In a similar vein, because this book is a work of journalism, it is not a statement of faith. I'm trying to describe the Church the way a sociologist might. I fully recognize that from a supernatural point of view, the lone trend that matters in Catholic life is God's will for the Church, which can always erupt in unpredictable ways. On this level, decisions about the Catholic future are forged not in dispassionate sociological analysis, but out of deep prayer and the spiritual effort to discern where the Holy Spirit is moving. Yet the Catholic understanding, put in its classic form in the thirteenth century by Saint Thomas Aquinas, is that grace builds on nature, it doesn't replace it. In other words, the descriptive observations about human realities in the Church offered here may not be the whole story, but they are nonetheless important preliminaries for spiritual reflection. They offer fruit for Catholic prayer, without any pretense of rendering it unnecessary.

In the interest of full disclosure, I should confess that I veer into prescriptive territory in the book's conclusion—not in terms of whether these trends are good or bad, but rather in urging Catholics to think and act in new ways in order to adapt successfully to this "upside-down" situation. This is one final point of resemblance between my book and Friedman's *The World Is Flat*. Friedman's list of drivers shaping a flat world is basically descriptive, but he's unabashedly enthusiastic about globalization. Similarly, I make no bones about my sympathy for Catholicism. I want to see the Church harness its resources to respond to the perils and promise of the twenty-first century, because I believe Catholicism has a potentially transformative contribution to offer that no other global actor can replicate. I don't pretend to know how to accomplish this, but I think I know how *not* to do it, which is to allow the Church's resources and energy to be consumed in stale internal debates. Tribalism will not be an adaptive behavior in the twenty-first-century Church.

I suppose I'm trying to strike a balance between leaving readers free to decide what to think, but at the same time encouraging them to think big.

Maybe a quick story will help explain the difference. Some time ago, I spent an afternoon discussing these trends with a couple hundred priests and pastoral workers in the Archdiocese of Seattle, at the invitation of Archbishop Alex Brunett. After I had finished, Brunett got up and told the crowd that in his opinion, an outlook he called "Trends Catholicism" offers a "hopeful vision for the future of the Church." I was a bit taken aback, since my intent was to describe trends, not to create one of my own. I wondered if I had gone off track someplace, and was now coming off as a prophet or reformer rather than a journalist. Upon reflection, however, I think I know what Archbishop Brunett meant. Reading about these trends won't tell you who's right or wrong in Church debates, but it does point to a broader horizon than the narrow set that is often seen as "issues in the Church." This book may not be prescriptive, but it is an invitation to perspective.

Printed in the United States
by Baker & Taylor Publisher Services